D0706455

Heroic Legends
of the North

GARLAND REFERENCE LIBRARY OF THE HUMANITIES
VOLUME 1403

THE DEATH OF SIEGFRIED (From Lienhart Scheubel's *Heldenbuch*, 15th century)
MS 15478, Folio 291 recto, Austrian National Library, Vienna.

Heroic Legends of the North

An Introduction to the Nibelung and Dietrich Cycles

Edward R. Haymes
Susann T. Samples

Garland Publishing, Inc.
New York and London
1996

Library of Congress Cataloging-in-Publication Data

Haymes, Edward, 1940–
    Heroic legends of the North : an introduction to the Nibelung and
Dietrich cycles / by Edward R. Haymes and Susann T. Samples.
        p.   cm. — (Garland reference library of the humanities ; vol. 1403)
    Includes bibliographical references and index.
    ISBN 0-8153-0033-6 (alk. paper)
    1. German poetry—Middle High German, 1050–1500—History and
criticism. 2. Epic poetry, German—History and criticism. 3. Old Norse
poetry—History and criticism. 4. Nibelungen—Legends—History and
criticism. 5. Dietrich, von Bern—Legends—History and criticism.
    I. Samples, Susann T. II. Title. III. Series.
    PT204.H38   1996
    830—dc20   96–5800
                                                     CIP

Cover illustration: *Sigurd Stabbing the Dragon Fáfnir* (from the Hylestad Stave
Church) Museum of National Antiquities, Oslo, Norway.

Printed on acid-free, 250-year-life paper
Manufactured in the United States of America

Contents

Preface	ix
A Note on Languages and Alphabets	x
Chronological Chart	xi
Abbreviations	xix
PART ONE: BACKGROUND	1
The Germanic Legends	3
The Medieval Literary Versions	5
The Hero, Heroic Poetry, and the Heroic Age	7
The Germanic Peoples and Their Heroic Tradition	8
Germanic Among the European Language Families	8
The Germanic Peoples	9
The Heroic Legends	11
Formation and Transmission of Heroic Legend	11
The First Stage: Eyewitness Reports	12
The Second Stage: Oral Epic Poetry	12
The Third Stage: Medieval Literature	13
Historical Background	15
The Roman Empire in the Fourth, Fifth, and Sixth Centuries	15
Ermanaric	18
The Burgundians on the Rhine	18
Attila	19
Theoderic the Great	20
Brünhild	21
Historical Sources	25
Primary Historical Sources	25
Lex Burgundionum	25

Jordanes	25
Gregory the Great	26
Gregory of Tours	26
Gesta Theoderici	27
Medieval Chronicles	29
Quedlinburg Annals	29
Frutolf von Michelsberg	31
Kaiserchronik	32
Other High Medieval Historical Sources	33
Oral Transmission	35
Epic Theory from the Nineteenth Century	35
Oral Poetry	37
Germanic Oral Narrative Poetry	39
The Common Form	40
The Development of the Middle High German Form	42
The Special Case of Old Norse	43
The Oral Transmission of Germanic Heroic Legend	45
PART TWO: LITERARY WORKS	51
Literary Works	53
Table of Motifs	54
Traces in Early Literature	57
Deor and *Widsiþ*	57
Wulf and Eadwacer	59
Beowulf	59
Walther and Hildegund	60
Waltharius	61
Waldere	62
Walther und Hildegunt	63
Valtari (in the *Þiðrekssaga*)	63
Wayland (Wieland, Velent) the Smith	63
Völundarkviða	63
Velent's Story (from the *Þiðrekssaga*)	64
The Dietrich Legend	67
Þiðrekssaga af Bern (The Saga of Þiðrek of Bern)	68
Hildebrandslied, Older and Younger	75
Das Buch von Bern (Dietrichs Flucht)	77
Rabenschlacht	79
Alpharts Tod	81

The poems in *Bernerton* 82

   Virginal 82

   Eckenliet 84

   Ekka (in the *Þiðrekssaga*) 87

   Sigenot 87

   Goldemar 89

  Biterolf und Dietleip 89

  Laurin 92

  Walberan 94

  Dietrich und Wenzelan 95

  Der Wunderer 96

  Ermenríkes Dôt 97

  Heldenbuch Prose 98

The Nibelung Legend 101

  Nibelungenlied 101

  Diu Klage 111

  Sigurð's Youth and Murder in the *Þiðrekssaga* 113

  Völsungasaga 114

  Nornagests Þáttr 117

  Niflunga saga in the *Þiðrekssaga* 118

  Poetic Edda 119

   Helgi Hundingsbani 120

   Sigurð and Brynhild 121

   Guðrún 123

   Oddrun 124

   Atli 124

   Hamðismál 126

  Snorra Edda 126

  Rosengarten zu Worms 127

  Das Lied vom Hürnen Seyfrid 129

Related Legends 133

  Wolfdietrich-Ortnit 133

   Ortnit 133

   Wolfdietrich D(B) 134

   Wolfdietrich A 135

   Wolfdietrich C 135

  Kudrun 136

  Rother 140

Glossary of Names 145

Index 159

Preface

Most English-speakers have a vague knowledge, probably derived directly or indirectly from Wagner, about the Nibelung legend, while the legend of Dietrich of Bern, certainly the most popular heroic material in medieval Germany, is largely unknown west of the English Channel. This book sets out to provide information for the general reader curious about these legendary matters and for the student setting out to find an entry into an often impenetrable secondary literature. The authors have sought to provide reliable information about the texts themselves and bibliographical guidance that will point the way into the published research on them.

This book sets out to trace its two major legendary topics from their historical roots during the last centuries of the Roman Empire to the medieval texts that make them known to us. There is no attempt to reconstruct lost literary versions or, except as an aid to orientation, to retell the stories in modern form. We have also decided to end the book with the last medieval versions of the material. A treatment of the Nibelung material from the eighteenth century to the present would be fascinating, but it would have unbalanced this book.

Many of the medieval texts have never been translated into English or even modern German. For this reason we have included a synopsis of each work so that the reader can form an idea of the content of the literary works in question.

There are many directions a study of Germanic heroic legend could have taken, but we have chosen a text-oriented approach that does very little in the way of situating the works in their social and political historical background. We have avoided theoretical issues that would have carried us beyond the scope of a handy orientation for readers and students. We have, however, included much in our bibliographical listings that will take the reader into the theoretical questions surrounding the study of these works.

One area of theory we could not avoid is the theory of oral poetic composition. This was necessary because few of our texts would have come into being without oral transmission and because the legends themselves are the product of an oral culture. Insofar as the theory of oral composition is still controversial, we have tried to cite scholarship offering views different from those presented here.

The nature of the material and its attendant scholarship makes it inevitable that a large amount of the bibliographical material cited here is in German. Although every effort has been made to find texts and secondary literature in English, we have chosen to include much of the recent and classic treatment of this area among German-speaking scholars.

Both authors have worked on the entire book, so that a clear division of responsibility is impossible, but the initial work on various parts of the book was parceled out in a way to make the best use of the authors' different backgrounds. The introductory matter and the sections on Old English, Old Norse, Old High German, and Latin texts were drafted by Edward Haymes, while the studies of Middle High German literature were prepared by Susann Samples. The authors are grateful to their colleagues and friends who have read the manuscript in various stages of development and offered useful suggestions and corrections. Acknowledgments are due Laura Blanchard and Mary Gustavson Small for many useful suggestions based on an early draft and to Bernard Bachrach, Bruce Beatie, and Stephanie Van D'Elden for reading through a penultimate draft. The authors remain responsible for any errors, of course, but these colleagues and friends have saved us from many a gaffe. Edward Haymes has been enabled to carry out some of the work on this book through a sabbatical leave from Cleveland State University and a grant from the Alexander von Humboldt Foundation in Bonn.

A NOTE ON LANGUAGES AND ALPHABETS

The literary works and historical sources discussed in this book are written in many different languages: Latin, Old and Middle High German, Old English, and Old Norse. Old English and Old Norse use several letters in addition to the usual Latin alphabet used for modern English. The most common of these are Þ and ð, both of which represent "th" sounds. Modern Icelandic uses the Þ to represent the voiceless sound in "thin" and ð to represent the voiced sound in "this." Old Norse texts generally follow this usage. Old English texts seem to use the two letters without differentiation. Most vowel sounds in all the languages used follow the pattern of Latin or modern German. An acute accent (´) is used in Old Norse to mark vowel length. Dieresis ("Umlaut" as in *ü*ber) is used in Norse and German to mark the rounding of vowels.

When discussing Germanic legend (i.e. legend known beyond a single national literature) we have used the modern German spelling of the names, since they are best known in that form. In the discussion of specific literary sources, we have used the spellings found in the best editions. When discussing historical figures, the most usual spelling found in historical literature in English is generally used. We have indicated the few departures from this practice in footnotes.

CHRONOLOGICAL CHART

This book covers more than a thousand years of poorly mapped history. In order to give our readers some help in finding their way through this wilderness, we have provided a chronological table that puts most of the events and most of the literary works discussed here in a European and world context. We have not tried to include the very late works that are found only in printed materials of the fifteenth and sixteenth centuries, since the dating of these works is problematic at best.

The selection of external events and literary works in the table is not intended to be complete, but only to provide orientation points for the general reader.

All dates are A.D. unless otherwise indicated.

World History	Germanic History
Han Dynasty in China (200 B.C.–220 A.D.)	Germanic settlement in northern Europe (c. 1000 B.C.–c. 100 B.C.)
Axumite cities in Ethiopia (c. 300 B.C–400 A.D.)	
Roman Empire (27 B.C. – 476 A.D.) Olmec and Chavín culture (1–1000)	Battle at Teutoburg Forest (c.9)
Gupta Dynasty in India (320–540)	Death of Ermanaric (375)
"Barbarian" invasion of Roman Empire (300–600)	Burgundians become allied troops to Rome (413)
Mayan culture (300–900)	Destruction of Burgundians by Roman and Hunnish Army (436)
Fall of Western Empire (476) Eastern Empire continues until 1453.	Huns stopped at Battle of Châlon (451) Death of Attila (453)
Muhammed (570–632)	Theoderic the Great (r.493–526) Clovis (r. 481–511)
T'ang Dynasty (618–907)	Merovingian Franks (486–751) Langobards in Italy (568–774)

Germanic Literature	World Literature
	Homer (8th cent. B.C.)
	Virgil (70–19 B.C.)
Gothic translation of Bible (c. 369)	Plays and poetry of Kalidasa (320–540)
Jordanes *History of the Goths* (551)	Boethius *Consolation of Philosophy* (524)
Gregory of Tours *History of the Franks* (–594)	
Widsiþ (late 7th century?)	

WORLD HISTORY	GERMANIC HISTORY
Arab Caliphates (661–1258)	Carolingian Dynasty (751–911)
Moslem defeat at Tours (732)	Charlemagne (768–814)
Kingdom of Ghana (c.700–1000)	
	Treaty of Verdun (843)
	Harald Fairhair (Norway, c. 870–930) Settlement of Iceland (c. 870)
Sung Dynasty (960–1279)	Alfred the Great (871–899) Saxon Dynasty in Germany (919–1024)
	Otto the Great (936–973) Christianization of Iceland (1000)
	Franconian Dynasty in Germany (1024–1125)
First Crusade (1095–1099)	Norrman Conquest (1066) Henry IV at Canossa (1077)
	Hohenstaufen Dynasty in Germany (1138–1254)
Kingdom of Mali (c.1100–1300) Genghis Khan (1167–1227)	Frederick Barbarossa (1152–1190)

GERMANIC LITERATURE	WORLD LITERATURE
	Bede *Ecclesiastical History of the English People* (731)
Hildebrandslied (c. 810–830)	Chinese poet Tu Fu (d. 770)
Heliand (c. 830)	
Ludwigslied (881)	
Waltharius (late 9th century?)	
Beowulf (c. 1000?)	*Genji Monogatari* (c. 1000)
	Chanson de Roland (c. 1100)
	Cantar del mio Cid (c. 1150).
	Chrétien de Troyes (c. 1160–1195)
Kaiserchronik (c. 1150) *Rother* (c.1150)	Marie de France (late 12th cent.)

WORLD HISTORY	GERMANIC HISTORY
Pope Innocent III (1198–1216)	Philip of Swabia (1198–1208)
	Otto IV (1208–1212)
	Magna Carta (1215)
	Frederick II (1212–1250)
	Hákon the Old (Norway, 1216–1263)
Yüan Dynasty (1260–1360)	
	Interregnum in Germany (1254–1263)
	Iceland joined to Norway (1264)

GERMANIC LITERATURE	WORLD LITERATURE
Hartmann von Aue (1170–1215)	
Nibelungenlied (c.1200)	
Gottfried von Straßburg	
Tristan (c. 1210)	
Wolfram von Eschenbach *Parzival*	
(c.1200–1210)	
Walther von der Vogelweide	Guillaume de Lorris, *Roman de la Rose,*
(1170–1230)	(c. 1237)
Diu Klage (c.1220)	
Snorri Sturluson *Prose Edda* (c.1220)	
Kudrun (1230–1240)	
Eckenlied (c.1250)	
Laurin (c.1250)	
Walberan (c.1250)	
Dietrich und Wenzelan (c.1250)	
Rosengarten zu Worms (c.1250)	
Thidrekssaga (c.1250)	
Alpharts Tod (c.1250)	
Sigenot (c.1250)	
Goldemar (c.1250)	
Buch von Bern (after 1250)	Saadi *The Fruit Garden* (c. 1257)
Rabenschlacht (after 1250)	
Virginal (after 1250)	
Biterolf und Dietleip (c. 1260)	
Poetic Edda (c. 1250)	
Völsungasaga (c. 1270)	

Abbreviations

ABäG	*Amsterdamer Beiträge zur älteren Germanistik.*
AGSN	*'Waz sider da geschach:' American-German Studies on the Nibelungenlied.* Eds. Werner Wunderlich and Ulrich Müller. Göppingen: Kümmerle, 1992.
BGDSL	*Beiträge zur Geschichte der deutschen Sprache und Literatur*
DVLG	*Deutsche Vierteljahresschrift für Literaturwissenschaft und Geistesgeschichte*
HH	*Heldensage und Heldendichtung im Germanischen.* ed. Heinrich Beck. Ergänzungsbände zum Reallexikon der Germanischen Altertumskunde 2. Berlin: de Gruyter, 1988.
HS	*Hohenemser Studien zum Nibelungenlied,* a special number of *Montfort: Vierteljahresschrift für Geschichte und Gegenwart Vorarlbergs,* 32 (1980). Pagination follows that of the single volume.
I Nibelunghi	*Colloquio Italo-Germanico sulla tema I Nibelunghi.* Atti dei convegni Lincei. Rome: Accademia Nazionale dei Lincei, 1974.
JEGP	*Journal of English and Germanic Philology*
JFI	*Journal of the Folklore Institute*
MGH	*Monumenta Germaniae Historica*
MLN	*Modern Language Notes*
MLR	*Modern Language Review*
PN	*Nibelungenlied und Klage: Sage und Geschichte, Struktur und Gattung: Passauer Nibelungengespräche 1985.* Ed Fritz Peter Knapp. Heidelberg: Winter, 1987.
PSMA	*Poetry in the Scandinavian Middle Ages: The Seventh International Saga Conference.* Ed. Teresa Pároli. Spoleto: Presso la sede del Centro Studia, 1990.
WW	*Wirkendes Wort*
ZDA	*Zeitschrift für deutsches Altertum und deutsche Literatur*
ZDP	*Zeitschrift für deutsche Philologie*

Part One:

BACKGROUND

CHAPTER 1

The Germanic Legends

The legend of Dietrich of Bern was medieval Germany's closest parallel to the legends of King Arthur in Britain and Charlemagne in France. Dietrich became the central figure in a wide variety of stories, most of which have absolutely no connection to the historical figure on whom Dietrich is based, the Ostrogothic king Theoderic the Great (c.453–526)[1] The Dietrich of legend is associated with the Italian city Verona, the name of which appears in medieval texts as "Bern," a name which has no connection to the present Swiss capital. The historical Theodoric made his capital in Ravenna, where his mausoleum can still be seen.

The story medieval audiences considered to be historical told of Dietrich's exile from his rightful lands, his thirty years with Attila the Hun, and his eventual return. Far more popular, however, were the fantastic adventures that featured Dietrich and his chief vassal, Hildebrand, in conflict with giants, dwarfs, and dragons.

The "Nibelung" legend actually combines several stories. The first of these involves the youth, marriage, and murder of Siegfried. There is no known historical source for Siegfried and his story, although there have been numerous attempts to associate him with various historical figures. The thirteenth-century poets and their audiences knew that Siegfried was raised in the wilds by a smith, that he killed a dragon and gained a great treasure, that he had some relationship to the supernatural princess Brünhild, that he violated that relationship and married the courtly princess Kriemhild, sister of Gunther, Gernot, and Giselher. As a condition for being allowed to marry Kriemhild, he helped Gunther win Brünhild. The tension between the two queens, Kriemhild and Brünhild, led to Siegfried's murder.

The second story has to do with Kriemhild's later marriage to Attila the Hun. Attila invited his brothers-in-law to a great feast and killed them along with all

---

[1] In the following the name Dietrich will be used to refer to the legendary figure and Theoderic to refer to the historical king. All of the legendary figures referred to in this introduction are identified in the Glossary of Names at the end of this book.

their entourage when they would not give up Siegfried's treasure. There are two mutually exclusive versions of this story, but the result is the same. In the one version Kriemhild invited her brothers in order to gain vengeance for Siegfried. In the other she killed Attila and all of his men in order to avenge her brothers, whom Attila had invited out of avarice.

These sketchy outlines are already problematic, since the different versions available in medieval texts vary so much. Many readers will have Wagner's version of the stories in the back of their minds as well. Instead of trying to harmonize the versions into a single unified legend, we will present the medieval stories in all their diversity. Some of the differences result from the different historical situations out of which the versions come. A simple example involves the number of players in each version. The German *Nibelungenlied* was written around 1200 against the background of German imperial politics, and the final battle brings more than twenty thousand men to their death. In one of the Norse versions of the Attila story, the *Atlamál*, which may have been composed somewhat earlier on the lonely shores of Greenland, only two members of Kriemhild's family come to Attila's family to meet their death.

It is also difficult to say why these particular legends became the backbone of medieval Germanic traditional storytelling. We have evidence that the medieval storytellers knew other stories, but these are the ones that formed the nexus of legendary history. As the Middle Ages progressed, most legendary material was somehow integrated into the Nibelung and Dietrich framework. The story of Wieland the smith, for example, becomes a part of the Dietrich legend when Wieland's son Witige becomes a member of Dietrich's court. Finally the two legends are combined in the *Nibelungenlied* and the *Þiðrekssaga* so that the Nibelung legend becomes a part of Dietrich's career.

The one element most of the stories have in common is conflict within families. If it is not present in the sources, it is added within the poetic tradition. The oldest surviving legendary poem in any Germanic language (the *Hildebrandslied*) tells of a battle, presumably to the death, between father and son. Dietrich's enemy is usually portrayed as his paternal uncle, although there is no historical basis for this idea. Siegfried is killed by his in-laws.

The literary presentations make it clear that there were two very strong bonds within Germanic society, those of blood relationship and those to the lord of the war-band. The most powerful tragic situation in the society must have been conflict between these two kinds of loyalty. We can imagine the tellers of these stories in oral tradition playing heavily on this kind of conflict in order to sharpen the effect of the stories, much as Shakespeare personalized the conflicts within the Wars of the Roses to make his history plays powerful on the human as well as on the historical level. The conflicts that drive the Nibelung and Dietrich legends are as universal as those that drive the Greek tragedies or modern soap operas. It is the individual poetic representation in the medieval works of literature that makes these legends special and it is those medieval works of literary art that will occupy much of our attention in what follows. At the same time we cannot lose track of the tradition and the way the various works relate to it.

THE MEDIEVAL LITERARY VERSIONS

The first connected written version of the Nibelung legend is the *Nibelungenlied*, composed in southern Germany around 1200, and the first connected written version of the story of Dietrich is the *Þiðrekssaga af Bern*, compiled in Norway approximately a half-century later. Both assume something like the form of the legend presented below.

From thirteenth-century Iceland we have a collection of heroic poems about the Nibelung legends known as the *Poetic Edda*.[2] The story of Siegfried's family is also told in a later (fourteenth-century) prose narrative, also from Iceland, called the *Völsungasaga*. There are written traces of Germanic heroic legend prior to these high medieval literary works, but they do not actually tell the stories, the sources merely refer to them. An example of this is the reference to the legend of Sigmund in the Old English epic *Beowulf* discussed below on p. 60. In the following chapters we shall look at the evidence pointing to earlier versions of the legends that emerges from historical documents from the fifth to the twelfth century.

When we speak of the Nibelung legend and particularly of the Dietrich legend we are actually describing a wide range of stories, most of which originally had nothing to do with each other. The *Þiðrekssaga* in particular brings together many different stories, including the Nibelung legend itself, by relating them to the single figure of Dietrich of Bern. The ease with which poets could refer to these stories makes it clear that not only the singers of tales but also their audiences knew the outline of what we might call a "heroic history" of the Germanic past. We shall explore this heroic history as it presents itself to us in many very different written versions.

Perhaps it will make the task of sorting out the many different versions of our legends somewhat easier if we lay out in some detail the course of the legendary "history" that gives structure to the medieval literary versions. Each individual medieval poem or saga takes its place within this framework. Any medieval author attempting a Dietrich or Nibelung poem would know where the events of that poem would fit into the "history." This outline resembles the *Þiðrekssaga* because that is virtually the only attempt in medieval literature to cover the whole story from beginning to end. (The names follow the modern German forms.)

---

[2] The *Poetic Edda* also contains mythological poems about the Norse gods and their history. The section dealing with human events, however, is almost entirely devoted to stories of the Völsungs, the family of Siegfried/Sigurð.

Dietrich of Bern rules over his kingdom in northern Italy. The young king's fame spreads far and wide and he attracts the greatest heroes of his time to his court. He is eventually involved in a power struggle with his uncle Ermanrich, king of Rome. Ermanrich drives Dietrich and his men from his kingdom. Dietrich and most of his heroes find refuge at the court of the king of Hunland, Etzel (Attila). (Hunland is located variously in northern and eastern Europe.) After many years of exile Dietrich makes an attempt to retake his kingdom. He is victorious but the loss of Etzel's young sons and his own brother in the battle so demoralizes him that he returns to Hunland in apparent defeat.

While Dietrich is establishing himself as the foremost king of his time, Young Siegfried is being raised by a smith in the woods. He kills a dragon and wins a vast treasure. He then finds a warrior princess named Brünhild who predicts his future. The two heroic figures agree to marry.

Meanwhile the brothers Gunther, Giselher, and Gernot have established themselves at Worms on the Rhine as kings of the Burgundians (also called Nibelungs). Young Siegfried arrives at their court and seeks the hand of their sister Kriemhild. Gunther agrees to the match if Siegfried will help him win the warrior maiden Brünhild. Siegfried does so, violating his earlier oath to marry Brünhild. Brünhild eventually manages to incite some members of Gunther's court to kill Siegfried. The brothers plot against Siegfried and kill him by stabbing him in the back with a spear. The murder takes place by a spring in the forest (or in the hero's bed). In some versions it is Hagen who kills Siegfried, in others it is Gernot (who is killed by the dying hero).

The widowed Kriemhild marries Etzel (Attila) and invites her brothers to a festival that turns into a slaughter as Etzel seeks to find out where Siegfried's treasure has been hidden. Dietrich and his men are eventually brought into the battle and they take part on Etzel's side. After all the Burgundian kings are killed, Kriemhild exacts vengeance on Etzel for killing her brothers. (In the *Nibelungenlied* she exacts vengeance on her brothers for the murder of her husband, and Etzel is virtually blameless in the matter.)

Several years after the slaughter of the Burgundians, Dietrich decides to return to his kingdom and retake it from Ermanrich. As the two armies face each other, Dietrich's weapons-master Hildebrand encounters his son in single combat and is forced to kill him (or is reconciled with him). Dietrich recovers his kingdom and reigns for many years before being spirited off to Hell on the back of a magnificent black horse that appears next to the pool where Dietrich had been bathing. The age of heroes is at an end.

This is more or less the backbone of the story as it existed in oral tradition from the twelfth to the fifteenth century. We have ignored the stories that violate the basic structure here,[3] but we will certainly discuss them as we move from a general consideration of the legendary world to a discussion of the individual works that transmit that world to us.

As we shall see below in our treatment of the *Völsungasaga* and the *Poetic Edda*, there was a northern branch of this tradition, mainly in Iceland, that emphasized Siegfried's family much more than the Burgundians and expanded a number of episodes far beyond what we see above. The summary of the *Völsungasaga* on pp. 114ff. shows the outlines of the Northern versions.

THE HERO, HEROIC POETRY, AND THE HEROIC AGE

Virtually all the poetry and prose discussed in this book belongs to the category generally called "heroic" poetry. The center of heroic poetry is the extraordinary individual, the hero, who stands above his contemporaries in physical and moral strength. There may be slight differences in the code of behavior expected of heroes in different cultures, but physical courage and strength seem to be common to all of them. Some cultures place more emphasis on the mental ability of the hero, his ability to outwit his enemies (Odysseus, Leminkäinen), but this is probably a secondary phenomenon and it is by no means universal.

Heroes are the products of narrative. This means that the study of literature that is identified as heroic literature must be to some extent a study of the transformation of a historical human being into a hero. The process is, of course, lost to us in most cases described in this book, but we can observe the widespread existence of hero patterns in literatures around the world.

A number of scholars have observed the similarities in biography among heroes in many different literatures. Archer Taylor has given a convenient summary of these patterns in his essay "The Biographical Pattern in Heroic Literature." We can observe that many heroes have a questionable or marvelous birth and youth. Siegfried's birth is told in several different ways in different sources, but most versions include his youth as an apprentice smith in the forest where he eventually kills a dragon. Hagen is said to be born as the result of a visitation of his royal mother by an incubus.

Heroic behavior can lead to disaster as well as success, and much heroic narrative is tragic in its tone and outcome. Achilles, Leonidas, Hagen (in the *Nibelungenlied*), Roland, Custer, and Davy Crockett all share the tragic qualities

---

[3] There are, for example, many stories of Dietrich's youth, such as the *Eckenlied* and the *Virginal*, that do not clearly fit into the generally accepted biography of Dietrich the king.

that mark the doomed hero. They are men of great courage—in fact they seem to mock death—and they know that they are doomed to die. They can only be overcome by overwhelming forces, and their deaths often inspire their respective peoples to vengeance and victory. Siegfried is, as we shall see, something of an exception to most of these generalizations, but the general notion of hero applies to him as well as to the others.

In his study of the development of the Custer legend, Bruce Rosenberg has shown that the hero is developed not in his actual deeds, but in the narratives of those deeds. Custer's story quickly took the form of what Rosenberg calls the "epic of defeat" as it made its way into newspaper accounts and popular books on the battle. The facts of the battle fitted themselves quickly into the narrative pattern expected of a heroic defeat, and soon Custer's Last Stand was a part of the heroic tradition of the United States.

There are numerous explanations for the similarities among heroic stories around the world. They have been seen as continuous narrative traditions, as expressions of archetypal story patterns, as expressions of the human condition, and so on. What is important for our study here is to recognize that these patterns exist and that they shape heroic stories as they make their way from history into narrative art.

One of the most extensive studies of the hero archetype is by the comparative mythologist Joseph Campbell in his book *The Hero With a Thousand Faces*. Campbell's book is easily available, so we will not repeat his conclusions here. The important point for our study is that heroes are a product of narrative, not of deeds and events. Many persons have performed heroic deeds, but they become heroes only if their stories are told in heroic form. This heroic form may be epic poetry or television reportage, but it must present the actions of the hero in a form the audience will recognize as heroic.

THE GERMANIC PEOPLES AND THEIR HEROIC TRADITION

The Nibelung and Dietrich legends are the product of a long process of transmission that reaches from the events of the fourth, fifth, and sixth centuries to the literary works of the thirteenth, fourteenth, and fifteenth centuries. Some parts of the stories are based on recognizable historical events, while others cannot be identified with any recorded events or personalities. In order to understand the place of Germanic legend in European literary history, we must first locate the Germanic peoples in early European history.

Germanic Among the European Language Families

The Germanic peoples entered recorded history during the last millennium B.C. and established themselves throughout much of what is now Central and Eastern Europe. They were speakers of a family of Indo-European languages that was clearly separated from the Italic (Latin) spoken in Italy, the Greek spoken throughout the Hellenic Empire, and the Celtic languages spoken throughout most of Western Europe and the British Isles at the time.

All of these European language families are related as members of the Indo-European language family, and so, we presume, are most of the peoples who spoke them. Scholars disagree on the existence of a single common Indo-European parent language, but there is no disagreement on the relatively close relationship of the languages spoken traditionally from Iceland to India. Some scholars have suggested a common fund of myths and legends among all the Indo-European peoples going back to the time when a single language was spoken, while others have argued for contamination spreading the legends from one people to another at a later date.

When we narrow our focus to a language group within the Indo-European family, such as the Germanic, the task becomes easier, because there are clearly common legends that have spread throughout the group. The Nibelung and Dietrich legends form the most important complex that was known down through the Middle Ages throughout the parts of Europe in which Germanic languages were and are spoken.

The Germanic Peoples

Before proceeding we need to clarify the two common terms for this family of peoples. In modern usage Germanic and Teutonic refer to the same grouping of peoples. "Germanic" is derived from a Latin term of the Classical period of undetermined origin. "Teutonic" is derived from the Latin name for a population group first mentioned in historical sources as originating in what is now Denmark. This name is presumed to be derived from the Germanic root *theod[4] meaning "the people," the same root from which the German word *Deutsch* and the Italian *Tedesco* (both meaning "German" in the modern sense) are derived. These synonyms are used by scholars and others to designate the same groups of peoples, the linguistic ancestors of today's Germans, Dutch, English, Scandinavians, and so on.[5]

Roman historians provide us with tantalizing glimpses of the *Germani* as they became known during the early Empire. The little book *Germania*[6] by Tacitus is

---

[4] We will follow the established practice of historical linguists of marking unattested (i.e. reconstructed) forms with an asterisk.

[5] In the following we will refer to the members of these population groups that spoke Germanic languages either as *Germani* (using the Latin word) or as Germanic peoples. We will not adopt the practice common among historians of referring to Goths, Franks, Burgundians, and so on of the late Roman imperial period as "Germans." This term will be reserved for the ancestors of modern Germans in the Middle Ages, i.e. from the Carolingian period on. We will, of course, retain the usage of passages quoted from other sources.

[6] Throughout this book we will follow Tacitus's example and refer to the totality of the Germanic peoples (and their descendants) together as "Germania." This unity is suggested by

the best known of these materials. We need to read Tacitus with a grain of salt because his main purpose was exposing the decadence of the Roman Empire rather than giving a clear picture of the *Germani*, whom he knew only through second-hand reports. He had no reason, however, to invent his few short references to Germanic poetry, which portray an oral epic of clearly historical bent.

> In the traditional songs which form their only record of the past the Germans celebrate an earth-born god called Tuisto. His son Mannus is supposed to be the fountain-head of their race and himself to have begotten three sons who gave their names to three groups of tribes. . . .
> (Tacitus, 102)

Tacitus also mentions a fear-inducing war chant called *barditus* or *baritus*, although he makes no suggestion that there were any texts, historical or otherwise, attached to them.

The stories treated below generally emanate from a somewhat later period, the so-called Period of Migrations (*Völkerwanderungszeit*) that began in the fourth century and continued into the sixth. During this period virtually every Germanic people changed its position on the map. The Goths[7] of southeastern Europe in particular swept across southern Europe, establishing themselves in kingdoms in southern Gaul (Visigoths), Spain (Visigoths), and Italy (Ostrogoths). Several Gothic leaders of the fourth to sixth century (e.g. Ermanaric, Theoderic) found their way into the legends we know from literature written in the twelfth to the sixteenth century. The Burgundians, a Germanic people that may have originated on the island Bornholm (the names is supposed to derive from "Borgundarholm") in the Baltic Sea, moved first to the shores of the Rhine and then, following the great battle that is reflected in the Nibelung legends, to their present location in Burgundy. The Alamans and Franks moved from the North Sea through what is now Germany to establish themselves in what is now northern France, Switzerland, and southwest Germany.

The Huns, a nomadic folk from Asia, entered the picture during the last third of the fourth century. This group was led at its peak by Attila (d. 451), a man whose name has become synonymous with ferocity and ruthlessness. This name was not his real one, however. It is a Germanic nickname meaning "Little

---

the close relationship of the languages and by the spread of traditional stories throughout the area. It is not meant to suggest a single group of peoples linked by blood. Many "non-Germanic" individuals (and even groupings) were absorbed into the linguistic community in the course of late antiquity and the early Middle Ages.

[7] The term "Goth" has become problematic in recent research. It denotes the Visigoths and the Ostrogoths and occasionally other groups who allied themselves with them. For a discussion of the terminology and references to recent literature see Wolfram, *History of the Goths*, 19–35.

Father." It seems clear from the legends that Attila had a very different and far more positive image among the Germanic peoples he encountered than he did in the Church-centered Latin histories that inform our school history books.

The Germanic tribes gradually formed into the major groupings we know from later history. The leading group in the West was the Frankish kingdom, first united under Clovis (r. 481–511) in the late fifth century. The Frankish custom of dividing the holdings of a leader, including the king, among the male heirs led to a fluid shape for the Frankish kingdom until it passed into the kingdoms that were to become France in the West and the Holy Roman Empire of the Germans in the East in the ninth century.

We shall not attempt to recount the fate of each of the Germanic tribes during the period of migrations. In the first place it is far too complex a matter, and in the second there is a great deal of uncertainty about the facts.[8] We shall, however, recount the probable historical backgrounds of several of the stories.

THE HEROIC LEGENDS

A literalist view of history has difficulties with a heroic history in which historical personages from different centuries appear side by side. Dietrich appears in the legend as a guest of Attila, who certainly died (453) at about the time the Gothic King Theoderic was born (c. 451). Hagen, the killer of Siegfried at Gunther's court, is a friend of Dietrich in the legends, while the historical Gundaharius (and his brothers) died in 436, more than a decade before Theoderic's birth. Theoderic's historical opponent Odoacer, who died in 473, is replaced in virtually all medieval versions by Ermanaric, who died in 375, three-quarters of a century before Theoderic was born. Clearly the medieval legends are not much use as historical sources.

Still we are on a better footing in seeking historical roots for our Germanic legends than the students of Arthurian legends with theirs. We can identify the historical figures behind many of our figures with relative ease, while the historical Arthur remains a tantalizing mystery.

Formation and Transmission of Heroic Legend

It would be a mistake to confuse the process of identifying historical personages in our stories with an interpretation of the legends or of the literary works that transmit the legends. We are dealing with at least three levels of story formation here: (1) eyewitness reports of the historical events, (2) oral heroic poetry based on the historical events, and (3) written literary adaptations of the oral heroic poetry. Parallel to (2), the oral epic poetry, were probably some form of reports circulating among people who had head about the historical events. These

---

[8] For examples of this complexity see Wolfram, *History of the Goths*, and James, *The Franks*.

reports are perhaps the most obscure element in the transmission of history. One such report is described in the dialogues of Gregory the Great (see below p. 26), but it narrates what was already historical legend. These reports and the historically based oral poetry make up what we will be calling "oral tradition." The non-poetic reports were still subject to the distortions characteristic of oral narrative, so that they are no more intrinsically reliable as sources of "history" than were the more "literary" songs. As we shall see, historical writing from the Middle Ages used oral tradition as a source along with the written histories available to them. This is an interesting process in itself, and we will be looking at it in more detail as we consider the ancient and medieval historical sources that treat our materials. What interests us here is the development of historically based narrative, mainly in the verse form of heroic epic. Let us look in a little more detail at the three stages involved.

The First Stage: Eyewitness Reports

As soon as the events took place there were reports circulating among the communities involved. Some of these may have circulated in report form for a long time before being written down (if, indeed, they ever were). We know from modern examples how unreliable eyewitness reports can be, yet they are the most direct source of information about historical events.[9]

The Second Stage: Oral Epic Poetry

If the events were appropriately heroic, these reports quickly found their way into oral poems, heroic narratives that idealized the events and their participants. This oral poetry represents the second level of story formation. The period of oral transmission is in many ways the most important part of the history of heroic legends. It is in the form of oral epic poetry that historical events combined with traditional heroic patterns to form the stories we would recognize as the Nibelung and Dietrich legends. During the period up to about 1050–1100 the stories were transmitted in the alliterative verse-form we find in virtually all Germanic languages. This form will be described in more detail in the chapter on oral transmission.

Heroic poetry in this verse form was composed by aristocratic singers among the warriors in the small warrior bands known in modern English only through their Latin designation *comitatus*. The comitatus consisted of warriors bound by personal loyalty to a war leader. We have a remarkable literary depiction of life within the comitatus in the scenes at Hrothgar's court in *Beowulf*. The passages are too long to quote here, but we find the warriors surrounding their leader, the

---

[9] For a general discussion of the problems of oral tradition as historical record, see Vansina, *Oral Tradition as History*.

lady of the hall passing among them with refreshment, and the *scop*, or singer of tales, regaling them with stories from their heroic past. These tales have the double function of keeping the deeds of past warriors alive and of providing illustrations of exemplary behavior for the living warriors.

An important point of contention within the study of Germanic heroic tradition is the question of the stability of the text. We know from comparative studies that the contents of heroic songs are tightly bound by tradition. No singer would dare knowingly change the major events of a story from the past, but each performance is not so much a repetition of all past performances as it is a re-creation. The poems exist in a tension between tradition and the exigencies of living composition. Each singer has a wide repertoire of stereotyped scenes, secondary figures, descriptions, and so on that can find their way into virtually any heroic song. The language is also formulaic. There is scarcely a verse that does not have countless parallels elsewhere within the song or within the wider tradition. The combination of formulaic language and type-scenes allows singers to produce narratives of considerable breadth without memorizing them word for word. This mode of performance, half tradition-bound and half improvised, is almost certainly the way our heroic stories were passed down from generation to generation.[10]

The use of formulaic and type-scene elements in the transmission of these stories meant that they all tended toward the typical. Only the most powerful images could survive the decades of oral performance without becoming another typical motif or type-scene. Siegfried's death by a spear in the back is variously set in the woods by a spring and in the hero's bed, but the very specific element of a spear through the back remains through all versions. At the same time Siegfried appears as a medieval knight in the *Nibelungenlied* and as a Norse warrior in the *Völsungasaga* and the poems of the *Edda*. We shall have occasion to refer to the leveling that takes place in all traditional narrative as we look at specific texts derived from the oral tradition.

The Third Stage: Medieval Literature

The third stage of our stories is the artistic formation of the orally transmitted legends into the works of medieval literature we know. Although all these works represent a reception of an oral tradition, they also represent the more or less effective reshaping efforts of a literary artist. Without question, the greatest of these was the anonymous *Nibelungenlied* poet of thirteenth-century Bavaria. His poem deals with thoroughly contemporary social and political concerns having to do with the transformation of chivalry and the legitimacy of dynastic power as much as it does with the ancient stories of the murder of Siegfried and the fall of

---

[10] The best description of the operation of an oral epic tradition remains Lord, *The Singer of Tales*.

the Burgundians. No other literary work derived from Germanic heroic legend composed in the High Middle Ages can match the artistic power of the *Nibelungenlied*, but all literary treatments of heroic materials transform their oral-traditional sources in an attempt to make them worthy of being preserved on parchment. The compiler of the *Þiðrekssaga*, for example, arranges his materials in such a way as to produce a monkish world history in which a heroic paradise is destroyed by the pernicious desire for women. Although it is not always clear what the motivation for a specific re-formation of legend is, it is doubtful that any medieval collector of ancient stories had the kind of antiquarian interest we feel when approaching these legends today.

LITERATURE CITED AND FURTHER READING

The Nibelungenlied. Tr. Arthur T. Hatto. Baltimore: Penguin, 1965. The most accessible English translation.

Poems of the Elder Edda. Tr. Patricia Terry. Philadelphia: University of Pennsylvania Press, 1990.

The Saga of Thidrek of Bern. Tr. Edward R Haymes. New York: Garland, 1988.

Campbell, Joseph. *Hero With a Thousand Faces.* Cleveland: World, 1956.

Foley, John Miles. *The Theory of Oral Composition: History and Methodology.* Bloomington: Indiana University Press, 1988.

Hoffmann, Werner. *Mittelhochdeutsche Heldendichtung..* Berlin: Schmidt, 1974. Excellent introduction to all Middle High German heroic poetry. Extensive bibliography.

James, Edward. *The Franks.* Cambridge: Blackwell, 1988.

Lord, Albert Bates. *The Singer of Tales.* Cambridge, MA: Harvard University Press, 1960. The essential primary source for the theory of oral formulaic composition.

Tacitus, Cornelius. *The Agricola and the Germania.* Tr. H Mattingly and S. A. Handford. Harmondsworth, Middlesex: Penguin, 1970.

Taylor, Archer. "The Biographical Pattern in Traditional Narrative." *JFI* 1 (1964): 121–9.

Todd, Malcolm. *The Early Germans.* Cambridge: Blackwell, 1992.

Vansina, Jan. *Oral Tradition as History.* Madison: University of Wisconsin Press, 1985.

Wolfram, Herwig. *History of the Goths.* Tr. Thomas J. Dunlap. Berkeley: University of California Press, 1988.

CHAPTER 2

Historical Background

Many events and details of the Germanic legends treated in this book have their roots in historical events. These events are no longer easy to reconstruct, since the historical sources from late antiquity are scarce and contradictory.[1] The main historical events we need to consider take place during the period of "barbarian" invasions of the Roman Empire from the fourth to the sixth century. In this chapter we shall consider them in a roughly chronological sequence.

THE ROMAN EMPIRE IN THE FOURTH, FIFTH, AND SIXTH CENTURIES

In the year 476 the last "Roman" emperor Romulus Augustulus was deposed. This relatively unimportant event has provided historians with a convenient date for the "Fall of the Roman Empire." (This simplification also ignores the fact that the "Roman Empire" continued in Constantinople for another thousand years.) The decline of the Western Roman Empire was, however, scarcely something that could be observed in the day-to-day life of most of the people involved. The city dwellers carried on their businesses and trades, and the numerous landholders and their farmworkers tried to provide enough for their own needs and for the taxes levied by the cities. The ordinary people paid little attention to who was ruling them, since they had no say in the matter. They were primarily interested in survival and avoiding being plundered. Any leader who could offer protection against marauding armies would be welcome. This helps to explain the success of many of the so-called barbarian kings, such as Theoderic and Clovis, who were often generous with those they had conquered. In addition, the conquest of a region did not usually involve much more than a defeat of the defending army and a replacement of the military magnates in charge. The greatest damage to the civilian population was generally done by the army itself as it passed through a region, feeding itself on the stores the locals

---

[1] A critical overview of the most important sources can be found in Goffart.

had planned to use through the winter and picking up any gold, silver, or glass trinkets that might strike their fancy.

The Germanic invaders remained a minority of the population as a whole, and, although they left their mark in many areas, their success did not really lead to the establishment of Germanic states on the ground formerly occupied by the Roman Empire. The invading "hordes" are reported to have numbered at most 50,000–100,000 people, while the established Roman population numbered in the millions. At the time of Theoderic's rule over Italy, the general population was a mixture of every people that had ever lived, fought, or been enslaved in Italy, and the Ostrogothic king made full use of the existing Roman bureaucracy. He was, in fact, sent to Italy as an officer of the [Eastern] Emperor to return Italy to Imperial rule. As late as the Carolingian period there was capital to be made of a pretense that the Empire still existed and that the Frankish king Carolus Magnus (Charlemagne, r. 768–814) could be crowned in Rome as its emperor in the year 800 and recognized as such by the Eastern Emperor reigning at Constantinople.[2] Germanic kings occupied the office of Roman Emperor intermittently until 1805.

The survival of Vulgar Latin as the major language in most of these areas is an indication of the numerical proportions between the Germanic-speaking Goths, Burgundians, Franks, or members of other, smaller groupings, such as the Gepids on the one side and the local population on the other. The Germanic languages contributed a few words, having mainly to do with war and with political administration and a few place-names in the wide areas they ruled, but by the eighth century Gothic, Lombard, and the other Germanic languages spoken south of the Alps had completely disappeared. Only in those areas where the Germanic population was numerically superior to the Latin-speaking colonials do we find Germanic languages spoken. The linguistic border in the eighth century was relatively close to where it is today, running through the middle of Belgium, along the Vosges mountains of Alsace, and through the Alpine valleys of today's Switzerland and northern Italy.

The adoption and spread of Christianity throughout the Empire was also a major factor in this period of history. The Council of Nicaea defined orthodox Catholic Christianity in 325, making all those with doctrinal differences into heretics. The strongest "heresy" in the regions concerning us here was that of Arius (256?–336), who taught that Christ was created by God and was thus not coeval with the deity as taught in the Catholic doctrine of the Trinity. The vast majority of Goths, Burgundians, and other Germanic invaders were at least

---

[2] Whether the gain was for Charlemagne or for the Church is still a matter of debate. In many ways the Roman Church functioned as a "successor state" of the Western Empire, and its use of the Imperial coronation as a device to influence secular rulers is an important part of medieval history, but this development is peripheral to the matters that concern us in this chapter.

nominally Arian Christians by the time they entered Roman territory. The tension between the Arianism of the invaders and the Catholicism of the Roman population probably slowed the integration of the Germanic minorities into the Roman majorities, but it did not prevent it. The adoption of Catholic Christianity by the Frank king Clovis in 496 was a major factor in the success both of the Roman Church and of the Frank kingdom.

The Empire was much weakened by the division into two parts, and the armies of the barbarians often found themselves in the service of one half of the Empire against the other. The period is one of great complexity, and it is not necessary to recapitulate Gibbon's *Decline and Fall of the Roman Empire* here in order to understand the historical events that gave rise to heroic legends.

Although there had been considerable jockeying for position in the Balkans during the fourth century, the first successful invasion of Italy was by the Visigoths under Alaric in the first decade of the fifth century. This climaxed in the "Sack of Rome" in 409–410. Alaric's death in 410 robbed the movement of its momentum, and the Visigoths reoriented their attention to what is now Southern France and Spain. They established a kingdom in Toulouse that lasted a few decades and later established a kingdom in Spain that lasted until the Muslim invasion in the early eighth century.

The invasion of the Empire by a confederation of barbarians dominated by the Huns under Attila was brought to a stop in the battle of Châlons in 451. The connections between the Huns and the Goths is a matter of considerable controversy. The next few decades saw the end of the Western Empire mentioned above and the installation of a Germanic king, Odoacer, in Italy.

The Ostrogoths under Theoderic were sent by the Eastern Emperor Zeno to take the Italian kingdom of Odoacer in 493. After defeating and murdering Odoacer, Theoderic established himself as king in Ravenna. He reigned very successfully until his death in 526. His successors were unsuccessful in fighting off attempts by Byzantium to retake Italy in the middle of the sixth century, and the Ostrogothic kingdom was eventually destroyed.

The Lombards made use of the resulting power vacuum in 568 and invaded Italy, establishing a kingdom that lasted until it was finally defeated by Charlemagne and incorporated into the Carolingian kingdom of the Franks in 774. Although the Lombards play no identifiable role in the origination of the surviving Nibelung and Dietrich legends, they may have played a role in its later formation, transmission, and dissemination.[3]

The Franks were a loose federation of Germanic warrior bands that gradually coalesced into a group that could be unified by Clovis at the beginning of the

---

[3] The Lombard king Rothari was apparently the source of the name of the eponymous hero of the poem *König Rother*, discussed below, p.140, but there is no appparent echo of the historical king in the poem's story. The bridewinning tale of an earlier Lombard king, Authari, may have been attached to Rothari to provide the kernel of this story.

sixth century. Clovis and Theoderic were contemporaries and sometime rivals, but they managed to maintain a balance of power that prevented the Franks from evicting the Goths from Southern Gaul and Italy.

ERMANARIC

Ermanaric was a king of the Ostrogoths during the second half of the fourth century. Jordanes (see below, p. 25) reports that he extended the domain of the Ostrogoths from the Black Sea to the Baltic before being defeated by the Huns. He is important to heroic legend because a story that is told of him found its way eventually into the *Hamðismál* of the *Poetic Edda* and the *Völsungasaga*. Jordanes speaks of the "faithless tribe of the Rosomoni" who brought Ermanaric to his end. The king had had a woman of this tribe ripped apart by horses because of her husband's "flight," one assumes either desertion or a joining of the other side. The brothers of the woman, Ammius and Sarus, attacked the king and left him with a severe wound in the side. The Huns used the king's incapacity to attack and defeat the Ostrogoths. The king, "who could bear neither the pain of his wound nor the defeat by the Huns," died in his "110th year." Ammianus Marcelinus, who lived much closer in time to the events, does not refer to the Rosomoni, but he describes Ermanaric's death as a result of the "horror of the impending dangers[. H]e put an end to his fear of these great perils by a voluntary death."[4] Historians have suggested both suicide and ritual regicide. Whatever his age, he probably died in 375. Beyond the cryptic narrative in Jordanes, there is little historical information from which to construct a life of Ermanaric.

THE BURGUNDIANS ON THE RHINE

After several centuries of wandering from the Baltic to central Europe, an East Germanic tribe known as the Burgundians established themselves in 413 as *foederati,* or troops allied to the Romans, on the Rhine. It is possible that their capital (if one can use such a word in this context) was Worms, but this is far from certain. In 435 the Burgundians attempted to extend their influence into the region of modern Belgium, where they were stopped by the Roman general Aëtius. The Burgundian army was then virtually destroyed in a battle with the Huns in 436. All of the royal family were killed in this battle, in which 20,000 Burgundians are said to have fallen. After these events the tribe resumed its wandering until the Romans settled them in the Savoy, the region we associate today with the name Burgundy. Later Burgundian tradition speaks of kings named Gundaharius, Gislaharius, Godomar, and Gibica. All of these names appear in later versions of the Nibelung saga. Gundaharius is clearly Gunther/Gunnar and Gislaharius is Giselher. Godomar may reappear as the

---

[4] Ammianus Marcelinus xxx. 3, 2.

Norse Guttorm, and Gibica appears as Gibech/Gjuki, the father of the other three in both Norse and German legend (the *Nibelungenlied*, however, changes his name to Dancrat). Virtually nothing more is known about the Burgundians on the Rhine.

ATTILA

Attila[5] is much better documented than Ermanaric or the Burgundians, but the information about him is still sketchy. The Huns were an Asiatic nomadic folk active in the region north of the Black Sea during the fourth century. They subjugated the Ostrogoths under Ermanaric to a large extent around 375. Two generations later, under Attila, they swept through what is now Austria and southern Germany until they met Aëtius at the battle of the Catalaunian Fields (Châlon) in 451. The battle was inconclusive, but the Huns were stopped in their westward surge. Until the death of Attila (453) the Huns played an important role in the military politics of the northern reaches of the Roman Empire.

Attila had been dead for almost a century when Jordanes penned his famous description of the Hun leader in 551, but it is the oldest physical description we have. It is possible that the description derives from Priscus, who did see Attila face to face. Jordanes is known to have used his history as a source and this description may have been in the portions that have otherwise been lost.[6]

> He was a man born to shake the races of the world, a terror to all lands, who in some way or other frightened everyone by the dread report noised abroad about him, for he was haughty in his carriage, casting his eyes about him on all sides so that the proud man's power was to be seen in the very movements of his body. A lover of war, he was personally restrained in action, most impressive in counsel, gracious to suppliants, and generous to those to whom he had once given his trust. He was short of stature with a broad chest, massive head, and small eyes. His beard was thin and sprinkled with grey, his nose flat, and his complexion swarthy, showing thus the signs of his origins.[7]

This description is not entirely negative, and it probably reflects the ambivalent attitude of Attila's Germanic neighbors and sometime allies. He was both feared and respected by Germanic and Roman opponents, and he could be a valuable ally. There were positive and negative characteristics enough to feed one-sided portrayals of his career on both sides.

---

[5] This name should be emphasized on the first syllable, but most English speakers accent the second and make it rhyme with villa.

[6] Cf. "Einleitung" in Jordanis Gotengeschichte, tr. Wilhelm Martens (Essen: Phaidon, 1986), 11.

[7] Quoted in Gordon, *The Age of Attila*, 61.

Attila does not seem to have been involved in the defeat of the Burgundians described above, but the presence of Huns in the opposing army would have been enough to associate him with the defeat in the popular mind. In all medieval literary versions of the fall of the Burgundians, Attila plays the role of opponent to Gunther and his brothers.

The one event in Attila's life that did find its way into the heroic tradition was his death. Jordanes reports that Attila died of a hemorrhage (probably nothing worse than a serious nosebleed from which he could have drowned) during his bridal night with a young Germanic woman named Ildico. When his attendants broke into the bridal chamber the next day, they found their leader dead in a pool of blood and the woman weeping. Very soon the story was abroad that the woman had killed Attila as vengeance for kinsmen.

THEODERIC THE GREAT

After Attila's death the Huns soon ceased to be a major force in Europe. The Ostrogoths, who had been subjugated by and allied with the Huns, began to establish their power in the lower Danube region near the Black Sea. One of three brothers who led this resurgence was Thiudimer, whose son, Theoderic,[8] grew up as a hostage at the imperial court in Constantinople. We can assume that he enjoyed the best education of his time and that he was as comfortable in the Roman civilization of late antiquity as he was among his Gothic countrymen. When he reached his majority, Theoderic assumed an important role in the Ostrogothic army. After defeating his major rival for power in the region, a man also named Theoderic (who is differentiated by being called Theoderic Strabo, "the Squinter"), Theoderic led his armies against Odoacer[9] in Northern Italy. He was sent on this mission by the emperor Zeno with the idea of returning Italy to Imperial control. He defeated Odoacer and subsequently murdered him with his own hands.[10] From 493 on he was undisputed king in Italy and over a wide region including eventually even the Visigothic kingdom in Southwestern Gaul and Spain. There is considerable evidence that his reign was one of the more bearable periods for the civilian population of the region during the centuries following the fall of the Western Empire. Shortly before his death in 526, Theoderic was misled by slanders to imprison and eventually execute the

---

[8] Many history books in English spell this name Theodoric, presumably under the influence of the Greek-derived name Theodore. There is no connection between the two names, and the spelling used here reflects that of the Latin sources, which usually Latinize the name as Theodericus. The name should actually be stressed on the initial -e- rather than the following -o-, but, as in the case of Attila, this is probably too much to hope for.

[9] Also spelled Odovacer. He was a member of another East Germanic tribe, the Sciri, and had been set up as king of Italy after the last Roman emperor, Augustulus, was deposed in 476.

[10] The scene is narrated in gory detail by John of Antioch. See the translation in Gordon, *The Age of Attila*, 182f.

philosopher Boethius (who wrote his *Consolation of Philosophy* in prison) and Boethius's father-in-law, Symmachus. He also had Pope John I imprisoned for failing to carry out a mission to his satisfaction. The Pope died while in prison, so his death was also blamed on Theoderic. The murders of Odoacer at the beginning of his reign and of Boethius at the end have left a somewhat bloodthirsty image of a man who was among the more capable rulers during an era that was otherwise sadly lacking in good leadership.

Theoderic's reputation was further blackened for succeeding generations by his adherence to what had become the religion of the Goths, the Arian heresy. Orthodox Roman Catholicism saw the Gothic adherence to this sect as one more piece of evidence that they were barbarians and beyond the pale of civilization. Most of our historical material from the period comes from the pens of Catholic historians who were opposed to the Goths because of their heresy. The major exception is the *Getica* by Jordanes, a Goth of the later sixth century. He was an orthodox Catholic, but his sympathies are generally with his people. This book will be discussed in the next chapter.

At the same time a clerical tradition against Theoderic was being established, the oral tradition of heroic poetry spread an entirely different image of the Ostrogothic king. In the poetic versions Odoacer became a usurper who had forced Theoderic into exile and the conquest became a reconquest of lands legally his. Eventually Odoacer[11] was replaced in the story by Ermanaric, a king who presumably had a much more unsavory reputation in the oral tradition, and the legend of Theoderic gradually became the story we know from the later Middle Ages.

BRÜNHILD

The Merovingian Franks maintained a custom of dividing a king's holdings among his sons. After the uniting of the Franks under Clovis (r.482–511), the large kingdom (extending over most of modern France and beyond) was divided among his four sons. The youngest son of Clovis, Chlothar I, ruled over a united Frankish kingdom after his brothers had died. Chlothar's death in 561 led to a renewed division into four parts, each ruled by one of Chlothar's sons. The wars and treacheries within the family would carry us far beyond the scope of this sketch. Two of the four kings, Chilperic and Sigibert, are the main figures in the struggle that seems to have contributed to the Nibelung legend.

Chilperic held the smallest of the four kingdoms but was spurred by ambition (and almost certainly by his concubine, and later wife, Fredegund) to scheme against his brothers and to try by all means military and political to expand his territory. Chilperic's brother Sigibert sought and won the Visigothic

---

[11] The early ninth-century *Hildebrandslied*, the sole Old High German relic of heroic epic, still speaks of "Otachre" as Dietrich's opponent.

princess from Spain named Brunichildis, usually referred to in our histories as Brünhild. Chilperic tried to match his brother by seeking and marrying Brünhild's sister Galsuintha. Gregory of Tours reports that Fredegund had Galsuintha murdered shortly after her arrival. Fredegund was, in any case, clearly back in charge of matters at Chilperic's court.

Sigibert, for his part, was successful in strengthening his power and even brought heathen Germanic troops from across the Rhine to attack Chilperic. At the height of his military success, Sigibert was murdered, and Gregory of Tours again blames Fredegund. When Sigibert's older brother had died, his kingdom had been divided among the remaining brothers. Sigibert, however, had a young son named Childebert and the kingdom was passed on to him, much to the chagrin of Chilperic and Fredegund, who had hoped to add Sigibert's kingdom to their own. When Childebert reached his majority, he ruled with the support and advice of his mother, Brünhild. Chilperic died a few years later and Fredegund managed to rule in his place. Shortly after her husband's death she revealed that she was pregnant with Chilperic's child. He was named Chlothar II and Fredegund later ruled as his regent. Many years after her death in 597, Chlothar finally managed to capture Brünhild and have her drawn and quartered (613). Brünhild must have been close to seventy at that time. Gregory of Tours saw much of the political evil of his age as the result of Fredegund's machinations, and there is a good chance that he is right in many of the cases. The two powerful women, Fredegund and Brünhild, were certainly among the most interesting figures of their age, and it would be indeed strange if their deeds had not found their way into some kind of popular narrative.

The events of this period of Merovingian history provide at least one name (Brünhild) and several examples of intra-family intrigue and violence that could be incorporated into heroic legend. The name Sigibert is also the only 'sigi-' name in a story that probably did influence the development of the legend, but it would require a great deal of rearranging to make him into Siegfried. If, however, the legend-makers switched Brünhild and Fredegund (as they seem to have), the identification of Sigibert with Siegfried becomes somewhat less problematic. The replacement of Odoacer with the totally unrelated Ermanaric in the Dietrich legend demonstrates how easily figures can change places in legends.

SOURCES AND FURTHER READING

Ammianus Marcellinus. Tr. John G. Rolfe. Cambridge, MA: Harvard University Press, 1938.

Bachrach, Bernard S. "The Hun Army at the Battle of Chalons (451): An Essay in Military Demography." *Ethnogenese und Überlieferung: Angewandte Methoden der Frühmittelalterforschung.* Ed. Karl Brunner and Brigitte Merta. Vienna: Oldenbourg, 1994. 59–67.

Brady, Caroline. *The Legends of Ermanaric.* Berkeley: University of California Press, 1943.

Burns, Thomas S. *A History of the Ostrogoths.* Bloomington: Indiana University Press, 1984.

Goffart, Walter. *The Narrators of Barbarian History (AD 550–800): Jordanes, Gregory of Tours, Bede, and Paul the Deacon.* Princeton: Princeton University Press, 1988.

Gordon, C. D. *The Age of Attila: Fifth Century Byzantium and the Barbarians.* Ann Arbor: University of Michigan Press, 1960.

James, Edward. *The Franks.* Cambridge: Blackwell, 1988.

Musset, Lucien. *The Germanic Invasions: The Making of Europe AD 400–600.* Tr. Edward James and Columba James. University Park: Pennsylvania State University Press, 1975.

Todd, Malcolm. *The Early Germans.* Cambridge: Blackwell, 1992.

Wolfram, Herwig. *History of the Goths.* Tr. Thomas J. Dunlap. Berkeley: University of California Press, 1988.

CHAPTER 3
Historical Sources

PRIMARY HISTORICAL SOURCES

In this chapter only a selection of those historical sources that touch on our subject matter will be described. The term "historical sources" refers to documents that were understood by their authors to be histories. This is not the place to go into questions of historiography, but the writing of history consisted then as now of collecting information about the past. Written information was generally given precedence, but we must keep in mind that ancient and medieval historians often considered oral tradition, including not only narrative reports, but also poetically formed material, to be a reliable source for information. Scholars have discovered more than one "heroic lay" hidden in the Latin prose of these texts.[1]

Lex Burgundionum

During the reign of Theoderic the Great the Burgundians were led by a king named Gundobad. One of his contributions was the first book of laws for the people, which would be of little interest to us if this book had not contained the names of some of the kings who preceded him. These names are given in the forms *Gibica, Godomar, Gislaharius,* and *Gundaharius.* All of these names appear in one form or another in numerous versions of the Nibelung legend. See the Glossary of Names under Gibech, Guttorm, Giselher, and Gunther.

Jordanes

Cassiodorus was a high official in the government of Theoderic the Great, and his history of the Goths would presumably have been a great treasure of Germanic history if it had survived. Jordanes, a Goth at the court in Constantinople, wrote his own history of the Goths based on Cassiodorus's

---

[1] See, for example, Andersson, *Preface*, 7.

work, which he claims to have had in his possession for only three days. He must have had a very good memory to be able to reconstruct as much as he did, but it remains an unreliable text.[2] It is, however, the only source we have for many events in Gothic history, such as the story of Ermanaric's difficulties with the Rosomoni. Jordanes's *Getica*, as it is called in Latin, was composed in 551.

Gregory the Great

Pope Gregory I wrote a number of *Dialogues* in the years 592–594. One of these retells an incident that had been passed on to an acquaintance over several generations. The original narrator had been an official who had been sent with others to Sicily to collect taxes. On the island Lipari they were told that King Theoderic was dead. A hermit told them what he had seen the day before: "Yesterday at the ninth hour he was led here without belt or shoes and with bound hands between Pope John and the patrician Symmachus and thrown into the crater of the volcano nearby." The travelers noted the date and discovered that it was precisely the death-day of the king.

The transmission of this story is probably typical of much oral tradition in a period of limited literacy and even more limited availability of expensive writing materials. Pope Gregory was told the story by a certain Julian, who was an official of the Roman Church and who had died seven years before the incident was written down. Julian had heard the incident from the father of his father-in-law, who had been the tax official in the story. Most such transmission is not so well documented. A recent study,[3] however, has cast the authorship of the *Dialogi* into question, so that the well-established provenance of this story might be only a fable itself.

Gregory of Tours

Gregory of Tours (c. 539–594) became bishop of Tours in 573 during the reign of King Sigibert. He wrote numerous works of Church history, and his *Ten Books of History*, widely known as the *History of the Franks*, is the richest source of information about the first century of Merovingian Gaul. He had a powerful ecclesiastical bias against the violent and treacherous world around him, and he praised Guntram as the one king of the Franks who stayed above most of the feuding between the houses of Chilperic and Sigibert. He attributes saintlike

---

[2] Just how unreliable is a matter of great contention. See Goffart for a discussion of the contention and a realistic assessment of Jordanes's reliability as a source for Cassiodorus. Many writers continue to quote Jordanes as if they were dealing with Cassiodorus. See Theodore M. Andersson, "Cassiodorus and the Gothic Legend of Ermanaric," *Euphorion* 57 (1963): 28-43.

[3] Clark, who also cites the questionable theology of the scene, which interprets the volcano as the actual mouth of Hell, 645-646.

qualities to the king and tells of miracles brought about by the king while he was still alive.

For the period after Gregory's death we are dependent on a chronicler whom later historians called Fredegar. "Fredegar" assembled materials from several different sources to make up a history of the world. He began his history of the Franks with a summary of Gregory and then continues the history from the last decade of the sixth century on.[4] His chronicle is the major source for the last days of Fredegund and Brünhild as well as the so-called *Gesta Theoderici*.

Gesta Theoderici

A fascinating glimpse of the early development of a legendary history of Theoderic is provided in the life of the Gothic king included in Fredegar's chronicle.[5] This text was incorporated in revised and expanded versions in later writers' histories, so that we have three texts that vary strongly from one another but are clearly versions of the same history. Since this text is not well known and is unavailable in German or English translation, we are including a more extensive synopsis of this interesting document than of some others.[6]

> The childless patrician couple Idatius and Eugenia have two servants from Macedonia, Theudorus and Lilia. They are in love, and when a child arrives they are allowed to wed. Lilia is supposed to tell her dream of the first night. She dreams that a tree grows from her and that it is so large that it touches the clouds. Her husband commands her to tell the dream differently: she should say she had seen a stallion and a mare, both of great beauty, and a foal followed them.
>
> A son is born. He is named Theoderic [Theudericus in original] and is adopted by the patrician couple, who raise him lovingly.
>
> After the death of the patrician couple, Theoderic is given military training by Emperor Leo. He is very popular with the Emperor and with the Senators.
>
> Finally, however, envy arises. The Senators seek a way to get rid of him through a command of the Emperor. Only Ptolomaeus remains a true friend who protects him. The Goths attack Rome, but then bow to Leo's command. The Romans and the Goths ask the Emperor for help against the continual attacks by Odoacer and others. Leo sends Theoderic to Rome, where he becomes *patricius*.

---

[4] The portion of "Fredegar" that functions as a continuation of Gregory is contained in Wallace-Hadrill.

[5] This text is unfortunately not in the portions translated by Wallace-Hadrill. It is available in the German translation of the entire work on 50–67.

[6] This synopsis of "Fredegar's" version is translated directly from Roswitha Wisniewski, *Mittelhochdeutsche Dietrichdichtung* (Stuttgart: Metzler, 1986), 61–64.

During the battles with Odoacer, Theoderic has to flee. His mother appears to him and calls on his courage because there is no escape. He battles, defeats, pursues, and kills Odoacer.

His enemies spread the word in Constantinople that he wishes to take over the Western Empire as king. Emperor Leo commands Theoderic to come. He comes with 12,000 Goths. The Senate plans to separate him from his men and kill him as soon as he enters the palace. Theoderic's friend Ptolomaeus warns him of the ambush. Instead of killing him, they decide to take him captive and report back to the Gothic camp that he has fallen in disfavor and deserves death. The Goths are supposed to determine whether he is to be beheaded or thrown to the wild beasts. Before this, however, Ptolomaeus had sent a boy with the message for the Goths to take the senators captive and use them to force the release of Theoderic. This is done with the four senators. Theoderic is freed and returns to Italy. There he fights with Avars and Huns.

One night Theoderic goes out of his camp with four men and encounters the Avar Xerxes. Theoderic commands his men to take him captive since he is alone. Xerxes, however, is able to kill all of Theoderic's men by feigning flight. Then Theoderic fights with him and takes him captive. He tries to win him over to his side but Xerxes refuses. Threats accomplish nothing. Theoderic frees him and he swims across the Danube. When he arrives on the other shore, he declares that he will now voluntarily follow Theoderic. He becomes Theoderic's best protector.

Renewed calumny causes Emperor Leo to command Theoderic to return to Constantinople. A boy is sent to Ptolomaeus, who—prevented by an oath from warning Theoderic outright—tells a fable: When the lion was elected king, the hart appeared to honor him. The lion seized the hart's antlers in order to capture and devour him. The hart fled, leaving the antlers behind. The fox was sent out to invite the hart to come back. He did so and was devoured by the lion. The fox managed to steal the hart's heart, which the lion particularly desired. Asked if he had stolen the heart, the fox said that the hart would not have returned if he had had one. Theoderic recognizes the sense of the fable and returns to Italy.

For forty years Theoderic rules in Italy over a kingdom that stretches from Pannonia to the Rhône and from the Tyrrhenian Sea to the Piedmontese Alps and Isère.

Alarich, the Visigothic king, and Clovis, the Frank king, are at war. At a peace conference the Gothic emissaries carry daggers instead of staves. The negotiations are broken off and Theoderic is supposed to bring about a peaceful settlement. He gives a solution that he is certain will not bring peace: a rider should be covered in gold up to the point of his lance. Alarich has no gold. Clovis defeats and kills Alarich and extends the Frank kingdom over Alarich's kingdom.

Theoderic condemns the innocent Pope Johannes to death and has the patrician Symmachus killed, also for no reason. Because of these crimes divine retribution strikes him and he is killed by his brother Geiserich. In the dialogues of St. Gregory it is told how Pope John and Symmachus lead the defeated Theoderic bound into a volcano in Sicily.

Although "Fredegar's" version of this text comes from only a little over a century after Theoderic's death, we can see clearly the working of traditional narrative patterns in restructuring the historical facts. This story may contain the germ of the exile story in the events leading up to the death of Odoacer. This is a valuable glance into the development of heroic legend at a point early enough in the process to retain many elements of historical fact.

MEDIEVAL CHRONICLES
As has already been noted, written sources are not the major carriers of heroic narrative through the Middle Ages, but there is a continuous interaction between various Latin (and vernacular) chronicles and contemporary orality. Some chroniclers criticize the oral narratives for their "historical" inaccuracy, while others attempt to integrate what they know of legendary history into the framework provided by such written sources as Jordanes. We have no way of knowing to what extent written chronicles influenced the course of oral tradition itself, but most literary works that make use of oral legend seem blissfully unaware of the criticism leveled at them in contemporary Latin chronicles or of the corrections they apply to the stories they are using. The chronicles themselves form a continuous tradition, each one adapting the material of several of its predecessors so that it is often difficult to tell what part of a chronicle is new and what part is from another source. The following examples are only selected stations in this tradition.

Quedlinburg Annals
The eleventh-century annals of Quedlinburg (a small city in Saxony-Anhalt about 45 miles northwest of Halle) survive only in a sixteenth-century copy. There is much debate about how much is original and how much is later interpolation. Most of the entries are in short sentences or even sentence fragments, so that it will probably remain impossible to determine finally what belonged to the original document, but recent research has restored much of what was earlier thought to be interpolated. Not only is it difficult to isolate genuine eleventh-century material from later interpolations, but the original text itself represents a compilation from many sources, including Bede's world chronicle.

The *Annales quedlinburgensis* remain valuable for our purposes because they form the earliest surviving chronicle to show extensive influence from the oral tradition that led to the vernacular literary works of the thirteenth century. The relatively brief passages involved are easier to quote in translation than to summarize:

[...] After the death of Bleda, his brother Attila devastated almost all of Gaul until, as promised by God, the patrician Egidius [Aëtius] and Thurismod, Gothic prince from Rennes [Toulouse?], drove him to flight. At that time Ermanric ruled over all the Goths; he was most skillful in fraud and most liberal in gifts. After the death of his only son, Frideric, by his own will, he hanged his nephews Embrica and Fritla. In the same way—incited by his nephew Odoacer—he drove his nephew Theoderic out of Verona and into exile with Attila. The patrician Aëtius, savior of the people in the East and terror to King Attila, was killed by Valentinian the younger. With him the kingdom in the West fell and it has up to now not been able to be reinstated.[. . .]

Zeno ruled seventeen years. Odoacer, king of the Goths, took Rome.

Anastasius ruled twenty-seven years. Bishop Fulgentius is proclaimed. The killing of Ermanric, the king of the Goths, by the brothers Hamidus, Serla, and Adacarus, whose father [Ermanric] had killed, cutting off his arms and legs in a foul manner, as was fitting. Theoderic, called the Amlung because his ancestor was called Amul, was judged the most powerful of the Goths. And this was Thideric of Bern, about whom the rustics once sang. Theoderic returned to the throne of the Goths with the help of King Attila and forced his cousin Odoacer out of Ravenna. Through the intervention of Attila, Odoacer was not killed but exiled. He was given a small holding near the confluence of the Albia [Elbe] and the Sala [Saale]. [. . .]

When Justinus had ruled nine years, Theoderic reigned over Rome, where he held the holy pontiff of the Romans John in prison in Ravenna until he died; he also killed the most illustrious consuls Symmachus and Boetius[sic]. The same Theoderic in truth died suddenly ninety-eight days after the death of Pope John; his grandson Athalric succeeded to his throne.

[There follows here a long story about the Thuringian king Irminfrid, after which we are told about Attila's death.]

Attila, king of the Huns and the terror of all Europe, was killed with a small knife by a certain girl, whom he had taken forcibly from her unfortunate father.

This chronicle brings Attila, Theoderic, Ermanaric, and even Odoacer together into one generation, clearly reflecting the chronology of legend. Attila is given an extremely long life so that all events of heroic legend take place within his lifetime.

The sentence in which we are told that Theoderic was the Dietrich of Bern, about whom the *rustici* once sang is often thought to be a late interpolation under the influence of the early fifteenth-century chronicle (in German) by Jakob Twinger von Königshofen, a member of a prominent Strasbourg family. Twinger's chronicle speaks of "Dietrich of Bern, about whom the peasants sing and tell so much." It would be easy to imagine how the phrase could have found its way into the manuscript tradition of the *Quedlinburg Annals*, but it should be mentioned that Twinger's chronicle draws on many sources, some of which drew ultimately on the *Quedlinburg Annals* as their sources. The source and age of the remark will never be resolved beyond doubt unless an early manuscript of the *Quedlinburg Annals* turns up. It is important here because it is one of the few references to the performance of Dietrich poems outside of the stories themselves.

A secondary problem is the appearance of both Odoacer and Ermanaric in the same narrative. Ermanaric has not yet clearly occupied the position of Dietrich's nemesis, but he is shown as a cruel ruler in the brief references to the killing of his son, Frideric, and the hanging of his nephews. He is also responsible for the expulsion of Dietrich from his lands in a sentence in which Odoacer appears as the evil advisor. The exile of Odoacer is unique to this source and seems to be there to link the stories to the geographical areas near Quedlinburg. This also seems to be the reason for the extensive interpolation about the Thuringian king Irminfrid.

Frutolf von Michelsberg

Frutolf was a priest at the monastery of Michelsberg in Bamberg. He died in 1103. His chronicle, which was widely read and copied in the later Middle Ages, draws on chronicle texts available to him (including some form of the *Quedlinburg Annals*), early histories (Jordanes, Gregory), and heroic legend, presumably received directly from oral tradition. He was disturbed by the problems of chronology that arose when the reports of Jordanes were placed alongside those of later chronicles and the "facts" of heroic legend. He realized that Ermanaric, Attila, and Theoderic could not possibly have been contemporaries but suggests that it was possible that other men bearing the same name as the historical figures could have lived at the time of Attila. Beyond pointing out the chronological problems he makes no attempt to harmonize the reports or to take sides in deciding who was right or wrong.

Frutolf is also responsible for introducing the story of Theoderic's end related by Gregory the Great (in which Theoderic is ushered into the mouth of a volcano by Pope John and Symmachus) into medieval German chronicle tradition.

Kaiserchronik

An anonymous German verse chronicle composed in Regensburg shortly after 1147, the *Kaiserchronik* is the first vernacular chronicle to tell a version of Dietrich's life. The author accepts the suggestions first put forward by Frutolf that another man named Dietrich had been a contemporary of Attila. The two Dietrichs are differentiated by calling the invented figure "old Dietrich."

The account begins with "Old Dietrich's" refusal to pay tribute to Attila, who is later said to have "drowned in his own blood." "Old Dietrich's" son is Dietmar, who defeats Attila's sons when they demand tribute from him. Later Dietmar's son Dietrich is given as hostage to the emperor Zeno as part of a peace settlement. We are told that he later took up the emperor's standard and forced many lands to pay him tribute.

The story then turns to Aëtius. After an unreasonable demand on the part of the empress that he come and pluck wool with her handmaidens, Aëtius turns to Styria, where he meets with Odoacer, whom he invites to come and rule Rome in defiance of Zeno. Odoacer advances to Rome, where he receives the crown. Zeno accepts Dietrich's offer to go and set things right. Dietrich assembles an army from all over the known world (from Russia to Africa), and it is said that except for Julius Caesar no one had ever assembled such an army, which is reported to have numbered 200,000 men. Aëtius leads the Romans, and the two armies meet before Ravenna, where Dietrich soon beheads Aëtius in battle. Dietrich besieges Odoacer in Ravenna until the latter challenges him to single combat, in spite of the fact that Dietrich is not legitimately born. Dietrich defeats him and takes the throne over Italy. Boethius and Seneca (Symmachus) and Pope John complain to Zeno that it is improper that an illegitimately born man should rule over Italy. Dietrich has John imprisoned in Pavia, where he starves to death. He is avenged when Pope John commands devils to carry Dietrich to the mountain Vulcan.

The account closes with this swipe at the legendary tradition: "Whoever maintains that Dietrich ever saw Etzel, let him look into the book and see that it was forty-three years after Etzel was buried in Ofen before Dietrich was born. He was raised in Greece, where he also achieved his knighthood, he was sent to Rome, and was buried in Vulcan. Here the lies must have an end." (14176–14187)

The poet overshoots the mark with his forty-three years, since it was only a matter of a year or two between Attila's death and Theoderic's birth, but he makes his point that the two were not contemporaries. Almost more important than the facts themselves is the insistence on the primacy of written historical records over the universally known Dietrich legends.

The *Kaiserchronik* differs from the Latin chronicles we have been considering in its lively presentation of history. In place of dry sequences of facts we find imagined dialogue carrying the most dramatic moments forward. There are no set scenes in the passage under consideration, but the characters break out into speeches reflecting their thoughts and course of action. The verse is rough and the rhymes frequently impure, as one would expect of a work composed at that point in the development of German narrative verse.

Other High Medieval Historical Sources
Most late medieval chronicles base their treatment of Dietrich on one or more of the earlier chronicles mentioned above. Frutolf is a major source for many assemblers of chronicles, and his version—more or less influenced by heroic legend—is probably the one most widely used. Additional elements are added from various sources as time goes on. The *Cologne Kings' Chronicle,* for example, reports the appearance of a giant phantom on a black horse along the banks of the Moselle who identified himself as Dietrich of Bern and warned of calamities that would be visited on the Empire. This apparition was reported to have taken place in 1197, some months before the death of the emperor Henry VI, an event that plunged the Empire into several years of unrest.

Many later chronicles tell some version of the story of Dietrich's being tossed into a volcano, and most seem concerned to emphasize that he will never return. The repeated emphasis on this point suggests that there was a widespread belief that Dietrich would return at a time of great need. This motif is, of course, attached elsewhere to Arthur, Charlemagne, and Barbarossa. The appearance of a gigantic ghost of Dietrich in the *Cologne Kings' Chronicle* mentioned above may be related to this expectation.

The version of the Dietrich's end we find in the *Þiðrekssaga* (Dietrich is carried away on the back of a mysterious black horse) leads naturally to his association with the Wild Hunt. This legend is widespread in Europe, and different historical and mythical figures are reported as the leader of the nocturnal hunt. In late medieval sources Dietrich is repeatedly mentioned as its leader.

SOURCES AND FURTHER READING
Clark, Francis. *The Pseudo-Gregorian Dialogues.* 2 vols. Leiden: Brill, 1987. Includes Latin text of the *Dialogi.*

"Fredegar." *Die vier Bücher der Chroniken des sogenannten Fredegar.* Tr. Andreas Kusternigg. Darmstadt: Wissenschaftliche Buchgesellschaft, 1982.

Goffart, Walter. *The Narrators of Barbarian History (AD 550–800): Jordanes, Gregory of Tours, Bede, and Paul the Deacon.* Princeton: Princeton University Press, 1988.

St. Gregory the Great. *Dialogues.* Tr. Odo John Zimmerman. New York: Fathers of the Church, 1959. A sometimes free translation. The passage concerning Theoderic occurs on 228.

Gregory of Tours. *History of the Franks.* Tr. Lewis Thorpe. Harmondsworth, Middlesex: Penguin, 1974.

Grimm, Wilhelm *Die deutsche Heldensage: Unter Hinzufügung der Nachträge von Karl Müllenhoff und Oskar Jänicke aus der Zeitschrift für deutsches Altertum.* Supplements by Karl Müllenhoff and Oskar Jänicke. 4th ed. Darmstadt: Wissenschaftliche Buchgesellschaft, 1957. Extensive collection of material from chronicles and other medieval texts referring to heroic legend. Contains the relevant passages of most of the texts under consideration in this chapter.

Gschwantler, Otto. "Frutolf von Michelsberg und die Heldensage." *Philologische Untersuchungen gewidmet Elfriede Stutz zum 65. Geburtstag.* Ed. Alfred Ebenbauer. Vienna: Braumüller, 1984. 196–211. Includes the Latin text of the relevant passages of Frutolf's chronicle.

————. "Die Heldensagen-Passagen in den Quedlinburger Annalen und in der Würzburger Chronik." *Linguistica et Philologica: Gedenkschrift für Björn Collinder.* Eds. Otto Gschwantler, Károly Rédei, and Hermann Reichert. Vienna: Braumüller, 1984. 135–181. Includes the Latin text of the relevant passages from the *Quedlinburg Annals* and the *Würzburg Chronicle.*

————. "Zeugnisse zur Dietrichsage in der Historiographie von 1100 bis gegen 1350." *HH,* 35–80. Overview of the treatment of the Dietrich legend in medieval German chronicles.

Jordanes. *The Gothic History of Jordanes in English Version.* Tr. Charles Christopher Mierow. 2d. ed. Princeton: Princeton University Press, 1915. Reprint. New York, 1960.

Kaiserchronik eines Regensburger Geistlichen. Ed. Edward Schröder. Hannover, 1892.

Stackmann, Karl. "Dietrich von Bern in der Kaiserchronik: Struktur als Anweisung zur Deutung." *Idee, Gestalt, Geschichte: Festschrift für Klaus Von See.* Ed. Gerd-Wolfgang Weber. Odense: Odense University Press, 1988. 137–142.

CHAPTER 4

Oral Transmission

This chapter will consist almost entirely of supposition and extrapolation. The oral transmission of Germanic heroic legend is entirely lost to us. We have a number of written documents that may be fairly close in form and content to the oral tradition, but we cannot be certain that any of them are literal transcriptions of oral texts. They have all gone through some kind of recomposition or editing on the part of the person who committed them to writing.

We are in something like the situation of paleontologists who reconstruct ancient animals and plants from the fossil imprints left in sedimentary rock. And like those scientists we can argue from the known to the unknown. The known consists of a rich collection of written narratives, mainly from the thirteenth century. These stories are connected by some kind of invisible cord to historical events of the fourth and fifth centuries. It is this invisible cord that is so fascinating. Theodore Andersson has remarked that "we know both too much and too little about the prototypes of the *Nibelungenlied*" (*Preface*, 105). We know too much about the oral tradition leading up to the medieval epic to simply leave it alone, and we know too little to reconstruct the missing pieces with any assurance of accuracy.

We do know a great deal more about the operation of oral poetic traditions than the scholars who established the study of Germanic heroic poetry in the nineteenth century. Before we speculate on the nature of the Germanic tradition, we need to review briefly both the ideas that formed traditional thinking on the subject and the evidence that has forced us to change the way we think about oral poetry.

EPIC THEORY FROM THE NINETEENTH CENTURY
One thing seemed clear to all scholars working on the problem of oral narrative beginning in the late eighteenth century. The poems composed without the help of writing had to be short, so that they could be memorized and passed on more or less verbatim from one singer to another. Most theorists imagined a form of

composition rather like that used by writers in which the poet would compose his work in private, writing it on his memory so to speak, and then present it as a completed masterpiece to his public.

There is even evidence for this sort of composition in the Old Norse saga of Egil Skallagrimsson. Egil was forced to compose a large poem in honor of his captor, Eirik Bloodaxe, in order to save his life. He spent the night in seclusion and was almost prevented from completing his task by the chirping of a particularly persistent bird outside his window. Egil's friend Arinbjörn eventually drove the bird away and Egil was able to complete the composition of his 144-line masterwork. Egil's poem was not an example of traditional heroic poetry, but rather of a specific kind of panegyric known today as skaldic poetry. When we return to the question of traditional composition, we will see how different oral epic narrative is from this kind of composition.

Early scholars had little or no opportunity to experience oral epic in performance. The closest thing to oral heroic epic available to most European scholars before the beginning of the twentieth century was the folk ballad. Since the folk ballad was the property of lower classes, it was never seriously considered as an exemplar of the kind of oral song that entertained medieval kings and princes.

After establishing (logically rather than empirically) that oral song lived only in relatively short memorized lays, scholars were faced with the fact that most early traditional poetry assumes the form of epic. The Homeric epics are the oldest narrative texts in Greek, but they were much too long for oral transmission according to the prevailing theory. In 1795 Friedrich August Wolf attempted to explain the development of the Homeric epics from shorter songs through a process of agglutination. The singers learned each of the short songs, and the epic was put together in writing by an editor who brought all of the traditional songs together. This notion was applied by Karl Lachmann to the *Nibelungenlied* in 1816 and formed the basis for the *Liedertheorie* that was virtually dogma on the subject throughout the nineteenth and early twentieth centuries. According to Lachmann the oral songs that made up the Nibelung legend were strung together by an editor like pearls on a string to form the epic poem we possess. The task of the scholar was to recognize the junctures between the individual songs. Wolf's and Lachmann's theory even inspired the Finnish scholar Elias Lönnrot to assemble short songs from the oral heroic tradition of his homeland into what is today considered the Finnish national epic, the *Kalevala*.

Most scholars dealing with Germanic epic today consider the new *Liedertheorie* developed by Andreas Heusler (*Lied und Epos in germanischer Sagendichtung*, 1905) to have marked a revolution in the study of medieval Germanic epic. Heusler based his work on the songs of the *Poetic Edda* and came to the conclusion that (oral) heroic songs did not stand in the same relation to (written) epics as pearls to a strand, but rather as saplings to a tree. According to Heusler's theory the short songs generally cover an entire story, and this story was simply increased by the addition of detail and sub-plots to achieve what Heusler called epic breadth. Lachmann saw the way from lay to epic as additive, one lay added to the next without major change. Heusler saw the way as expansive, each lay was expanded by the addition of detail and incident to make up an epic. There is doubtless some truth in Heusler's idea that the written epics were expanded versions of the material told in oral songs, but it is still based on a profound ignorance of the nature of oral epic poetry.

In spite of major differences in emphasis, all of the scholarly theories from Wolf to Heusler[1] had one important thing in common. They assumed that oral poetry had to consist of short songs that could be memorized. The *Hildebrandslied* and the poems of the *Poetic Edda* seemed to provide perfect examples. An additional point that Heusler invariably made was that each of these songs was the unique creative work of an individual poet. He held the idea of poetry composed by "the people" in great contempt and held any concept of collective authorship to be "romantic." Heusler's use of this term as a pejorative is ironic, because his idea of the individual creative artist in oral tradition is just as much a product of romantic thinking as the idea of *Volkspoesie*. Empirical studies of real oral epic have shown that the oral poet is dependent both on the collective tradition and on his own individual talents.

ORAL POETRY

The early twentieth century began to see the application of more than haphazard observation to the question of living oral epic. Inspired by the Croatian folklorist Matija Murko, the Homeric scholar Milman Parry and his assistant Albert B. Lord made an extensive study of oral poetry in performance in mainly Muslim areas of Yugoslavia beginning in the early 1930s. They recorded some 15,000 texts on phonograph records and were able to show that songs of the breadth and length of the Homeric epics could actually be produced by illiterate singers. Such long songs were not typical of oral performance, but the special situation of being able to record for as long as they wanted to without disturbance allowed exceptional singers to produce epics of over 12,000 lines. Comparative scholars have argued that the ancient or medieval situation of dictation might have inspired poets to surpass their traditions and produce the large book-length epics we know.

The most important realization to come out of these studies was that the songs were not memorized word for word, but rather that they were composed during performance using a highly formulaic poetic language that made the

---

[1] Heusler's picture of the oral-traditional Germanic *Heldenlied* is still influential. See Andersson, "Die Oral-Formulaic Poetry im Germanischen," and Ebenbauer, "Heldenlied," for contemporary examples of "Heuslerism."

production of "correct" verse lines almost easy. The singers maintained that they never changed a word in what they sang, but the recorded texts made it clear that no two texts were identical. Parry and Lord observed that a fixed memorized text was virtually an impossibility in this tradition.

There was also no "original" in our sense of an original work of art, and no "correct" text from which others somehow deviated. There was certainly a first performance of a new song on a given topic, but Lord observed that the first performance was seldom a very good song. The story had to find its way through countless performances into a traditional pattern using traditional motifs. Like the archetypes of Jung's psychology, the tradition provides a limited number of story patterns that are then given individual shape through the addition of specific elements from the historical event. The unique kernel of historical fact is often difficult to recognize in the complex weave of traditional song.

In place of the romantic notion that "the people" could somehow generate poetry spontaneously, the new theory made it clear that oral poetry was the product of individual singers working within a collective poetic tradition. The songs were composed in performance using language, formulas, motifs, and stories known to all singers. The singers were men[2] who had been exposed to the tradition from childhood on and who were somehow inspired to learn the art for themselves. Lord's famous study *The Singer of Tales* gives a complete picture of this tradition ranging from the formal nature of the poetry itself to the training and career of the individual singer. It is the basis for any study of oral poetry, even if some details of his theory cannot be applied without adjustment to other traditions. The Parry-Lord Theory, as it has come to be called, does not say how extensive oral narrative poetry—oral epic—*must* exist, but it does show how it *can* exist. If we find a widespread poetic tradition that exhibits the formulaic language and other traditional features of oral-formulaic epic composition, then the simplest, and therefore most likely, explanation is that the texts draw on a common oral epic tradition of the kind described by Parry and Lord.

The work of Parry and Lord emphasized oral composition in performance, but Lord was also at great pains to emphasize the necessary conservatism of the oral tradition. The individual singer might be able to add brilliance and detail to a song, but he could not make sweeping changes in its content. Any changes that took place in the substance of the songs as they were transmitted would have to have been so gradual that neither the singers nor the audience would be aware of them. This helps to explain the astounding level of stability of the stories as they spread through space and time.

After the flush of enthusiasm following the early publications using the "oral-formulaic theory," as it was called both by its proponents and its detractors, there

---

[2] In the South Slavic tradition the epic songs are the exclusive province of male singers. There is a specific genre known as "women's songs" that is lyric, not epic, in nature.

followed a period of sobering reconsideration during which some much-needed adjustment of terminology took place. Lord and his closest associates continued to equate "oral" with "oral-formulaic" and used the term to describe only the specific kind of oral epic discussed above. Ruth Finnegan and others have been quick to point out that there are many different kinds of pre-literate and thus "oral" poetry that do not fall into this category. The most usual contrast to the semi-improvisational style of the South Slavic oral epic is memorized verse of the kind we find in medieval Scandinavia. This is the kind of transmission the literary historians imagined in the first place, but it seems to be a much later development in the Germanic languages than they had imagined.

GERMANIC ORAL NARRATIVE POETRY

In the introductory chapter we quoted a passage from Tacitus that says that [oral] songs are the only form of history known to the Germani. We have no way of knowing what that poetry was like, but we can put together a picture of what was certainly a common Germanic poetic tradition in later centuries (perhaps 700– 1100) from the bits and pieces we have from the Carolingian period (c. 800) onward. Scraps of early inscriptions suggest that the verse form had been relatively stable for some centuries before that.

During most of the period in question virtually all narrative poetry was in the form of alliterative long-line verse of the kind we know best from its literary adoption in Old English poetry. We find the same form in Old High German, in Old Saxon, and—with some variations—in Old Norse poetry. A few lines from the Old English *Beowulf* will serve to illustrate the form.

```
. . .              Sigemunde gesprong
æfter death-dæge   dom unlytel,
syþan wiges heard  wyrm acwealde,
hordes hyrde.
```
Sigemund gained
after [his] death-day   great [lit. unlittle] fame,
since the battle-hardened man   killed the dragon,
the protector of the hoard.

In the first full line of our excerpt the *d* of *death-dæge* ties the first half-line to the *d* of *dom* in the second. This poetic linking of the beginning of words is called "alliteration." The second full line alliterates on *w*. This form of "rhyme" arises naturally within the Germanic languages, with their heavy stress on the first syllable of most words. There are four heavy stresses in each long line, at least two of which (one in each half-line) must carry alliterating syllables.

The presence of an identical verse form in Old English, Old Saxon, and Old High German poetry makes it probable that the alliterative long line we know from the Old English *Beowulf* (MS. from c. 1000), the Old High German *Hildebrandslied* (c. 800), and the Old Saxon *Heliand* (c. 840) was the standard unit of Germanic narrative verse. The same line occurs with some variance and grouped into stanzas in Old Norse heroic narrative, which was recorded in the thirteenth century. Although very little of the material we have in this verse form can be considered to be an unaltered representation of oral narrative in performance, the surviving texts are built on a formulaic language, a use of traditional motifs and type-scenes, and ancient traditional stories in a form highly reminiscent of South Slavic oral song. These characteristics allow us to make fairly confident statements about the shape and style of the oral tradition that generated these elements, since it is highly unlikely that they would arise in a purely written tradition of poetry.

The only text before the thirteenth century that completely fits into the range of this book is the Old High German *Hildebrandslied*. This text will be discussed in detail below, but it is important in the battle between what we can call the old theory (short songs with fixed texts) and the new theory (longer songs in an improvisational form—oral poetry). The length of the surviving fragment (some sixty-four lines) would seem to let us identify it easily as a short *Heldenlied* of the kind envisioned by both Lachmann and Heusler, but when we look at the density of the narrative, we see that it is quite "loose," full of repetitions and other signs of an improvisational style.[3] It shows clearly the form and style of German oral heroic poetry of the time. This text also locates the legend of Dietrich in Germany, probably in the south, around the year 800.

The Common Form

The poetic form described above is common to the earliest traces we have of narrative verse in various Germanic languages. This form was adopted for many purposes by the writers of Old English verse. We find heroic epic, elegy, biblical narrative, saints' lives, and many other genres using the same verse form. The different genres also make extensive use of formulaic language and even of formulaic themes and type-scenes that could scarcely have originated anywhere but in the native oral tradition. The Old English poetry we have in writing is almost certainly the product of literary composition, i.e. composition in writing, but its use of a language typical of oral poetry is powerful evidence for the existence of traditional poetry in that form.

We find confirmation of this supposition when we look at the verse form adopted by Old High German and Old Saxon writers on the Continent. The Old High German *Hildebrandslied* is the most important text in this connection, because it also represents heroic narrative in a form we can assume to be very

---

[3] The details of this argument are contained in Haymes, "Oral Poetry and the Germanic Heldenlied."

close to the oral original. The writings of Otfrid von Weissenburg (a ninth-century cleric, who wrote a life of Christ in Old High German verse), however, also make extensive use of the conventions of Germanic verse, although he adds a primitive sort of end-rhyme to the verses and tends to neglect the alliterative joining of half-lines as a result.

The Old Saxon *Heliand,* on the other hand, adopts the native Germanic verse form and its vocabulary almost without change to tell the story of Christ. The same is true of the Old Saxon *Genesis* that seems to be a source for an Old English poem on the same subject.

A number of scholars have put up a spirited resistance to the use of oral-formulaic theory to describe the Germanic heroic tradition. The most persuasive of these Neo-Heuslerians is probably Theodore Andersson, who has published several studies designed to show the irrelevance of the Parry-Lord theory to the Germanic past. He argues that the only work that shows the epic breadth we would attribute to an oral-formulaic tradition is *Beowulf* and that all other texts from the Germanic past fall into the category of short heroic lay. He admits the presence of formulas and type-scenes but denies their relevance to the question of oral-formulaic vs. memorized transmission. Many scholars have held fast to the idea of short memorized heroic lays in the Heusler mode without seriously confronting the questions raised by Heusler's many critics, not all of whom come from the oral-formulaic "camp," but Andersson is virtually the only one who has met the challenge of the oral theory head-on from a position of orthodox Heuslerism.

Andersson explains the broad epic style of *Beowulf* and the Old English biblical and hagiographic epic through the influence of Virgil and other classical models, while maintaining that the *Hildebrandslied, Waldere, Finnsburh,* and the poems of the *Poetic Edda* represent a tradition of short memorized lays of the kind postulated by Heusler.

Heusler did not limit himself to a discussion of the length and narrative density of the Germanic *Heldenlied.* He also attempted to describe the esthetic and generic nature of the lost poems. The songs used historical events as their matter, but the poets extracted the tragic essence from historical events and distilled them into concentrated works of art. According to this view, the heroic songs focused on the tragic kernel of the story and presented the events in the form of carefully structured scenes in which dialogue was the main element. The songs were no longer carriers of history, but artistic formulations of universal human conflict and tragedy.

With their focus on the "individual creative artist," Heusler's disciples must have seen the oral-formulaic theory with its emphasis on traditional composition as a return to the romantic heresy of *Volkspoesie,* the notion that the people as a whole could somehow collectively generate poetry. In fact some early oral-formulaic studies in medieval literature (such as Borghart) saw their work as just such a return to the generation of the Brothers Grimm. This is not the case at all. In fact Lord goes out of his way to show that the best songs are the work of exceptionally gifted singers, whose work often changed the way a song was transmitted by later generations. The individual poetic genius imagined by the post-romantic generation of Heusler is still a part of the oral tradition, but the individual contributions cannot be sorted out with the simplicity posited by Heusler.

In spite of spirited opposition on the part of Neo-Heuslerians, it is difficult to come to any other conclusion than that the Germanic peoples of Western Europe had a common tradition of oral-formulaic epic poetry during the period from the fifth to the eleventh century using the verse form, language, and motifs we find in the first written texts in Old English, Old High German, and Old Saxon. It is highly probable that this tradition was a continuation of the ancient songs referred to by Tacitus in the first century, although this will probably always remain an unprovable supposition.

The Development of the Middle High German Form

For some reason the individual traditions began to develop different traits at about the same time as the languages made their shift from the early medieval form (Old English, Old High German) to their high medieval form (Middle English, Middle High German). Germany showed the earliest tendency toward end-rhyme with the work of Otfrid von Weissenburg mentioned above. As early as the eleventh century we find evidence of what may have been end-rhymed oral narrative poetry (Metzner, *Balladendichtung*). By the end of the twelfth century end-rhymed stanzas had become the standard form of German heroic epic. The form we find in the *Nibelungenlied, Alpharts Tod*, the *Ortnit-Wolfdietrich* poems, and with some changes in the *Kudrun* and *Rabenschlacht* is almost certainly the form in which heroic stories were narrated in the oral tradition between c. 1150 and 1500. We still find the end-rhymed long lines arranged as two-line ballad strophes in the *Younger Hildebrandslied, Koninc Ermenríkes Dôt*, and the *Hürnen Seyfrid*, all of which were apparently first written down in the fifteenth and in some cases even the sixteenth century. The ballad strophe we observe here was in wide use throughout the Germanic world and is still used in many English and American ballads today.

The great mystery of the German strophe is its development during the time between the ninth and the twelfth centuries. We have no indication of how the change to end-rhyme found its way into vernacular poetry outside of clerical experiments such as those of Otfrid. We do find that virtually all German verse after the middle of the eleventh century is rhymed, although the Latin translation of the *Tanzlied von Kölbigk* is the closest thing to solid evidence of rhymed long lines before the *Nibelungenlied*, and many would question its value as proof of anything, since we only have the Latin translation and all German versions are reconstructions.

The Special Case of Old Norse

German theorists of the Heusler school delight in dividing the transmission of heroic legend into "bound" and "unbound" forms, by which they normally mean verse and prose. More recent work under the influence of the oral-poetry theory has shown us that verse is not always as "bound" as the Heuslerians would have it and that prose narrative may be almost as restricted by tradition and traditional form as verse. Medieval Scandinavia is the place where this can be observed most clearly.

Old Norse developed two forms of oral verbal art that were virtually unknown in the rest of Germania. The first of these was a tightly organized form of verse known as "skaldic" verse from the Old Norse word for poet, "skáld."[4] These verses were composed in stanzas in which virtually every aspect of the text was determined by rules about the number of syllables, internal rhyme, and so on. These poems were composed to praise great leaders, usually kings and earls after significant events, and most of them were quite short. A large number survive only in individual stanzas while a few are of considerable length. Egil's famous *drápa* known as *Höfuðlausn* ("Head Ransom") reaches the stately length of 144 lines. We have already mentioned the famous narrative in *Egilssaga Skallagrímssonar* of the composition of this poem. The tight organization of these verses required that they be memorized word for word, and the special gifts needed to compose and memorize such poems became the skills expected of court poets.

There is no way to be sure, but it seems likely that the demand for literal memorization required for skaldic verse drove out the freer style of poetic composition we have seen in Old English, Old High German, and Old Saxon poetry. In *The Singer of Tales* Albert Lord explored the effect of literacy on oral poets and discovered that the poets, when faced with written texts and the ability to read (and memorize) them, ceased to be oral poets in the traditional sense. They were no longer able to perform songs without memorizing them, and the art of oral composition quickly died out.

Faced with a "technique" of poetic composition every bit as alien to oral-formulaic composition as writing, the Old Norse version of the common Germanic tradition was apparently supplanted by two derivative forms: prose

---

[4] According to Richard Cleasby and Gudbrand Vigfusson, *An Icelandic-English Dictionary*, 2d Edition by William A. Craigie (Oxford: Clarendon, 1957), s.v. "skáld," the etymology of this word is disputed, but the editors of the dictionary lean toward a relation with English "scold" and German "schelten," a connection that points out the originally negative role of this poetry. By the tenth century skaldic poetry had become a special means of praise of rulers.

narrative and short memorized songs of heroic content. The former became the ground in which the great sagas of Iceland grew, and the latter became the songs of the *Poetic Edda.*

There was probably always a bit of "prose" retelling of heroic events, but it did not develop into an art form until the competing oral epic disappeared and left prose holding the narrative bag. The long winters and the annual Alþing (assembly) have often been cited as the environmental influences that provided an opportunity for the composition of the oral forerunners of the great sagas. The written sagas betray roots in genealogical narratives, stories transmitted to legitimize land holdings, and in heroic narratives about the early settlers of Iceland. There is no evidence that the Icelanders ever composed oral epic about the deeds of their Icelandic ancestors. There is plenty of circumstantial evidence, on the other hand, to show that extensive knowledge about the early history of Iceland was passed on in the form of oral prose narrative and that these prose narratives became the material out of which the great literary sagas of the thirteenth and fourteenth centuries were fashioned.

Skaldic poetry, on the other hand, demanded that the heroic and mythic stories of the Germanic past be kept in the mind of the audience. The skaldic style was richly allusive and required that the audience recognize references to many obscure episodes of Germanic myth and legend, including the Nibelung and Dietrich legends. One can only assume that the same skalds who showed such economy of means in their skaldic poetry found it necessary to recast the half-improvised traditional songs into short, compact retellings that could be memorized and passed down from poet to poet. The first fruits of this were probably the narrative songs of the kind best represented by the *Atlakviða* in the *Poetic Edda.* Here the traditional story is presented in relatively straightforward narrative with few "skaldic" mannerisms. Later poems such as the *Helreið Brynhildar* and the four Guðrún poems betray more "skaldic" characteristic and represent in some cases what can only be called a "fantasy on heroic themes."

Mythological materials were condensed into compendia such as the *Völuspá,* the Eddic lay that tells of the creation and destruction of the world, and the *Hávamál,* a sort of Eddic equivalent to the Old Testament *Proverbs.* If our hypothesis about their origin is correct, each of these poems was originally the work of a skald concerned to keep the stories he needed as background to his praise poetry before his public. Since many of these songs spent a century or two in oral transmission, it is probable that they also underwent some changes along the way, in spite of their more stable form.

By the middle of the thirteenth century, when the *Poetic Edda* was written down, some of the poetic tradition seems to have become fragmented. There are songs, such as the *Völundarkviða,* that are imbedded in some kind of explanatory prose while others stand on their own. It seems likely that some of the individual stanzas had lost their connection to a coherent story and so it was necessary to explain their place in the overall legend. There are two passages (*Frá dauða Sinfjötla* and *Dráp Niflunga*) that are entirely in prose. The *Völsungasaga* may be a more extensive version of the same thing in which the narrative is shifted almost entirely to prose and the verses are included almost as decoration. Most of the verses we have in the *Völsungasaga* are also contained in the *Poetic Edda* manuscript. The *Prose Edda* of Snorri Sturluson does much the same thing with mythological verse. It may well be that the usual home of Eddic poetry in the thirteenth century was imbedded in prose narrative. If the songs were regularly performed and understood by their audiences, there would have been no need for the kind of explanatory prose we find even in the Codex Regius manuscript of the *Poetic Edda*.

Snorri's *Prose Edda* shows clearly why a knowledge of mythological and heroic legend was necessary for the composition and understanding of skaldic poetry. Most of the book consists of retellings of traditional stories along with examples of the most common kennings associated with them. A kenning is a veiled reference to an object, usually associating it with a well-known incident in traditional lore. Since Fáfnir the dragon is depicted as sleeping on a bed of treasure, gold might be referred to simply as "Fáfnir's bed" or "the dragon's bed." Without a wide knowledge of traditional mythological and heroic stories, a poet of the thirteenth century would have been unable to unravel the complicated language of the older skaldic poetry and would have been equally unable to compose poetry of his own.

Iceland of the thirteenth century had many oral and literate genres. We can imagine that the oral tradition included narrative in prose, traditional songs embedded in explanatory prose, and some few songs that needed no such buttressing. The presence of relatively new songs in the *Poetic Edda* collection suggests that the composition of poems on ancient themes had by no means ceased at the time the songs were collected in writing, but these late songs are also those that are farthest from the style we have postulated as a common Germanic narrative style as found in Old English, Old High German, and Old Saxon poetry. It is possible that Scandinavia had always had a tendency toward shorter, more stable poems, but that cannot be demonstrated from the written documents that survive. We can only recognize that Scandinavia in general and Iceland in particular had developed a special style for the transmission of heroic legend that has no parallel elsewhere in Germania.

THE ORAL TRANSMISSION OF GERMANIC HEROIC LEGEND

We have virtually no traces of the tradition that must have carried Germanic legend from the fourth and fifth centuries to the ninth when elements of the stories find their way onto parchment in England and Germany, and pictorial and name evidence makes it apparent that they were also known in Scandinavia. We can only guess about the routes of transmission. The Goths did not maintain a linguistic community far into the Middle Ages. Virtually all descendants of the Goths (and their fellow East Germani, the Burgundians) spoke Latin by the end of the seventh century. In spite of their more thorough replacement of Roman institutions with Germanic ones, the Lombards soon followed them into linguistic oblivion. The Lombards shared a long border with the Bavarians, who had established themselves in the region between the Alps and the Danube. They seem to have had close connections with the Lombards (members of the Bavarian ducal house ruled the Lombards for several decades), and it is quite possible that the stories of Ermanaric, Theoderic, and Odoacer found their way into the Germanic heartland through this Alpine channel.[5]

Another probable route is the Frankish kingdom that bridged the distance from the Gothic-Roman south to the purely Germanic Rhineland. It is quite possible that the legends took both routes. The presence of Frankish names such as Brünhild[6] and Siegfried indicates that the Franks had at least some role in the transmission and development of the legends. There were many connections between the Gothic kingdoms and the Frankish kingdom during the fifth and sixth centuries, and the history of the Goths was known in some detail to Isidor of Seville in the Visigothic kingdom of Spain in the early seventh century.[7] In the Icelandic texts of the thirteenth and fourteenth centuries the figures of the Nibelung legend are referred to variously as Franks, Goths, and Huns with no recognizable pattern. Only the *Nibelungenlied* identifies the occupants of the Worms kingdom as Burgundians.

The Old English poem *Widsiþ* may give a clue to the propagation of Germanic legend. The poem tells of a poet who travels throughout the Germanic world and who knows about all of the stories we are discussing here. Such singers of tales may have wandered from the Mediterranean to Scandinavia bearing these stories in heroic song. The erratic travels of a "Widsiþ" would make the recognition of clear-cut patterns of dissemination impossible.

The one route heroic legend did not take was through written texts. It has been suggested that works like the *Nibelungenlied* were historical fiction built on chronicle knowledge about the past. Many scholars are uncomfortable with missing links in the written historical chain. We need to keep in mind, however, that the legends know much that is not in the chronicles and vice versa. The so-called historical sources, as we saw in the previous chapter, provide a very

---

[5] One scholar buttressed his argument for the Lombard connection to the point of translating the Old High German *Hildebrandslied* into his reconstruction of Lombard (Krogmann, *Hildebrandslied*).

[6] Brunichildis was a Gothic princess from Spain, but her story takes place among the Franks and it is in their histories that we find her name.

[7] Isidore avoids the kinds of stories that find their way into heroic legend. When he deviates from the straightforward listing of kings and events, it is usually to tell a pious story such as that of the Roman women who protected the wealth of St. Peter's church from the invading Goths under Alaric.

different image of the figures of heroic legend. For example, the legends have a largely positive view of Theoderic and Attila, both of whom were thoroughly damned in the clerical written tradition. Only in an oral tradition largely insulated from the written histories could the positive view of these two men we find in medieval epic come into being and survive.

The evidence points toward a northward migration of the heroic stories through traveling singers during the period from the sixth to the ninth century. The fact that we have almost no evidence of such migration other than the fact that it took place is troubling, but there is a general lack of information about most of Europe during this period. The earliest texts having to do with our topic (the Old English *Widsip* and the Old High German *Hildebrandslied*) both suggest extensive knowledge of the legendary history of the Goths and other Germanic tribes at the time they were written down. Oral dissemination is the simplest and most efficient explanation for the spread of Germanic legend, and the homogeneity of the tradition across wide geographical (and temporal) distances makes the use of oral-formulaic verse the likely vehicle of this transmission.

SOURCES AND FURTHER READING

Andersson, Theodore M. *A Preface to the Nibelungenlied.* Stanford: Stanford University Press, 1987.

———. "Die Oral-Formulaic Poetry im Germanischen." *HH*, 1–14.

Bäuml, Franz H. "Der Übergang mündlicher zur artes-bestimmten Literatur des Mittelalters. Gedanken und Bedenken." *Festschrift für Gerhard Eis.* Eds. Gundolf Keil et al. Stuttgart: Metzler, 1970, 1–10.

———. "From Illiteracy to Literacy: Prolegomena to a Study of the Nibelungenlied." *Forum for Modern Language Studies* 10 (1974): 248–259.

———, and Agnes M. Bruno. "Weiteres zur mündlichen Uberlieferung des Nibelungenliedes." *DVLG* 46 (1972): 479–493.

———, and Donald J. Ward. "Zur mündlichen Überlieferung des Nibelungenliedes." *DVLG* 41 (1967): 351–390.

Beck, Heinrich. "Eddaliedforschung heute: Bemerkungen zur Heldenlied-Diskussion." *Helden und Heldensage: Otto Gschwantler zum 60. Geburtstag.* Eds. Hermann Reichert and Günter Zimmermann. Vienna: Fassbaender, 1990. 1–24.

Borghart, K.H.R. *Das Nibelungenlied: Die Spuren mündlichen Ursprungs in schriftlicher Überlieferung.* Amsterdam: Rodopi, 1977. 162–163.

Bowra, Cecil Maurice *Heroic Poetry.* London: Macmillan, 1952.

Curschmann, Michael. "Oral Poetry in Mediaeval English, French, and German Literature: Some Notes on Recent Research." *Speculum* 42 (1967): 36–52.

———. "The Concept of the Formula as an Impediment to Our Understanding of Medieval Oral Poetry." *Medievalia et Humanistica* 8 (1977): 63–76.

Ebenbauer, Alfred. "Heldenlied und 'Historisches Lied' im Frühmittelalter—und davor." *HH*, 15–34.

Egil's Saga. Tr. Hermann Pálsson and Paul Edwards. Harmondsworth, Middlesex: Penguin, 1976.

Foley, John Miles *Oral-Formulaic Theory and Research: An Introduction and Annotated Bibliography.* New York: Garland, 1985.

———. *The Theory of Oral Composition: History and Methodology.* Bloomington: Indiana University Press, 1988.

Harris, Joseph. "Eddic Poetry as Oral Poetry: The Evidence of Parallel Passages in the Helgi Poems for Questions of Composition and Performance." *Edda: A Collection of Essays.* Eds. Robert J. Glendinning and Haraldur Bessason. Winnipeg: University of Manitoba Press, 1983, 210–242.

Haymes, Edward R. "Oral Poetry and the Germanic Heldenlied." *Rice University Studies* 62.2 (1976): 47–54.

———. *The Nibelungenlied: History and Interpretation.* Urbana: University of Illinois Press, 1986.

Heusler, Andreas *Lied und Epos in germanischer Sagendichtung.* Darmstadt: Ruhfus, 1905.

———. *Nibelungensage und Nibelungenlied.* Dortmund: Ruhfus, 1920.

Kellogg, Robert L. "The Prehistory of Eddic Poetry." *PSMA*, 187–199.

Krogmann, Willy *Das Hildebrandslied in der langobardischen Urfassung hergestellt.* Berlin: Schmidt, 1959.

Lachmann, Karl. *Über die ursprüngliche Gestalt des Gedichts von der Nibelungen Noth*, Berlin: Dümmler, 1816. Most easily found in *Das deutsche Versepos.* Ed. Walter Johannes Schröder. Darmstadt: Wissenschaftliche Buchgesellschaft, 1969. 1–82.

Lehmann, Winfred P. *The Development of Germanic Verse Form.* Austin: University of Texas Press, 1956.

Leyen, Friedrich von der. *Das Heldenliederbuch Karls des Großen.* Munich: Beck, 1954.

Lord, Albert Bates. "Avdo Mededovic, Guslar." *Journal of American Folklore* 69 (1956): 318–330.

———. *The Singer of Tales.* Cambridge, MA: Harvard University Press, 1960.

Lutz, Hans Dieter. "Vorüberlegungen und Versuche zur statistischen Beschreibung der Adjektiv-Substantiv-Verbindung im Mittelhochdeutschen." *DVLG* 49 (1975): 465–501.

———. "Zur Formelhaftigkeit mittelhochdeutscher Texte und zur 'theory of oral-formulaic composition.'" *DVLG* 48 (1974): 432–447.

Meier, John. *Werden und Leben des Volksepos.* Halle: Niemeyer, 1909. Repr. in *Das deutsche Versepos.* Ed. Walter Johannes Schröder. Darmstadt: Wissenschaftliche Buchgesellschaft, 1969. 143–181.

Metzner, Ernst Erich. *Zur frühesten Geschichte der europäischen Balladendichtung. Der Tanz in Kölbigk; legendarische Nachrichten, gesellschaftlicher Hintergrund, historische Voraussetzungen.* Frankfurt: Athenäum, 1972.

Parry, Milman *The Making of Homeric Verse.* Ed. Adam Parry. Oxford: Clarendon Press, 1971. All of Parry's work on Homeric and South Slavic poetry conveniently collected.

Reichert, Hermann. *Nibelungenlied und Nibelungensage.* Vienna: Böhlau, 1985.

Schröder, Werner. "Ist das germanische Heldenlied ein Phantom?" *ZDA* 120.3 (1991): 249–256.

Stein, Peter K. "Orendel 1512: Probleme und Möglichkeiten der Anwendung der theory of oral-formulaic poetry bei der literaturhistorischen Interpretation eines mittelhochdeutschen Textes." *HS*, 322–338.

Wolf, Alois. "Die Verschriftlichung von europäischen Heldensagen als mittelalterliches Kulturproblem." *HH*, 305–328.

Part Two:

LITERARY WORKS

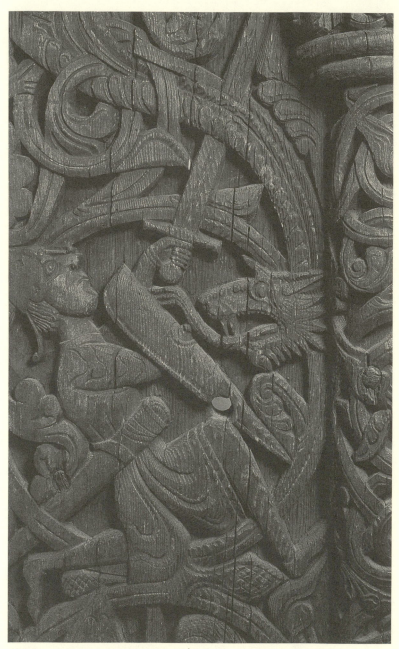

SIGURÐ STABBING THE DRAGON FÁFNIR (from the Hylestad Stave Church)
Museum of National Antiquities Oslo, Norway

CHAPTER 5

Literary Works

It is not possible here to talk about the many special characteristics that separate modern literature from medieval literature. A manuscript culture is fundamentally different from a print (or television, for that matter) culture, and the differences affect the formation and production of literary works at every level. The literature being discussed here is particularly special in its close dependency on oral tradition for both matter and style. It is probably this dependence on an oral background that led medieval authors of heroic materials to remain anonymous. Except for those few instances where an author is mentioned, all of the medieval literature described here is anonymous, and even in those few cases where an author's name appears, we know, with the exception of Snorri Sturluson, virtually nothing about the person named.

All medieval literature is transmitted in manuscript form, and only in the rarest of cases do we have a manuscript that can be considered authoritative. The discussion of different manuscript versions in the following sections will try to give an idea of the shifting basis of our modern texts. Any modern text is the product of a lot of choices, many of which are questionable, but without which we would have no modern editions at all.

Dating is also a problem. In some cases (e.g. *Beowulf*) the proposed dates range over centuries. In other cases, we can place a work within a few years, but there is almost always a considerable amount of guessing involved. Most of the Middle High German Dietrich poems, for example, were written sometime in the thirteenth century, but we have no real idea when. Even the sequencing of texts is usually questionable, since it is difficult to determine in most cases which text preceded another.

We have arranged the discussions under several general headings in order to bring some order into what is an inherently unruly collections of texts. The next chapter will deal with a number of works, generally quite early, that refer to the Nibelung or Dietrich stories or tell unrelated stories about characters from the primary legends. The main purpose of this chapter is to show the presence of the legends in the minds of Germanic storytellers from the ninth century to the thirteenth.

The next two chapters are devoted respectively to the Dietrich and Nibelung legends themselves in all the medieval narratives that are devoted completely to them.

A final chapter treats briefly several related legends that round out the legendary material of medieval Germany. The *Kudrun* is not explicitly related to any aspect of the Nibelung or Dietrich legends, but it obviously belongs to the same general tradition and some critics have suggested that it can be understood as something of a reaction to the catastrophic conclusion of the *Nibelungenlied.* The Wolfdietrich legends have a number of connections to the story of Dietrich, as does *König Rother.* Both narratives also have episodes that are attached to Dietrich himself in the *Þiðreksaga.*

There is relatively little secondary literature that covers this whole area. The standard literary histories of English, German, and Norse literature cover most of the works we discuss here within their own contexts. Hoffmann covers the Middle High German area well, and Wisniewski offers a relatively complete coverage of the literature having to do with the Dietrich poems. Two major works of medieval literature, *Beowulf* and the *Nibelungenlied,* are well covered in bibliographies and studies. The following list is generally limited to the bibliographical guides and literary histories, with preference given to works in English.

Clover, Carol J., and John Lindow, eds. *Old Norse–Icelandic Literature: A Critical Guide.* Ithaca: Cornell University Press, 1985.

Godden, Malcolm, and Michael Lapidge, eds. *The Cambridge Companion to Old English Literature.* Cambridge: Cambridge University Press, 1991.

Heinzle, Joachim. *Mittelhochdeutsche Dietrichepik.* Zurich: Artemis, 1978. Extensive documentation of manuscript and early print transmission of the so-called "fairy-tale Dietrich poems."

Hoffmann, Werner. *Mittelhochdeutsche Heldendichtung.* Berlin: Erich Schmidt, 1974.

Wisniewski, Roswitha. *Mittelalterliche Dietrichdichtung.* Stuttgart: Metzler, 1986.

Walshe, M. O'C. *Middle High German Literature: A Survey.* Cambridge, MA: Harvard University Press, 1962.

TABLE OF MOTIFS

On the following page is a table showing the occurrence of the important motifs of the Nibelung and Dietrich legends in some of the major literary works discussed in their respective chapters. Narratives that treat only one or two episodes are omitted.

Distribution of Motifs in the Major Literary Works

	Völsunga saga	Poetic Edda	Þiðreks-saga	Hildebrandslied	Nibelungenlied	Rosengarten	Biterolf und Dietleip	Buch von Bern	Rabenschlacht
Dietrich's Exile			x	x	x	x	x	x	x
Dietrich at Etzel's Court		x	x		x	x	x	x	x
Dietrich's Vassal Hildebrand			x	x	x	x	x	x	x
Siegfried's youth w = wild, c=courtly	w	w	w		c (and w)				
Siegfried kills a dragon F = Fáfnir, x=unnamed	F	F	x		x				
Siegfried's treasure	x	x	x		x				
Siegfried betrothed B = Brünhild, K = Kriemhild	B	B	B			K			
Siegfried's murder W = in woods, B = in bed	B	B and W	W		W				
Invitation to Feast E=Etzel, K=Kriemhild	E	E	E + K		K				
Kriemhilt avenges B=brothers, H=husband	B	B	H		H				

CHAPTER 6

Traces in Early Literature

A number of medieval literary texts mention elements of the Nibelung or Dietrich legend but are mainly devoted to other, usually legendary matters. We are including these works because they demonstrate the continued presence of the legends in the minds of authors (and presumably audiences) from the centuries preceding the first literary treatment of the legends as a whole.

DEOR AND *WIDSIÞ*

The Exeter Book, a late tenth-century manuscript collection of Old English verse, contains two poems that refer to our legends. One of them, *Deor*, is cast as a scop's lament on losing his job. According to the last strophe Deor has been replaced by a new poet named Heorrenda. He attempts to alleviate his suffering by comparing his own situation to unhappy situations from Germanic legend that turned out happily. He divides his poems into something like stanzas of varying length by inserting a refrain, "That has passed on, this too shall pass," after each story.

He begins by sketching the situation of Weland, referring mainly to his having been lamed by the king who is called here Niþhad. Most of the passage dwells on Weland's misery. The second "stanza" deals with Niþhad's daughter, here called Beaduhild. In the full story told in the Norse sources described below, Weland avenged himself on the king by killing his sons and dishonoring his daughter, and a version quite close to this seems to lie behind this reference. The poet remarks that Beaduhild was less grieved by her brothers' death than by her own pregnancy. We can assume that the "happy ending" was the birth of the hero Widia (Witege, Viðga), her son by Weland.

After reference to an obscure story that does not seem to be part of our complex, the poem refers to a story of Theoderic in two lines:

> Þeodric owned   for thirty winters
> the castle of the Mærings. That is known to many.

The thirty winters mentioned here agree with the exile of Theoderic as we know it from the *Hildebrandslied* and elsewhere, but there is no known connection between Theoderic the Great and any group known as "Maerings." Malone has argued that this Þeodric is not Theoderic the Goth but Theoderic the son of Clovis, who may have been the model for the German Wolfdietrich legends. He cites a Swedish runic inscription which also mentions a "ÞioðrikR" as the lord of the Maerings. The evidence is too slight to be certain of either solution. *Widsiþ* explicitly mentions "Þeodric" as a ruler of the Franks. If there were legends about both Theoderics, then it is quite possible that the Anglo-Saxon singers of tales confused them as well. They lacked even the reference tools we have for sorting out the historical background of their stories.

The next stanza refers to the misery of the people under the reign of the "wolfish" Eormanric, clearly a reference to the Ermanaric of legend. No specific events are cited here except that his people wished his downfall.

The last two "stanzas" meditate on the misery of exile and the specific situation of the poet. Frederick Norman has related the names given here to the Hagen-Hild-Hetel episode in the Middle High German *Kudrun*.

The second of the Exeter Book poems, *Widsiþ*, is cast as the report of a singer who visited the court of Eormanric (Ermanaric). The major part of the poem consists of lists of kings and tribes and the courts the singer had visited. In his edition Malone argues that the lists are much older than the frame story and that they make up the "oldest poem in the English language" (68). Unfortunately the lists do not generally go beyond such formulas as "X ruled over Y." We find many of the most important figures of our legends mentioned. Ætla (Attila) rules the Huns, Eormanric the Goths, Gifica (Gibica) the "Burgendan." Þeodric is mentioned as the ruler of the Franks, which may lend some additional weight to Malone's arguments that the Þeodric of Deor is Theoderic the son of Clovis and not the Ostrogothic king. The presence of the two poems in the same manuscript does not prove any relationship between the poems before they were copied, but it is probable that the two poets would have known essentially the same tradition.

The lists give tantalizing evidence of extensive knowledge of a "legendary history" on the part of Anglo-Saxon singers. A real singer would have had to live several centuries to have known all of the names mentioned, but this does not seem to have been a problem until literal-minded chroniclers of the later Middle Ages began to question the appearance of Ermanaric, Attila, and Theoderic at the same time. (See Frutolf of Michelsberg in the chapter on historical sources.)

There is a reference at the end of the main part of the poem to Wudga and Hama, who are described in battle and ruling over gold, men, and women. Wudga and Hama are probably Witege and Heime who appear together in many different medieval stories. See the discussion in the Glossary of Names.

Deor. Ed. Kemp Malone. 4th ed. New York: Appleton-Century-Crofts, 1966.

Norman, Frederick. "Problems in the Dating of Deor and Its Allusions." *Franciplegius: Medieval and Linguistic Studies in Honor of Francis Peabody Magoun, Jr.* Eds. Jess B. Bessinger, Jr., and Robert P. Creed. New York: New York University Press, 1965. 205–213.

Widsith. Ed. Kemp Malone. 2d Revised ed. Copenhagen: Rosenkilde and Bagger, 1962.

Chambers, R. W. *Widsith: A Study in Old English Heroic Legend*. Reprint (orig. 1912) ed. New York: Russell and Russell, 1965.

WULF AND EADWACER

This Old English poem, which follows *Deor* in the Exeter Book, may not belong in this book at all, but the name Eadwacer is equivalent to Odoacer, and at least one interpretation (Harris) has identified Wulf with Hildebrand, who is occasionally identified as a representative of the Wulfing clan. The poem is the plaint of a woman who seems to have been left behind by Wulf and is married against her will to Eadwacer. This would suggest a version of the story in which Hildebrand's wife had been forced to marry Odoacer after Hildebrand had been driven from the land along with his lord.

The Exeter Book. Ed. Elliott Van Kirk Dobbie. The Anglo-Saxon Poetic Records 3. Morningside Heights, NY: Columbia University Press, 1936. *Wulf and Eadwacer*, 179–180.

Harris, Joseph. "Hadubrand's Lament: On the Origin and Age of Elegy in Germanic." *HH*, 81–114.

BEOWULF

The Old English poem *Beowulf* survives in a single English manuscript from the late tenth or early eleventh century. There have been many attempts to date the poem itself, but they have all been called into question. The dating has moved from the seventh century to the eleventh without universal acceptance of any hypothesis. Current opinion leans more toward the later dating.[1]

The poem contains the broad heroic narration of two adventures in the career of the Geatish warrior-king Beowulf. In the first of these stories he journeys to Denmark to rid King Hroþgar's hall, Heorot, of the murderous visitations of the monstrous giant Grendel. After killing the monster, Beowulf still has to kill Grendel's mother, who seeks vengeance for her son's death.

---

[1] Chase, *Dating*, brings together recent scholarly opinion. See also Kiernan, *Beowulf*, who argues for an eleventh-century date both for the manuscript and the poem. Serious objections to Kiernan's method are raised in the review by John D. Niles in *Speculum* 58 (1983): 765-767. Niles, however, accepts a relatively late date for the poem.

During the celebration following the monsters' deaths, the court poet at Hroþgar's court compares Beowulf's achievements to those of several heroes of the past, including Sigmund, to whom the dragon-killing that usually belongs to Siegfried/Sigurð is attributed. Sigmund is also described as wandering about with his son Fitela, who is the Sinfjötli of the *Poetic Edda* and the *Völsungasaga*. As a reward for his killing of Grendel Beowulf receives a rich collar that is compared to a necklace of the "Brosings." The necklace is featured in a brief story involving Hama (Heime), who in some unspecified way gained the enmity of Eormanric. There are no new details except that we are told that Hama "chose eternal reward," which is probably no more than a euphemism for death.[2]

In the second part of the poem Beowulf has reigned over his people for fifty years and is suddenly faced with a monster infestation of his own. A dragon has been awakened from its sleep by a treasure-hunter and is ravaging the countryside. There is no one among the young warriors of the land who will face the monster. The aged Beowulf kills it but receives his own death-wound in the process. The poem concludes with Beowulf's funeral.

EDITION AND TRANSLATION

Klaeber, Fr[iedrich], ed. *Beowulf and the Fight at Finnsburh.* Boston: Heath, 1922. Standard Edition.

Alexander, Michael, tr. *Beowulf: A Verse Translation.* Harmondsworth, Middlesex:: Penguin, 1973.

STUDIES

Andersson, Theodore M. "The Dating of Beowulf." *University of Toronto Quarterly* (1983): 288–301.

Benson, Larry D. "The Pagan Coloring of Beowulf." *Beowulf: Basic Readings.* Ed. Peter S. Baker. New York: Garland, 1995. 35–50.

Chase, Colin, ed. *The Dating of Beowulf.* Toronto: University of Toronto Press, 1981.

Hasenfratz, Robert J. *Beowulf Scholarship: An Annotated Bibliography, 1979-1990.* New York: Garland, 1993.

Kiernan, Kevin S. *Beowulf and the Beowulf Manuscript.* New Brunswick, NJ: Rutgers University Press, 1981.

Short, Douglas D. *Beowulf Scholarship: An Annotated Bibliography.* New York: Garland, 1980.

WALTHER AND HILDEGUND

The story of Walther and Hildegund is not a necessary part of the Nibelung or Dietrich legends, but it does involve both Attila and Gunther, and it is included

---

[2] Malone, ed., *Widsith*, 160-161.

in the *Þiðrekssaga af Bern* and is mentioned in the *Nibelungenlied.* There were at least four medieval versions of the story (including that in the *Þiðrekssaga*).

Waltharius

This Latin poem may be the oldest written version of the story, since the latest date suggested for its composition is about 930. The poem was apparently written by a monk for the amusement of his brothers, since he addresses his audience as "fratres" in the first line of the narrative. A brief dedication to a bishop named Erkambald seems to identify its author as a Brother Gerald. There is also, however, an eleventh-century reference to a Latin poem about "Waltharius manu fortis" ("Walther of the strong hand") that was supposed to have been written by Ekkehard of St. Gall. There is no way of achieving certainty about the identity of the poet using the evidence we have.

Waltharius, Hagano (Hagen), and Hiltgunt (Hildegund) are noble hostages given by their parents to secure a peace with Attila. They grow up together at the Hunnish court and become close friends. Hiltgunt and Waltharius had already been betrothed by their parents before they were given as hostages. Hagano escapes and returns to his king Guntharius (Gunther) in Worms. Hagano and Guntharius are here referred to as Franks rather than Burgundians, but the situation is virtually the same as the one we know from the *Nibelungenlied.*

Waltharius distinguishes himself as a warrior for Attila, and the Huns are concerned to retain him in that role. For his part Waltharius wishes only to escape with Hiltgunt and return to his homeland. He plots an elaborate escape that involves getting the whole Hunnish court drunk and having Hiltgunt collect the treasures that had been given along with them as a pledge of peace. The two steal off into the night and are not missed until it is too late to catch them.

Walther and Hiltgunt cross the Rhine near Worms and pay for their trip with some fish. This fish finds its way onto the king's table and Guntharius demands to know where it comes from since it is of a variety that does not come from that region. The ferryman tells of the couple he had set over the Rhine. Gunther is filled with avarice and, over Hagano's objections, sets out with eleven men (including Hagano) to separate Waltharius from his gold.

The "Franks" catch up with Waltharius in the Vosges mountains, where he is able to find an easily defensible spot where he can meet his attackers one at a time. In the course of a long day he kills all of them but Guntharius and Hagano. The two ride off planning to ambush Waltharius when he leaves his position. Waltharius and Hiltgunt remain in the mountain pass overnight and emerge the next day, only to be ambushed by Guntharius and Hagano. Waltharius reproaches Hagano for violating their vows of friendship, and Hagano says that he is now forced to take vengeance for one of his relatives who had been slain the day before.

A fierce fight follows in which Hagano is several times required to rescue his king from certain death. Waltharius strikes off the king's leg, Hagano cuts off Waltharius's right hand, and Waltharius finally lands a blow that cuts out Hagano's eye. The severe wounds bring the fight to an end, and the three men sit around drinking wine and making scurrilous jokes about their wounds as Hiltgunt binds them.

The story is told with skill and a sense of irony born of a familiarity with classical literature. The traditional characters and narrative patterns are clearly drawn from Germanic tradition, but the treatment is learned and witty rather than heroic.

EDITIONS AND TRANSLATIONS

Kratz, Dennis M., ed. and tr. *Waltharius and Ruodlieb.* New York: Garland, 1984. Includes extensive bibliography.

Smyser, H.M., and F.P.Magoun, Jr. *Walter of Aquitaine: Materials for the Study of His Legend.* New London: Connecticut College, 1950. Contains translations of all versions of the Walther legend.

Waldere

The Old English version of the story of Waldere (Walther) and Hildiguþ (Hildegunt) exists in two brief fragments of what must have been a poem of considerable length. The first is apparently an exhortation on the part of Hildiguþ during the early part of the battle. She says that Weland's handiwork, the sword Mimming, has never failed any man. The second fragment tells something of the history of the sword Mimming, that Þeodric had given it to Widia (Witege), the son of Weland, along with a great treasure. Guðhere (Gunther) is here correctly identified as the "friend [i.e. lord] of the Burgundians." The fragment concludes with Waldere's praise of his own armor. There is much talk of treasure and possessions in the two fragments, which is only appropriate in a poem that describes a battle over treasure.

The Old English text of *Waldere* is included in Klaeber's edition of *Beowulf.*

TRANSLATION

Alexander, Michael, tr. *The Earliest English Poems*. Harmondsworth, Middlesex: Penguin, 1966. Also includes translations of *Deor* and *Widsiþ*.

Walther und Hildegunt

Like the Old English version, the Middle High German poem exists only in a few fragments. There are fragments of at least two manuscripts that had been used in the binding of later books. The cutting and sewing process has left many illegible passages in the fragments as they survive.

Although there is insufficient material in the fragments to allow a reconstruction of the Middle High German poem, we can be sure that it was a literary work of "epic" breadth. The poem is written in stanzas very much like those used in the *Nibelungenlied* and *Kudrun*. We can observe a filling out of courtly detail very much like what we find in the *Nibelungenlied*. The largest of the fragments is a portion of the homecoming of Walther and Hildegund, a scene that is lacking in all other versions of the story. The fragments of a second manuscript also seem to contain a scene that is missing from the other versions. Hagen informs Walther that he had been betrothed from infancy to Hildegund. This occurs before Hagen's departure from Etzel's court.

An English translation of the fragments is found in Smyser and Magoun cited above under *Waltharius*.

Eckerth, W. *Das Waltherlied. Gedicht in mhd. Sprache.* Halle: Niemeyer, 1909. This is actually the edition of a modern poem in Middle High German by Eckerth based on the Latin *Waltharius*, but he includes the text of the Middle High German fragments on 70–79.

Valtari (in the *Þiðrekssaga*)

Here the emphasis is on the bridewinning story. Högni leads the Hunnish troops pursuing the young couple. Valtari is able to fight them off effectively, and they give up the pursuit. There is no fight with Gunnar in this version.

WAYLAND (WIELAND, VELENT) THE SMITH

Völundarkviða

The Old Norse poem is preserved in the mythological portion of the *Poetic Edda*, although it does not involve the gods directly. We can only guess why it was included in this section.

The lay is introduced by a prose narrative in which Völund and his brothers Slagfiðr and Egil capture and marry three Valkyries. After nine years the three escape and fly away. Slagfiðr and Egil go out in search of their mates, while

Völund remains at home working in his smithy. King Níðuð has him captured and brought to his court.

The lay proper retells some of the matter told in the prose introduction and goes on to tell the story we associate with Völund. The king has him hamstrung and placed on an island so that the smith will have to work for him. Völund kills the sons of the king and makes drinking cups out of their skulls. Later he ravishes the king's daughter and makes her pregnant. Although it is not mentioned explicitly in this text, we know from the *Þiðrekssaga* that he makes artificial wings of feathers that allow him to escape. The text of the lay only mentions that he rose into the air. He flies before the king to tell him what he has done, and the lay ends with the king's daughter's lament.

In the course of the poem Völund is referred to twice as *vísi álfa*, or "leader of elves," and his ability to fly is never explained. From these points and many external associations of smiths with dwarfs and other supernatural beings, Kaaren Grimstad ("Revenge") argues that, at least as far as the *Völundarkviða* is concerned, Völund is some kind of elf or dwarf with supernatural powers. She suggests that the poem is built around a kind of initiation involving torture and mistreatment from which the dwarf/elf/smith rises with renewed power. She suggests a comparison with *Grímnismál*, in which Óðin appears disguised at a king's court, is captured and tortured, after which he identifies himself, bringing about the death of the king and the installation of his son in his place.

If Völund is a supernatural being, then it is perhaps understandable why the poem is found in the mythological section of the *Poetic Edda* rather than the heroic. The other versions of the Weland story do not suggest supernatural powers for the smith himself, and the *Þiðrekssaga* attempts a "realistic" explanation by describing the feather coat Velent makes with the help of his brother Egil. It is impossible to rule out influence from the Daedalus legend in this case, since it was known through Ovid and others throughout Europe.

For text and general criticism of the *Poetic Edda*, see the introductory section below, p. 119.

Grimstad, Kaaren. "The Revenge of Völundr." *Edda: A Collection of Essays.* Eds. Robert J. Glendinning and Haraldur Bessason. Winnipeg: University of Manitoba Press, 1983. 187–209.

Velent's Story (from the *Þiðrekssaga*)
In the *Þiðrekssaga* Velent is mainly important as the smith of the sword Mimung and as the father of Viðga.

Velent appears at Niðung's court as a castaway, and after numerous trials he becomes the king's smith. The king hamstrings him after a trumped-up charge is brought against him, and the remainder of the story is very much as in the *Völundarkviða*, except that he has his brother Egil's help to make artificial wings so that he can fly away. In this version there is no indication of supernatural powers beyond his extraordinary abilities as a craftsman.

In the *Þiðrekssaga* Velent's brother Egil plays a much larger role. He comes to the court of King Niðung, where he has to undergo the test later associated with Wilhelm Tell. He has to shoot an apple off his young son's head, after which he tells the king that the other arrows he has were for him (the king) if he had struck his son. He hunts birds to provide the feathers for Velent's artificial wings and gives the device a test flight. When Velent flies away, the king demands that Egil shoot him down. Egil shoots a bladder Velent is carrying filled with the blood of the murdered princes, so the king thinks he has wounded Velent when he sees blood flowing from him.

CHAPTER 7

The Dietrich Legend

With the exception of the *Þiðrekssaga,* which combines both types, the medieval treatment of Dietrich falls roughly into two main categories: the "historical" poems, which follow the legendary history of Dietrich, and the "fairy tale" poems (*märchenhafte Dietrichepik*), which tell of Dietrich's fights with dragons, giants, and dwarfs with no solid anchoring in the established legendary history. Since the dividing line is not clear, we will not attempt to reflect it in our presentation, following instead a roughly chronological arrangement of the works.

The following literature covers the Dietrich legend in general or a number of different works together.

Boer, R. C. *Die Sagen von Ermanarich und Dietrich von Bern.* Halle: Waisenhaus, 1910.

Boor, Helmut de. "Die Heldennamen in der historischen Dietrichdichtung." *ZDA* 78 (1941): 234–267.

Curschmann, Michael. "Dichtung über Heldendichtung: Bemerkungen zur Dietrichepik des 13. Jahrhunderts." *Jahrbuch für Internationale Germanistik: Akten des V. Internationalen Germanisten-Kongresses, Cambridge 1975* (1976): 17–27.

Firestone, Ruth H. Hartzell *Elements of Traditional Structure in the Couplet Epics of the Late Middle High German Dietrich Cycle.* Göppingen: Kümmerle, 1975. Analysis following folktale methodology of Vladimir Propp.

Gottzmann, Carola *Heldendichtung des 13. Jahrhunderts. Siegfried—Dietrich—Ortnit.* Frankfurt: Lang, 1987.

Heinzle, Joachim. "Dietrich von Bern." *Epische Stoffe des Mittelalters.* Eds. Volker Mertens and Ulrich Müller. Stuttgart: Kröner, 1984. 141–155.

———. *Mittelhochdeutsche Dietrichepik.* Zurich: Artemis, 1978.

Jiriczek, Otto Luitpold Karl. "Dietrich von Bern und sein Sagenkreis." *Deutsche Heldensagen.* Vol. 1. Strassburg: Trübner, 1898.

Jones, George Fenwick. "Dietrich von Bern as a Literary Symbol." *PMLA* 67 (1952): 1094–102.

Laurien, Hanna-Renate. *Stilelemente der historischen Dietrichepen*. Dissertation Microfilm. Freie Universität Berlin: 1951.

Mohr, Wolfgang. "Dietrich von Bern." *ZDA* 80 (1944): 117–155.

Patzig, Hermann. *Dietrich von Bern und sein Sagenkreis*. Dortmund: Ruhfus, 1917.

Plötzeneder, Gisela. *Die Gestalt Dietrichs von Bern in der deutschen Dichtung und Sage des frühen und hohen Mittelalters*. Unpublished dissertation, Innsbruck, 1955.

Pütz, Horst P. *Studien zur Dietrichsage. Mythisierung und Dämonisierung Theoderics des Großen*. Unpublished dissertation, Vienna 1969.

Wessels, P. B. "Dietrichepik und Südtiroler Erzählkunst." *ZDP* 85 (1966): 345–369.

Zimmermann, Hans Joachim. *Theoderic der Große—Dietrich von Bern. Die geschichtlichen und sagenhaften Quellen des Mittelalters*. Unpublished dissertation, Bonn, 1972.

Zink, Georges *Les légendes héroiques de Dietrich et d'Ermrich dans les littératures germaniques*. Lyon: IAC, 1950.

ÞIÐREKSSAGA AF BERN (THE SAGA OF ÞIÐREK OF BERN)

This extensive saga is a compilation of virtually all known stories of Dietrich, including many that are only marginally a part of the story of Dietrich himself. It was probably assembled in the mid-thirteenth century at the court of the Norwegian king Hákon the Old (r. 1216–1263), where many continental literary works found their way into Norse. This ordering of the narratives provides the only connected story of the life and career of Dietrich we have. All other medieval narratives having to do with Dietrich treat a single episode or group of episodes. The title *Þiðrekssaga* refers to the work as a whole, although the individual books are also referred to as "sagas."

The saga begins with the story of Þiðrek's grandfather, Sir Samson, who is known in no other sources. Samson abducts the daughter of his lord, and in the process of fighting off his pursuers kills both his lord and his king. He assumes the rank of both and rules in Salerno.

Samson passes his kingdom on to his older son, Erminrek. Samson's last conquest in Bern (Verona) is passed on to the younger son, Þetmar, who in turn passes it on to his son, Þiðrek. Þiðrek establishes himself early through adventures as a hero. He gains Hildibrand as weapons-master and surrogate father.

[The main manuscript of the saga interrupts the story of Þiðrek here with a series of stories that belong later in the saga. See the stories of Vilkinus and Attila below.]

About a third of the saga is devoted to the youthful adventures of a whole series of heroes: Heimir (Heime), Velent (Wieland), Viðga (Witige), Ekka (Ecke), Þetleif (Dietleip), and Ömlung (Amelung), all of whom join Þiðrek in a kind of Germanic Round Table. The story of young Sigurð (Siegfried) is told to introduce him. At the end of this first major section there is a great feast at Þiðrek's hall in which each of the heroes is described physically along with his armor. The heroes then embark on a campaign in Bertangaland (Brittany), where each of the heroes fights a duel with a member of the court of a king named Isung. Sigurð appears among Isung's knights and duels with Þiðrek, who defeats him. Þiðrek and his men are recognized as the greatest warriors in the known world.

The second major section of the saga is devoted to a series of adventures involving women as the object of bridewinning, seduction, or rape. The first of these is Sigurð's winning of Grimhild (Kriemhild), the sister of Gunnar (Gunther), and his agreement to help win his former betrothed, Brynhild (Brünhild), for Gunnar. In a second adventure Herburt (Herbort) sets out to win Hild, the daughter of King Artus, for Þiðrek. He succeeds but falls in love with her himself and runs off with her. (This is obviously a parody of the Tristan legend.) The bridewinning stories of Osantrix and Attila followed in the original version of the manuscript. A later editor has moved them to an earlier point because the stories predate the time of Þiðrek. The story of Valtari (Walther) and Hildigunn (Hildegund) follows the establishment of Attila as the king of Hunland. Apollonius of Tira is the name applied to the hero of a thoroughly conventional bridewinning romance. Apollonius's brother Iron is the main figure of a story having to do with a faithful wife who is jealous of her husband's passion for hunting, and a later story in which Iron seduces the wife of Aki Ömlungatrausti, an adventure that leads to his death.

The turning point of the story comes in the final story of this sequence, in which Erminrek's (Ermanaric) trusted advisor Sifka avenges the rape of his wife by his lord by destroying everything that is dear to the king. He manages to make the king guilty in each of these episodes. The pinnacle of this series is Erminrek's forcing his nephew Þiðrek and his men into exile after Sifka had convinced the king that Þiðrek had been withholding tribute.

The final third of the saga deals with Þiðrek's exile at Attila's court. During the first section Þiðrek aids his host in many battles. Þiðrek then sets out to retake his kingdom. He is successful on the battlefield, but the deaths of his younger brother, Þether (Diether), and the sons of Attila so demoralize him that he returns to Attila without taking his lands.

The story of the killing of Sigurð is inserted at this point, leading to the largest homogeneous section of the work, the "Saga of the Niflungs," which tells essentially the same story as the last third of the *Nibelungenlied.*

The major differences lie in the motivation (here Attila invites the Burgundian brothers out of avarice) and in the details of the conclusion. In the saga Þiðrek fatally wounds Högni (Hagen) (who is able to father a son to avenge him during his last night alive), and, after the carnage is over, it is Þiðrek who kills Grimhild.

Þiðrek and Hildibrand return to Italy to recover their kingdom. With the help of Hildibrand's son Alibrand they are able to defeat Sifka and retake not only their own holdings, but those of Erminrek, who had died horribly in his bed in the meantime. After the death of his wife, Herrad, Þiðrek wins a bride by killing a dragon that had killed the woman's husband. There are a few final adventures involving mainly Heimir, who retires briefly to a monastery before being killed by a giant. It is clear that the age of heroes is at an end. Þiðrek is carried off by a mysterious black horse, presumably to Hell, although the narrator suggests that he had been able to call on the Virgin in time to save his soul.

Almost all of the Germanic heroic stories we know from Middle High German and other sources find their way into this massive compilation. Some stories here we know only from oblique references elsewhere, and a few stories, such as the initial story of Þiðrek's grandfather Samson, seem to have been simply cobbled together from motifs derived from other heroic tales. Many names from unrelated medieval sources find their way into the narrative. We find a king named Artus (Arthur), who has a son named Apollonius (of Tira). There is a surrogate bridewinning narrative involving a knight named Tristram (who is not, however, the wooer). The narrative pattern of the Middle High German poem *Der Rosengarten zu Worms*, involving a sequence of single combats as a combination tournament and battle, is used in an entirely different context in the saga. The compiler of the saga made extensive use of virtually everything known to him about the Germanic legendary past along with many motifs and names from other sources as well.

The saga even uses folktale motifs we associate now with entirely different legends. In the saga of Velent the Smith, for example, we find the story associated with Wilhelm Tell, in which a father has to shoot an apple off his son's head. The manuscript was written some forty or fifty years before the historical Wilhelm Tell's birth in about 1290, so this is clearly a wandering motif in European folklore that only later became attached to the Swiss hero.

We know nothing about the compiler of the collection. A cleric seems probable for a number of reasons, not the least of which was that there were very few literate lay persons in Norway at the time. The Norse version of the Tristan legend, *Tristrams saga ok Isönd*, names as its translator/adapter a certain Brother Robert. None of the other texts adapted from French or German sources names its author. If the author of our saga was not himself a priest, he had enjoyed clerical education, perhaps in Germany. Certainly he betrays again and again a clerical turn of mind, as we shall see in our analysis of the arrangement of materials below.

Theodore Andersson believes the compilation we have was actually made in Germany in the 1190s and translated into Norwegian in the middle of the thirteenth century (*Preface*, 52). There is little external evidence that speaks for or against this hypothesis, but the "Preface" of the saga itself maintains that "the saga is assembled from the stories of German men, and some of it comes from their verses, which were composed to entertain great men, and which were composed long ago, soon after the events that are told here" (Preface). To buttress the authority of his narrative, the saga-man says (in an epilogue to the Niflunga saga) that he has heard the stories told by men "who were born in Bremen or Münster, and none of them knew the others, but they all tell the story about the things that happened in that land the same way, and that is mostly according to the way things are told in old songs in the German language" (ch. 394). There is no compelling reason to doubt the words of the saga writer, especially since he would have been able to establish even greater authority for his text if he had referred simply to a "book in the German language." Written sources were generally held to be more reliable than oral ones, and the saga writer felt that he had to establish the correctness of the oral tradition by saying that "they all tell the story . . . the same way."

Compilations of this sort are not uncommon in Old Norse literature. Perhaps the best known is the history of the kings of Norway compiled by the Icelander Snorri Sturluson in the first half of the thirteenth century. This work is today known under the title *Heimskringla*. An even more similar collection of sagas having to do with Charlemagne is known as the *Karlamagnussaga*. The only other collection having to do with the common Germanic past treated in this book is the *Völsungasaga*. The dry narrative of most of the *Þiðrekssaga* may be more reflective of chronicle writing than of heroic poetry, but, as we have seen in the case of ancient historiography, the two genres are hardly mutually exclusive.

The material is arranged in a roughly chronological fashion around the career of Dietrich, but there is more than a little evidence that the real organizing principle is a thematic one. The stories seem to have been arranged to tell of the rise and fall of a heroic paradise modeled on the biblical story of the Fall. The preface goes to considerable length to place the history of Þiðrek within world history. The saga author correctly locates him in the time after Constantine and later betrays more than a little knowledge of the negative clerical tradition about Theoderic, but he goes out of the way to blunt its impact. He invents a conversion of the hero from the Arian heresy to orthodox Catholicism later in his life and seeks to whitewash the clerical legend of the king's being carried directly to Hell on the back of a mysterious black horse believed to be the Devil himself in disguise.

Edward Haymes has suggested ("Bridewinning") that the *Þiðreksaga* was structured to show the destructive power of a lust for women on a pure brotherhood of heroes. The first third of the saga contains a number of opportunities for Þiðrek and some of his men to become involved with women, but these entanglements are always avoided and the heroes assembled at the great banquet are all, at least theoretically, virgins. The middle portion of the saga is completely devoted to stories in which the desire for women has dire consequences. This section leads up to the rape of Sifka's wife and the resulting destruction of Erminrek's happiness. Þiðrek is an innocent victim of Sifka's revenge and thus indirectly of Erminrek's lust. The final third of the saga is devoted to a gradual destruction of the heroic age, as one hero after another finds his death. The history of Þiðrek of Bern becomes a sort of demonstration of the Fall of Man. As the original sin of Adam was frequently portrayed as the result of his carnal desire for Eve and of her seductive ability to make him disobey God's command, so the fall of the Age of Heroes is portrayed as resulting from the carnal desire of these heroes for women. The Norwegian or Icelander who arranged these materials into the *Þiðrekssaga* we know certainly thought like a priest, whether he was in holy orders or not.

The oldest manuscript we have of the saga, a Norwegian parchment of the thirteenth century, seems to bear the signs of an attempt to reorder the materials to match the chronological order of events. The bridewinning stories of Osantrix and Attila (which take place a generation before the youth of Þiðrek) have been moved from their thematically appropriate place within the sequence of bridewinning stories to a place early in the story, where they come before the stories of Velent and Viðga. This rearrangement hurts the overall sense of the saga because it leaves the story of Valtari and Hildigunn, which proceeds from the story of Attila, standing alone in the middle of the bridewinning section without any connection to the story of Þiðrek. Fortunately the rearrangement was left unfinished and we can clearly see where the stories of Osantrix and Attila belong. The manuscript lacks a beginning and an end. These have been supplied by two later Icelandic paper manuscripts. There is also a Swedish adaptation of the saga dating from the fourteenth century.

EDITIONS AND TRANSLATIONS

Die Geschichte Thidreks von Bern. Tr. Fine Erichsen. Jena: Diederichs, 1924. German translation.

Saga Didriks konungs af Bern. Ed. C.R.Unger. Kristiania, 1853.

The Saga of Thidrek of Bern. Tr. Edward R. Haymes. New York: Garland, 1988. English translation.

Þiðreks Saga af Bern. Ed Guðni Jónsson. 2 vols. Reykjavík: Íslendingasagnaútgafan, 1954. Edition in standardized Old Icelandic orthography.

Þiðreks Saga af Bern. Ed. Henrik Bertelsen. 2 vols. Copenhagen: Møller, 1905–1911. Critical edition based on oldest manuscript.

(Swedish Version)

Sagan om Didrik af Bern. Efter svenska handskrifter utgifven. Ed. Gunnar Olof Hyltén-Cavallius. Stockholm, 1850.

Die Didriks-Chronik oder die Svava: Das Leben König Didriks von Bern und die Niflungen. Tr. Heinz Ritter-Schaumburg. St. Goar: Reichl, 1989. German translation.

STUDIES

Andersson, Theodore M. "The Epic Source of Niflunga Saga and the Nibelungenlied." *Arkiv för nordisk filologi* 88 (1973): 1–54.

―――. "An Interpretation of Thidreks saga." In *Structure and Meaning in Old Norse Literature: New Approaches to Textual Analysis and Literary Criticism of Edda and Saga Narrative.* Eds. John Lindow, Lars Lönnroth, and Gerd Wolfgang Weber. Odense, 1986. Maintains that the saga was composed in German in Soest (Westphalia) and later translated into Norse. Includes an extensive bibliography.

―――. *The Legend of Brynhild.* Ithaca: Cornell University Press, 1980.

―――. "Niflunga saga in the Light of German and Danish Materials." *Medieval Scandinavia* 7 (1974): 22–30.

―――. *A Preface to the Nibelungenlied.* Stanford: Stanford University Press, 1987. Includes translations of extensive portions of the *Þiðrekssaga.*

Beck, Heinrich. "Zur Thidrekssaga-Diskussion." *ZDP* 112 (1993): 441–448.

Benedikt, Erich. "Die Überlieferungen vom Ende Dietrichs von Bern." *Festschrift für Dietrich Kralik.* Horn: Berger, 1954. 99–111.

Brady, Caroline. *The Legends of Ermanaric.* Berkeley: University of California Press, 1943.

Curschmann, Michael. "The Prologue of *Thidreks Saga:* Thirteenth-Century Reflections on Oral Traditional Literature." *Scandinavian Studies* 56 (1984): 140–151.

Droege, Karl. "Zur Siegfrieddichtung und Thidrekssaga." *ZDA* (1934): 83–100.

―――. "Zur Thidrekssaga." *ZDA* (1929): 3–46.

Ebel, Uwe. "Die Thidreks Saga als Dokument der norwegischen Literatur des dreizehnten Jahrhunderts." *Niederdeutsches Wort* 22 (1981): 1–11.

Forster, Leonard. "Die Thidrekssaga als hansische Literatur." *Sprachkontakt in der Hanse: Aspekte des Sprachausgleichs im Ostsee- und Nordseeraum.* Ed. P. Sture Ureland. Tübingen: Niemeyer, 1987. 43–50.

Frantzen, J.J.A.A. "Über den Stil der Thidrekssaga." *Neophilologus* 1 (1916): 196–209.

―――. "Über den Stil der Thidrekssaga." *Neophilolgus* 1 (1916): 267–282. Continuation of previous article.

Friese, Hans. *Thidrekssaga und Dietrichsepos: Untersuchungen zur inneren und äußeren Form.* Berlin: Mayer and Müller, 1914.

Frings, Theodor. *Herbort: Studien zur Thidrekssaga.* Leipzig: Hirzel, 1943.

Gutenbrunner, Siegfried. "Die Niflungasaga." *Arbeiten zur Skandinavistik.* Ed. Heinrich Beck. Frankfurt: Lang, 1985. 433–142.

Haupt, Waldemar. *Zur niederdeutschen Dietrichsage*. Berlin: Mayer and Müller, 1914.

Haymes, Edward R. "The Bridewinning, Seduction and Rape Sequence in the *Thidrekssaga*." in *höhem príse: A* Festschrift *in Honor of Ernst S. Dick*. Ed. Winder McConnell. Göppingen: Kümmerle, 1989, 145–152.

Hempel, Heinrich. "Die Handschriftenverhältnisse der Thidrikssaga." *BGDSL* (1923): 414–445.

————. "Sächsische Nibelungendichtung und sächsischer Ursprung der Thidrekssaga." In *Edda, Skalden, Saga: Festschrift zum 70. Geburtstag von Felix Genzmer*. Heidelberg: Winter, 1952. 138–156. Maintains the *Þiðrekssaga* was composed in Lower Saxony. Collects evidence for Saxon Dietrich poetry.

Heusler, Andreas. *Nibelungensage und Nibelungenlied*. Dortmund: Ruhfus, 1921. The *locus classicus* for the *ältere Not*, the lost German epic on which both "The Saga of the Niflungs" and the *Nibelungenlied* seem to be based.

Hofmann, Dietrich. "Zur Lebensform mündlicher Erzähldichtung des Mittelalters im deutschen und niederländischen Sprachgebiet: Zeugnisse der Thidreks Saga und anderer Quellen." In *Niederdeutsche Beiträge: Festschrift für Felix Wortmann zum 70. Geburtstag*. Ed. Jan Goossens. Cologne: Böhlau, 1976. 191–215.

Hugus, Frank. "*Blómstrvallasaga* and *Þiðriks saga af Bern*." *Scandinavian Studies* 46 (1974): 151–165.

Hünnerkopf, Richard. "Die Rothersage in Der Thidrekssaga." *BGDSL* 45 (1921): 291–297.

Kralik, Dietrich von. *Die Überlieferung und Entstehung der Thidrekssaga*. Halle: Niemeyer, 1931. Close analysis of the apparent revisions that took place in assembling the saga in MS. Mb.

Krogmann, Willy. "Zur Handschriftenfrage der Thidrekssaga." *BGDSL* (1927): 140–142.

Lohse, Gerhart. "Die Beziehungen zwischen der Thidrekssaga und den Handschriften des Nibelungenliedes." *BGDSL (T)* 81 (1959): 295–347.

Marold, Edith. "Dietrich als Sinnbild der Superbia." *Arbeiten zur Skandinavistik*. Ed. Heinrich Beck. Frankfurt: Lang, 1985. 443–486.

McTurk, Rory. "The Relationship of *Ragnars Saga Loðbrókar* to Þiðriks saga af Bern." Eds. Einar G. Péttursson and Jónas Kristjánsson. *Sjötíu Ritgerðir helgaðir Jakobi Benediktsyni 20 juli 1977*, 2 vols. Reykjavík: Stofnun Arna Magnússonar, 1977. Vol 2, 568–585.

Mundt, Marina. "Observations on the Influence of Thidriks saga on Icelandic Saga Writing." *Proceedings of the First International Saga Conference. University of Edinburgh, 1971*. Eds. Peter Foote, Hermann Pálsson, and Desmond Slay. London: Viking Society for Northern Research, 1973. 335–359. Argues for early date of saga in order to make influence on certain Icelandic sagas possible.

Paff, William J. *The Geographical and Ethnic Names in the Thidriks Saga: A Study in Germanic Heroic Legend*. 's-Gravenhage: Mouton, 1959. Includes a great deal of information about the stories and their sources.

Panzer, Friedrich. *Studien zum Nibelungenliede*. Frankfurt, 1945.

Patzig, Hermann. *Dietrich von Bern und sein Sagenkreis*. Dortmund: Ruhfus, 1917.

Pütz, Horst P. "Heimes Klosterepisode: Ein Beitrag zur Quellenfrage der Thidrekssaga." *ZDA* 100 (1971): 178–195.

Reichert, Hermann. *Heldensage und Rekonstruktion: Untersuchungen zur Thidrekssaga.* Vienna: Fassbaender, 1992.

Ritter-Schaumburg, Heinz *Die Nibelungen zogen nordwärts.* Munich: Herbig, 1981. Relates the historical events of the Nibelung legend to the questionable geography of the *Þiðrekssaga* rather than that of the *Nibelungenlied.*

Stephens, W. E. D. "*Þiðriksaga* and *Eckenlied.*" *London Mediaeval Studies* 1 (1937–1939): 84–92.

Unwerth, Wolf von. "Ostacia und Kâra." *BGDSL* 40 (1914): 160–162.

Wisniewski, Roswitha. *Die Darstellung des Niflungenunterganges in der Thidrekssaga.* Tübingen: Niemeyer, 1961.

Wyss, Ulrich. "Struktur der Thidrekssaga." *Acta Germanica: Jahrbuch des Südafrikanischen Germanistenverbandes* 13 (1980): 69–86.

HILDEBRANDSLIED, OLDER AND YOUNGER

The Old High German *Hildebrandslied* was written down in the early ninth century on the flyleaves of a Latin manuscript. The surviving fragment consists of some sixty-five[1] alliterative long lines. Linguistically the text betrays a mixture of Upper and Lower German forms, suggesting an Upper German source and a Low German scribe or vice versa. The usual assumption is that the surviving text was written down in a monastery along the linguistic border between High and Low German, probably Fulda.

Like the language, the text is uneven. There are moments of moving magnificence beside passages that have resisted all attempts to interpret or emend.

The poem begins with an identification of the two warriors and their preparations to meet in single combat between their respective armies. Hildebrand speaks first and asks the younger man's identity. Hadubrand tells of his father, Hildebrand, who had left him behind as an infant thirty years earlier. Hildebrand tells him that he has never begun an action with such a close relative. He removes an arm-ring and offers it to the younger man. Hadubrand accuses him of trying to trick him with the gift so that he can stab him with his spear. He concludes his speech with the statement: "Dead is Hildebrand, the son of Heribrand." Hildebrand breaks out in a cry of woe that a great calamity is about to take place. Either his own child will kill him or he will kill the young man. Hadubrand accuses Hildebrand of cowardice, and the two men throw

---

[1] The line count depends on the editorial treatment of several fragmentary lines.

their spears. They close and fight with swords, hewing their shields into small pieces. At this point the fragment breaks off.

It is a dogma of Germanic studies that this poem ends with the death of the son. There is also an Old Norse poem, usually referred to as "Hildebrand's Death-Song," in which Hildebrand laments having killed his son. There is, however, a second medieval version of this story that is found both in a late ballad-like version known as the "Younger Hildebrandslied" and in the *Þiðrekssaga af Bern*. In this later version the father overpowers the son and forces him to recognize that he is indeed who he says he is. The story concludes at the table of the mother, who recognizes her long-lost husband only after he provides her with a token of his identity. This version survives in High and Low German printed versions from the late fifteenth and early sixteenth centuries.

EDITIONS

Braune, Wilhelm. *Althochdeutsches Lesebuch*. Halle: Niemeyer, 1875. Many later editions. Most commonly cited edition of *Hildebrandslied*

Meier, John, ed. *Deutsche Volkslieder: Balladen*. Berlin: de Gruyter, 1935. The "Jüngeres Hildebrandslied" is on 1–21.

Edda. Die Lieder des Codex Regius. Ed.Gustav Neckel. 4th. ed. rev. by Hans Kuhn. Heidelberg: Winter, 1962. Includes "Hildebrands Sterbelied," ("Hildebrand's Death Song") as an appendix, 313-314.

CRITICAL WRITINGS AND RELATED WORKS

D'Alquen, Richard. "The Lay of Hildebrand: An Old Dutch Contribution to German Literature." *Canadian Journal of Netherlandic Studies/Revue Canadienne d'Etudes Néerlandaises* 4–5.2 (1983): 37–43.

Ebbinghaus, Ernst A. "'Forn her ostar gihuet...'" *Neophilologus* 72 (1988): 238–243.

Ebel, Uwe. "Historizität und Kodifizierung: Überlegungen zu einem zentralen Aspekt des germanischen Heldenliedes." *Althochdeutsch*. Eds. Rolf Bergmann, Heinrich Tiefenbach, and Karl Stackmann. Vol. 1. *Grammatik: Glossen und Texte*. Heidelberg: Winter, 1987. 685–714.

Gronvik, Ottar. "Sunufatarungo." *Gedenkschrift für Ingerid Dal*. Eds. Cathrine Fabricius-Hansen and Kurt-Erich Schondorf. Tübingen: Niemeyer, 1988. 39–53.

Harris, Joseph. "Hadubrand's Lament: On the Origin and Age of Elegy in Germanic." *HH*, 81–114.

Klare, Andreas. "Die Niederschrift des Hildebrandsliedes als Zufall." *Leuvense Bijdragen* 82 (1993): 433–443.

Krogmann, Willy *Das Hildebrandslied in der langobardischen Urfassung hergestellt*. Berlin: Schmidt, 1959.

McDonald, William C. "Too Softly a Gift of Treasure: A Rereading of the Old High German Hildebrandslied." *Euphorion* 78.1 (1984): 1–16.

Meier, Hans-Heinrich. "Die Schlacht im Hildebrandslied." *ZDA* 119 (1990): 127–138.

Renoir, Alain. "Oral-Formulaic Rhetoric: An Approach to Image and Message in Medieval Poetry." *Medieval Texts and Contemporary Readers*. Eds. Laurie A Finke and Martin B. Shichtman. Ithaca: Cornell University Press, 1987. 234–253.

————. "Repetition, Oral Formualaic Style, and Affective Impact in Mediaeval Poetry: A Tentative Illustration." *Comparative Research on Oral Traditions*. Ed. John Miles Foley. Columbus, OH: Slavica, 1987. 533–548.

Stutz, Elfriede. "Hadebrant and Alebrant." *Beiträge zur Namenforschung* 19 (1984): 261–274.

Tyler, Lee Edgar. "The Heroic Oath of Hildebrand." *De Gustibus: Essays for Alain Renoir*. Eds. John Miles Foley, J. Chris. Womack, and Whitney A. Womack. New York: Garland, 1992. 551–585.

Vries, Jan de. "Das Motiv des Vater-Sohn-Kampfes im Hildebrandslied." *Zur germanisch-deutschen Heldensage*. Ed. Karl Hauck. Darmstadt: Wissenschaftliche Buchgesellschaft, 1965. 248–284.

DAS BUCH VON BERN (DIETRICHS FLUCHT)

This anonymous poem was probably written down sometime after the middle of the thirteenth century. It deals with two recurring and important themes of the Dietrich legends: Dietrich's exile and Dietrich's attempt to recapture his lands with the assistance of Etzel's men.

The poem begins with an account of the illustrious ancestors of Dietrich von Bern and sets the stage for the recurring conflict between Dietrich and his kinsman Emmerich.

Emmerich, brother to Dietrich's father, Dietmar, covets the young Dietrich's lands and assembles a great army to lay waste to them. Dietrich's forces take Emmerich's by surprise and are victorious, but later Emmerich's forces are able to capture several of Dietrich's most valued warriors (Hildebrand and Wolfhart, among others). Dietrich is compelled to give up his re-conquered lands to save his men. Dietrich journeys to Etzel's court, where Helche, Etzel's gracious wife, and Rüedeger become his staunchest allies. Dietrich pledges fealty to Etzel, who, in turn, promises to help him.

Upon receiving news that Bern has been retaken by his forces, Dietrich returns to his lands. Another skirmish occurs and Emmerich retreats. Dietrich entrusts Raben [Ravenna] to Witege and returns to Etzel's court. Witege betrays Dietrich, who must once again assemble a mighty force to fight Emmerich. The ensuing battle is bloody and intense. Dietrich is victorious, but Emmerich again manages to escape. After reoccupying his kingdom, Dietrich returns to Etzel's court.

In contrast to the other poems in the Dietrich cycle, the *Buch von Bern* devotes nearly one quarter of its narrative to Dietrich's ancestors.

Within the context of the various Dietrich poems, the *Buch von Bern* is noteworthy in that it depicts the circumstances behind Dietrich's exile and his alliance with Etzel, two popular and recurring motifs in the Dietrich legend. The *Buch von Bern* also portrays the theme of the conflict within ruling families (Dietrich and Emmerich) and its effect on the state. This familial conflict is a typical feature in medieval Germanic story telling.

Here the emphasis is on feudal order based on loyalty, which types the various figures accordingly. As the designated hero Dietrich embodies the virtue of loyalty in his speeches and actions. His strong and praiseworthy loyalty is reflected and affirmed by his bravery, generosity, and unrestrained manifestations of grief. He gives up his hard-won lands without hesitation for the safe return of his captured warriors. Similarly Dietrich's circle of warriors displays a staunch and unwavering loyalty to their lord. By contrast Emmerich is disloyal and bears the ignominious epithet *ungetriuwe* (unfaithful). His traditional role of villain is intensified in this poem, where he is portrayed as having *no* redeeming qualities—he is cowardly and greedy. Emmerich is surrounded by similarly negative figures: Sibeche, Witege, and Heime, whose treachery is a recurring motif in many of the Dietrich poems.

The narrative alternates between Dietrich's exile and his troops' successful battles against Emmerich. The numerous and detailed battle scenes hold a special fascination for the poet, who takes delight in describing the carnage.

Finally there is also an extremely flattering portrait of Etzel and Helche. The characterization of Helche is especially noteworthy, since she is a visible and active female figure. Her fierce loyalty to Dietrich prompts her to provide Dietrich not only with goods and men but also with a wife.

Das Buch von Bern appears together with the *Rabenschlacht* in four medieval manuscripts, two from the fourteenth century (one now lost), and one each from the fifteenth and sixteenth centuries. All of the manuscripts are collections that include other works beyond the two heroic narratives.

EDITION

Dietrichs Flucht. Ed. Ernst Martin. *Deutsches Heldenbuch.* 5 vols. Berlin: Weidmann, 1866. Vol. 2, 57–215. Reprinted 1967 and 1975.

STUDIES

Bindheim, Dietlind. *Die Dialogtechnik in Dietrichs Flucht und die Rabenschlacht. Eine vergleichende Untersuchung der beiden Epen.* Unpublished dissertation, Munich, 1966.

Leitzmann, Albert. "Dietrichs Flucht und Rabenschlacht." *ZDP* 51 (1926): 46–91.

Premerstein, Richard von *Dietrichs Flucht und die Rabenschlacht. Eine Untersuchung über die äußere und innere Entwicklung der Sagenstoffe.* Gießen: Schmitz, 1957.

Voorwinden, Norbert. "Das intendierte Publikum von 'Dietrichs Flucht' und 'Rabenschlacht.'" *2. Pöchlarner Heldenliedgespräch. Die historische Dietrichepik.* Ed. Klaus Zatloukal. Vienna: Fassbaender, 1992. 79–102.

Wagner, Norbert. "Ein Aquitanier in der Dietrichepik." *ZDA* 114 (1985): 92–95.

RABENSCHLACHT

This poem may have existed in an earlier version before *Buch von Bern*, but its dating is commonly accepted to be in the last half of the thirteenth century. Its opening lines appear to take up the narrative where the *Buch von Bern* ends.

Dietrich is in exile at Etzel's court and about to marry Herrat when he receives news of Emmerich's renewed attacks on his kingdom. Wedding preparations and festivities alternate with battle and war preparations. Once again Helche, Etzel, and Rüedeger are unstinting in their loyalty to Dietrich. After amassing a great force Dietrich departs with Helche's two young sons, but only after promising that they will remain under his protection.

Before engaging in combat with Emmerich's forces, Dietrich leaves the two young princes in the care of an elderly warrior, Elson, at Bern. However, the youths along with Diether, Dietrich's younger brother, secretly leave the safety of the city in search of battle. The three youths encounter Witege, who is challenged by Diether. All three young warriors are killed by Witege.

Meanwhile the two great armies meet and Dietrich's forces are triumphant. The victory, however, is quickly overshadowed by the deaths of the three youths. After a great display of mourning Dietrich returns to Etzel's court, where, with Rüedeger's assistance, he is eventually reconciled with Helche and Etzel.

The two poems, *Buch von Bern* and *Rabenschlacht*, share a number of features. Foremost is the recurring theme of conflict within the ruling families, exemplified in the struggle between Dietrich and his kinsman Emmerich. In both poems loyalty and disloyalty form a central theme, and the portraits of Dietrich and Emmerich are essentially black and white. Both poems have the customary lists of warriors. The warriors on the opposing sides form a familiar *Nibelungenlied* constellation. Among Dietrich's men are Hildebrand, Wolfhart, Dietleip, and Rüedeger; among Emmerich's are Sibeche, Witege, Heime, Gunther, Gernot, and Hagen. The figure of Sibeche can be linked with that of Sifka in the *Þiðrekssaga*.

Both poems indulge in hyperbole in their portrayal of the large armies. In the *Buch von Bern* Dietrich commands a force of 150,000 ("anderhalp hundert tûsent man," 8040) and in *Rabenschlacht* Emmerich has over 200,000 men (480–499). An entire generation of warriors is destroyed as thousands perish. Intense and uncontrolled grieving is also typical of both poems.

In spite of these similarities major differences exist. Werner Hoffmann has argued that the poet of the *Buch von Bern* had a better knowledge of geography and of military operations than the poet of *Rabenschlacht*. The dialogue is structured differently and the two poems are written in two different verse forms. *Buch von Bern* is in rhymed couplets while *Rabenschlacht* is in a strophic form distantly related to that of the *Nibelungenlied*. *Rabenschlacht* appears to be drawn from an earlier narrative concentrating on Etzel's two sons, and therefore Emmerich is much more in the background.

Within the narrative context of the Dietrich cycle, the *Rabenschlacht* appears to set the stage for the events of the *Nibelungenlied*. Rüedeger assumes a more important and familiar role at Etzel's court. As noted earlier, he is largely responsible for bringing about the reconciliation between Helche and Dietrich.

Both poems' treatment of Christianity merits our attention. In the course of *Buch von Bern* and *Rabenschlacht* the main figures tend to employ God's name or to call upon him for assistance with regularity. Upon closer examination, however, this Christianity is essentially superficial; the world of these two poems is not God-oriented. Indeed, with their emphasis on revenge and immoderation (the unrestrained blood-letting and grief), these works in effect reject the basic tenets not only of Christianity but also of courtly knighthood.

See the notice on manuscript transmission under *Das Buch von Bern* above for a description of the manuscripts preserving this work.

EDITIONS

Rabenschlacht. Ed. Ernst Martin. *Deutsches Heldenbuch*. 5 vols. Berlin: Weidmann, 1866. Vol. 2, 219–326.

Die Rabenschlacht nach dem altdeutschen Heldengedicht. Ed. Ludwig Buckmann. Leipzig: Reclam, 1887–1890.

STUDIES

Leitzmann, Albert. "Dietrichs Flucht und Rabenschlacht." *ZDP* 51 (1926): 46–91.

Premerstein, Richard von. *Dietrichs Flucht und die Rabenschlacht. Eine Untersuchung über die äußere und innere Entwicklung der Sagenstoffe*. Gießen: Schmitz, 1957.

Steche, Theodor. *Das Rabenschlachtgedicht, Das Buch von Bern und die Entwicklung der Dietrichsage*. Greifswald: Bamber, 1939.

Voorwinden, Norbert. "Das intendierte Publikum von 'Dietrichs Flucht' und 'Rabenschlacht.'" 2. *Pöchlarner Heldenliedgespräch. Die historische Dietrichepik*. Ed. Klaus Zatloukal. Vienna: Fassbaender, 1992. 79–102.

This poem in the same strophic verse from as the *Nibelungenlied* was probably written down in the middle of the thirteenth century.

The emperor Emmerich decides to take back the lands of his vassal and kinsman Dietrich. This message is delivered by Heime, whom Dietrich accuses of disloyalty. Dietrich refuses to be driven off and consults with his men, and together they draw up a list of allies. Alphart, a young, unproven knight, wishes to engage Emmerich's guard. Though initially unwilling, Dietrich grants the youth his request. His kinsman Hildebrand rides out after him in an attempt to dissuade him, but after Alphart defeats him, he, too, allows the lad to pursue his quest.

Alphart fights valiantly, defeating scores of Emmerich's warriors. Hearing of this, Emmerich commands Heime to combat Alphart. Witege secretly rides out behind his friend. When Heime later falls before Alphart's mighty sword, Witege joins in the fight. Alphart is eventually overcome and slain by the two warriors together.

The death of such a young and gallant warrior becomes a rallying cry as Hildebrand leads a group of Dietrich's allies into battle. They defeat Emmerich's forces, but the emperor is intent on punishing Dietrich, and another battle takes place before Worms in which Dietrich's men are again victorious. Emmerich and Sibech as well as Witege and Heime, however, manage to escape the carnage. There is much rejoicing in Bern before the warriors depart.

In light of its narrative *Alpharts Tod* (*Alphart's Death*) appears to occur near the beginning of the unending and popular cycle of conflicts between Dietrich and his kinsman Emmerich. It should be pointed out that Dietrich is not yet in exile, and thus his familiar alliance with Etzel is not portrayed. Moreover, in contrast to other poems dealing with the Dietrich legend, most notably *Buch von Bern* and *Rabenschlacht*, this poem does not depict Dietrich's flight.

The choice of Alphart as the hero has important implications for our understanding of this poem. First of all, Alphart is not one of the traditional warriors of the Dietrich circle; he does not even appear in the *Þiðrekssaga*. By contrast he is deemed important enough by the poet of *Buch von Bern* to be killed twice by two different opponents!

The figure of Alphart embodies the literary chivalric-knightly ethos of the thirteenth century. Alphart is depicted as the young, brave, and idealistic knight-warrior who sets out alone in search of an adventure, that is, combat with Emmerich's guard. In this poem the knightly ethos is most clearly visible in

Alphart's battle with Witege and Heime, two traditional villains of the Dietrich legend. While Alphart fights honorably, never taking advantage of his foes, Witege and Heime act in an uncourtly fashion: they both engage Alphart in combat at the same time. While Alphart's courtly conduct is praised, it is also shown to be flawed. Alphart's rigid adherence to the concept of knightly honor results in his own death. It would seem that Alphart's courtly world view is in dissonance with the grim reality of feudal order.

Alpharts Tod survives in a single manuscript from the fifteenth century.

EDITIONS

Alpharts Tod. Ed. Ernst Martin. *Deutsches Heldenbuch.* 5 vols. Berlin: Weidmann, 1866. Vol. 2, 3–54. Reprinted 1967 and 1975.

Zimmer, Uwe. *Studien zu "Alpharts Tod" nebst einem verbesserten Abdruck der Handschrift.* Göppingen: Kümmerle, 1972.

STUDIES

Behr, Hans-Joachim. "Der Held und seine Krieger oder über die Schwierigkeiten ein Gefolgsherr zu sein. Überlegungen zu 'Alpharts Tod.'" *2. Pöchlarner Heldenliedgespräch. Die historische Dietrichepik.* Ed. Klaus Zatloukal. Vienna: Fassbaender, 1992. 13–23.

Jiriczek, Otto Luitpold Karl. "Die innere Geschichte des Alphartliedes." *BGDSL* 16 (1892): 115–199.

Kettner, Emil. "Die Einheit des Alphartliedes." *ZDP* 31 (1899): 24–39.

Vogelsang, Heinz. *Studien zur Entstehungsgeschichte von Alpharts Tod.* Unpublished dissertation, Bern, 1949.

Zimmermann, Günter. "Wo beginnt der Übermut? Zu 'Alpharts Tod.'" *2. Pöchlarner Heldenliedgespräch. Die historische Dietrichepik.* Ed. Klaus Zatloukal. Vienna: Fassbaender, 1992. 165–182.

THE POEMS IN *BERNERTON*

The following four poems (*Virginal, Eckenliet, Sigenot,* and *Goldemar*) share the same strophic form, a complex thirteen-line stanza known as the *Bernerton*. In contrast to the other poems in the Dietrich cycle the author of *Goldemar* names himself in the poem: "von Kemenâten Albreht der tihte ditze maere" ("by Albrecht von Kemenaten, who wrote this story") (2,2). All four poems are dated in the middle of the thirteenth century, and some literary historians have held them all to be the work of a single author, provisionally identified as Albrecht von Kemenaten, about whom nothing else is known. The poems vary enough in quality and style to allow us to question seriously the idea of a single author, but there is no way to be sure.

Virginal

Hildebrand sets off with the young Dietrich in search of *aventiure* (adventure) (7,7). They separate. While Hildebrand rescues a maiden who is being carried off as tribute from the dwarf queen Virginal to the heathen Orkise, Dietrich fights a band of heathens. Hildebrand arrives in a timely fashion to help Dietrich defeat them. The maiden returns to Virginal, who promptly sends another messenger, the dwarf Bibung, to Dietrich and Hildebrand.

Hildebrand and Dietrich battle dragons. Rentwin is rescued from the mouth of a dragon by his great-uncle Hildebrand, and Dietrich slays another dragon. Rentwin's father, Helferich, appears and all journey to Helferich's kingdom of Arona. Bibung invites Dietrich and Hildebrand to Virginal's court at Jeraspunt. Bibung is forced to return again to make sure that the guests follow.

With Helferich's men Hildebrand and Dietrich finally set off, but Dietrich is separated and is overpowered by the giant Wicran and brought as a prisoner to Nitger in Muter. The others discover Dietrich is missing in Jeraspunt and make plans to rescue him.

Dietrich is befriended by Nitger's sister Ibelin, who helps him to send a messenger to Jeraspunt. Ibelin warns her brother of the impending attack. Two simultaneous preparations for Dietrich's rescue occur. While Imian of Hungary assembles Biterolf and Dietleip, Hildebrand journeys to Bern to bring back the Wulfings as well as Heime and Witege.

At Muter eleven single combats occur. Nitger is beaten and is made a vassal of Dietrich. After fighting with more giants Dietrich and his guests at last arrive at Jeraspunt, where a great celebration takes place. News arrives of a siege of Bern. Dietrich and guests set off for Bern, but the threat fails to materialize. Dietrich arrives triumphantly in the city and his guests depart.

Much discussion has focused on *Virginal's* structure. The poem appears to consist of three discernible stories. The first and probably the oldest deals with Dietrich's first adventure, where Dietrich appears as a youth. The second story depicts the Rentwin-dragon episode. The Muter episode harks back to an older tradition that recounts the imprisoning of Dietrich by giants and the rescuing of Dietrich by his men. One recurring and unifying motif is the separation of Dietrich from Hildebrand, which takes place in each of the three parts. The three stories are interwoven with the persistent attempts of Virginal (here represented by her messenger Bibung) to have Dietrich visit her court. The poem also contains repetitions, retellings of previous events, and discrepancies that can be attributed to various uncoordinated reworkings of the text.

The knightly influence in the poem is most apparent at the beginning and at the end of the poem. Hildebrand accompanies the young and unproven Dietrich so that his lord can experience adventure. One recurring motif present in this work is Dietrich's reluctance to serve ladies. Virginal's court is one, long festive scene replete with dancing, feasting, and tournaments. The poem also emphasizes the fantastic—the presence of dragons, giants, and dwarfs enables the heroes to shine all the more brightly.

There are three principal manuscripts: h, d, and w. After stanza 233 the versions differ from one another considerably. The popularity of *Virginal* can be attested to by its twelve manuscripts, many of which exist today only as fragments.

In some early editions *Virginal* appeared under the title "Dietrichs erste Ausfahrt" ("Dietrichs First Excursion"), and some of the critical literature retains this title.

EDITIONS

Virginal. Ed. Julius Zupitza. *Deutsches Heldenbuch*. 5 vols. Berlin: Weidmann, 1870. Vol. 5, 1–200. Reprinted 1968.

Dietrichs erste Ausfahrt. Ed. Franz Stark. Stuttgart, 1860.

STUDIES

Kraus, Carl von. "Virginal und Dietrichs Ausfahrt." *ZDA* 50 (1908): 1–123.

Kuhn, Hugo. "Virginal." *BGDSL* 71 (1949): 331–86, and in *Dichtung und Welt im Mittelalter*. Stuttgart: Metzler, 1959. 220–248.

Lunzer, Justus. "Über Dietrichs erste Ausfahrt." *ZDA* 43 (1899): 193–257.

———. "Zu Virginal und Dietrichs erster Ausfahrt." *27. Jahresbericht über das k.k, Franz Joseph-Gymnasium in Wien*. Vienna: Selbstverlag des Gymnasiums, 1901. i–xxxiii.

Schmidt, Ernst A. *Zur Entstehungsgeschichte und Verfasserfrage der Virginal*. Prague, 1906.

Wilmanns, W. "Über Virginal, Dietrich und seine Gesellen und Dietrichs erste Ausfahrt." *ZDA* 15 (1872): 294–309.

Eckenliet

Three warriors, Vasolt, Ecke, and Ebenrot, gather to recount great heroic deeds. Talk focuses on Dietrich of Bern, which prompts Ecke to seek out Dietrich in order to measure his own prowess. Three young queens are so enthralled by Dietrich and his legend that they agree to provide Ecke with magical armor. If he is successful in bringing Dietrich back to their court, he can choose one of them to be his wife. Too big for a horse, Ecke travels by foot to Bern, where the ever-wise Hildebrand attempts to dissuade him from his present folly. He enters a strange forest where he slays a *Meerwunder* (sea monster). He then encounters a knight who has been grievously wounded by Dietrich.

Finally Ecke catches up with Dietrich and challenges him. Ecke explains the origin of his magnificent armor in the hope of getting Dietrich to fight him. Dietrich refuses and chides him for his arrogance but reluctantly consents to do battle with him when faced with a probable loss of honor and reputation. Their battle is protracted and fierce. After numerous entreaties to God for assistance Dietrich finally overpowers the cocky Ecke. Fearing shame and dishonor, Ecke refuses to surrender and Dietrich slays him, then strips him of his armor, which is so big that he has to cut it down. This is a bitter victory for Dietrich, and he decides to seek out the three queens. His wounds are healed by a mysterious woman along the way. He then encounters Ecke's brother, Vasolt, who is hunting a woman. They fight, and Vasolt is forced to swear loyalty to Dietrich. Vasolt's man, a dwarf, and his people also pledge their allegiance to Dietrich. Dietrich and Vasolt continue their journey to the land of the three queens. Eggenot, a blood relative of Ecke and Vasolt, is also vanquished by Dietrich. Vasolt secretly plots revenge and leads Dietrich to his mother, Birkhilt, whose power stems from the Devil. After cleaving her in two, Dietrich is seriously challenged by her tree-swinging daughter, Uodelgart.[Here the manuscript E_2 ends abruptly.]

A popular motif found in this poem is Dietrich's reluctance to fight. On the one hand Dietrich appears as a larger-than-life figure whose fame prompts the giant Ecke to seek and fight him. On the other hand Dietrich is slow to fight and does so only to prevent loss of honor.

The characterization of Ecke functions to expose the presumed shortcomings of the knightly ethos. Ecke's great size provides some humor, preventing him from riding a horse, a universal perquisite of knighthood. The whole concept of *frouwendienst* (service of ladies) comes under attack when Ecke is further encouraged to seek out Dietrich for combat by the three queens. Thus the ensuing battle is a frivolous whim, an adventure. After his defeat Ecke is so concerned with his diminished honor in the eyes of his three queens that he chooses death, a stance that Dietrich, the consummate warrior, criticizes. The poem also depicts the demonic in Vasolt, Ecke's brother, who hunts a maiden like an animal. Their mother and sister are also evil and apparently supernatural.

Seven manuscripts and eleven printed copies exist. The earliest transmission is a single strophe found in the Codex Buranus from the first half of the thirteenth century. The oldest manuscript containing most of the text is E_2 (which the summary above follows). The manuscript found in the *Dresdener Heldenbuch* is important because it probably contains the original conclusion. In this version Dietrich throws the severed head of Ecke before the queens as a rejection of the courtly ideals of *aventiure* and *frouwendienst*.

There are at least three distinct versions, the version summarized above, the one in the *Dresdener Heldenbuch*, and the one found in the printed *Heldenbuch* (see *Heldenbuch Prose*, below, p. 97). The differences begin with the events following Vasolt's surrender to Dietrich (verse 245).

Of special interest among these is the E₇ version from the *Dresdener Heldenbuch*, in which Ecke is portrayed as a negative figure. After seeking out the three queens, Dietrich learns that he has rescued them from Ecke's tyranny.

More information about the manuscripts and the versions can be found in the treatments by Hoffmann and Heinzle.

EDITIONS

Ecken Liet. Ed. Julius Zupitza. *Deutsches Heldenbuch.* 5 vols. Berlin: Weidmann, 1870. Vol. 5, 219–264. Reprinted 1968.

Eckenlied. Ed. and tr. Francis B. Brévart. Stuttgart: Reclam, 1986. Includes facing-page modern German translation.

Eckenlied. Ed. Martin Wierschin. Tübingen: Niemeyer, 1974.

STUDIES

Bernreuther, Marie Luise. "Herausforderungsschema und Frauendienst im 'Eckenlied.'" *ZDA* 117 (1988): 173–201.

Boer, R. C. "Das Eckenlied und seine Quellen." *BGDSL* 32 (1907): 155–259.

Boor, Helmut de. "Zur Eckensage." *Mitteilungen der schlesischen Gesellschaft für Volkskunde* 23 (1922): 29–43.

Boos, G. "Studien über das Eckenlied." *BGDSL* 39 (1914): 135–174.

Brévart, Francis B. "Der Männervergleich im 'Eckenlied'." *ZDP* 103 (1984): 395–406.

———. "won mich hant vrouwan usgesant (L. 43,4): Des Helden Ausfahrt im Eckenlied." *Archiv für das Studium der Neueren Sprachen und Literaturen* 220 (1983): 268–284.

Flood, John L. "Dietrich von Bern and the Human Hunt." *Nottingham Mediaeval Studies* 17 (1973): 17–41.

Freiberg, Otto. "Die Quelle des Eckenliedes." *BGDSL* 29 (1904): 1–79.

Heinzle, Joachim *Mittelhochdeutsche Dietrichepik.* Zurich and Munich: Artemis, 1978.

Hoffmann, Werner *Mittelhochdeutsche Heldendichtung.* Grundlagen der Germanistik 14. Berlin: Erich Schmidt, 1974.

Kratz, Henry. "The Eckenlied and Its Analogues." *Spectrum Medii Aevi: Essays in Early German Literature in Honor of George Fenwick Jones.* Ed. William C. McDonald. Göppingen: Kümmerle, 1983. 231–255.

Lassbiegler, H. *Beiträge zur Geschichte der Eckendichtungen.* Bonn: Georgi, 1907.

Meyer, Matthias. "Zur Struktur des *Eckenliedes.*" *Jahrbuch der Reineke Gesellschaft* 2 (1992): 173–85.

Stephens, W. E. D. "*Þiðriksaga* and *Eckenlied.*" *London Mediaeval Studies* 1 (1937–1939): 84–92.

Vogt, Friedrich Hermann Traugott. "Zum Eckenlied." *ZDP* 25 (1893): 1–28.

Zingerle, I. V. "Die Heimat der Eckensage." *Germania* 1 (1856): 120–123.

Zink, Georges. "Eckes Kampf mit dem Meerwunder. Zu, Eckenlied L 52–54." *Mediaevalia litteraria: Festschrift für Helmet de Boor zum 80. Geburtstag.* Eds. Ursula Hennig and Herbert Kolb. Munich: Beck, 1971. 485–492.

Ekka (in the *Þiðrekssaga*)

Þiðrek sets out to regain his honor after having been defeated in single combat. He encounters Ekka, who is betrothed to the queen of Drekanflis. After a long resistance Þiðrek finally agrees to fight in the dark. Ekka strikes his sword against a stone generating sparks so that the two men can see each other. Ekka gets the better of his opponent, but Þiðrek's horse, Falke, realizes his master's predicament and, breaking his reins, attacks Ekka. After the horse has broken Ekka's back, Þiðrek cuts off his head. Þiðrek rides toward Drekanflis, where the queen sees that a strange man has on Ekka's armor. She commands mourning in the castle, and Ekka's men arm themselves to seek revenge. Þiðrek prudently rides away only to encounter Ekka's brother Fasolt, who disables his brother's killer with a single blow. When Þiðrek recovers his senses, he rides after Fasolt and challenges him to continue the battle. They fight until Fasolt is defeated and the two combatants swear blood-brotherhood.

The two ride off and soon encounter a dragon that is swallowing a knight, whom they rescue. This episode is clearly related to the Rentwin episode in the Middle High German *Virginal* described above.

The service of ladies so prominent in the Middle High German version is reduced to a mention of nine princesses, who play no role in the story. (Þiðrek does come back and marry one of the princesses later in the saga, but only after being disappointed in his desire to marry the daughter of King Artus.) His reluctance to fight is explained by his wounds, which were not yet completely healed, although there is something fairly close to cowardice in much of his behavior.

Sigenot

Dietrich awakens a sleeping giant, Sigenot, only to discover that he is intent on seeking vengeance on Dietrich, who had slain two of his kinspeople, Grim and his wife. Failing to dissuade the giant from this course of action, Dietrich fights but is overpowered and thrown into a cave by Sigenot.

Hildebrand appears in the forest and battles with Sigenot. Although initially overpowered by his opponent, Hildebrand is able to surprise the giant, cutting off Sigenot's left hand before slaying him.

After attempting unsuccessfully to rescue his lord (Hildebrand makes a rope out of his own clothing), Hildebrand encounters a sleeping dwarf, Eggerich, a vassal of Dietrich. With Eggerich's assistance, Hildebrand is able to find a ladder and Dietrich is finally rescued. Dietrich and Hildebrand return to Bern, where they are cordially received.

Two passages appear to connect *Sigenot* with *Eckenlied*. According to the narrator the time sequence is right after Dietrich's slaying of Ecke: "dar nâch er Ecken stach" ("after he slew Ecke") (1,13). The closing lines of *Sigenot* refer directly to *Eckenlied*: "sus hebet sich Ecken liet" ("so begins the song of Ecke") (44,13). However, *Sigenot*'s relationship to *Eckenlied* is tenuous at best. The two poems have little in common. While this particular incident is not recounted elsewhere in the Dietrich cycle, the *Þiðrekssaga* does indeed portray Dietrich's battle with Grim's wife. The author interjects some humor into the poem by portraying Hildebrand and Eggerich having their beards tugged. As a friendly and loyal dwarf, Eggerich is somewhat reminiscent of Laurin (see section on the poem of *Laurin* below, p. 92).

There are two standard renditions: *The Older Sigenot* and *The Younger Sigenot*. About one hundred years separate these two versions (1250–1350). The numerous extant copies of *The Younger Sigenot* attest to its continuing popularity. Indeed, *Sigenot* was frequently published during the early years of printing. The oldest manuscript of the *Older Sigenot* dates from the fourteenth century.

EDITION

Sigenot. Ed. Julius Zupitza. *Deutsches Heldenbuch*. 5 vols. Berlin: Weidmann, 1870. Vol. 5, 207–15. Reprinted 1968.

STUDIES

Benzing, Josef. "Eine unbekannte Ausgabe des Sigenot vom Ende des 15. Jahrhunderts." *Gutenberg Jahrbuch* (1964): 132–134.

Eis, Gerhard. "Zur Überlieferung des Jüngeren Sigenot." *ZDA* 78 (1941): 268–276.

Flood, John L. "Studien zur Überlieferung des Jüngeren Sigenot." *ZDA* 95 (1966): 42–79.

Matthey, Walther. "Der älteste Wiegendruck des Sigenot. Datierung, Bildschmuck, Nachwirkung." *Anzeiger des germanischen National-Museums 1954 bis 1959* (1960): 68–90.

Rosenfeld, Hellmut. "Ein neues handschriftliches Sigenot-Fragment." *ZDA* 96 (1967): 78–80.

Steinmeyer, E. "Das jüngere Gedicht vom Riesen Sigenot." *Altdeutsche Studien.* Berlin, 1871. 63–94.

Goldemar

Dietrich, a courageous and valiant warrior, learns about great giants in the forest. He sets off in search of them. At the mountain of Trûtmunt he catches sight of a lovely maiden and is immediately smitten by her. The maiden, however, is guarded by dwarfs who live in the mountain. Dietrich asks the dwarf king, Goldemar, to allow him see her. In the middle of Goldemar's reply, the text abruptly ends.

This poem has some similarities with *Laurin.* Most notably both depict a kingdom of dwarfs in a mountain that is guarded by giants. There is also a captive maiden who escapes defilement.

According to Werner Hoffmann (195–197), the author of *Goldemar* was reacting against the traditional image of Dietrich. Here Dietrich appears as the lovestruck suitor. This is a significant departure from the conventional portrait of Dietrich as a valiant and loyal warrior whose relations with ladies is polite but usually somewhat distant. Not surprisingly the focus of *Goldemar* is on *minne* (love), not on heroic deeds and battles.

The poem exists in a single fragmentary manuscript.

EDITION
Goldemar. Ed. Julius Zupitza. *Deutsches Heldenbuch.* 5 vols. Berlin: Weidmann, 1870. Vol. 5, 203– 204. Reprinted 1968.

STUDIES
Haupt, M. "Goldemar von Albrecht von Kemenaten." *ZDA* 6 (1848): 520–529.

Hoffmann, Werner *Mittelhochdeutsche Heldendichtung.* Berlin: Schmidt, 1974.

BITEROLF UND DIETLEIP
The poem in rhymed couplets was written between 1260 and 1270 by an anonymous Austrian poet. It has two main divisions: the pre-history of Biterolf and Dietleip with their separate journeys to Etzel's court and the combat at Worms with its preparations.

Biterolf is the ruler of a Spanish land whose capital is Toledo. He and his wife, Dietlint, have a son, Dietleip.

So taken is Biterolf with the fame of Etzel's court that he secretly leaves his wife, son, and kingdom to seek it out. He encounters a nephew, Walter of Kärlingen, and later meets Rüedeger. Finally he arrives at Etzel's court and swears fealty to him. Along with Rüedeger he falls prisoner to a rival of Etzel's but later is able to overcome Etzel's foes.

Years pass. Biterolf's son, Dietleip, now sets off to find his father. On his journey he encounters the Burgundians. Dietleip is forced to fight Hagen, Gernot, and Gunther—all of whom the inexperienced youth overcomes. He arrives at Etzel's court. In an ensuing battle father and son fight each other unknowingly, but the outcome is not tragic. Rüedeger is instrumental in reuniting Biterolf and Dietleip.

Attention then shifts to Dietleip's presumed insult at the hands of the Burgundians. Etzel is determined to avenge this wrong and assembles a great army under the command of Rüedeger. Rüedeger is sent as a messenger to Worms, where he is warmly received. The fighting has three phases: a tournament; an engagement between the two armies; and another battle stemming from Rüedeger's gift, a banner. Gunther concedes defeat and a reconciliation occurs. Biterolf and Dietleip receive Steiermark from Etzel.

Like the poet of the *Klage* the poet of *Biterolf und Dietleip* appears to be reacting to the *Nibelungenlied*. Whereas the former recast the chief figures, the *Biterolf und Dietleip* poet focuses on the role of knighthood. Thus the impetus for narrative action at the beginning of the poem is Biterolf's fervent wish to see *ritterschaft* (knighthood) (405) at Etzel's court, which functions much like Arthur's court: its renown making it a model and a magnet for aspiring knights.

The emphasis on knighthood is reflected in the more prominent role of Rüedeger, who exudes courtliness. This courtly ethos is evidenced by Rüedeger's role as peacemaker in the poem. He is thus responsible for reuniting the father and son. Later Rüedeger acts as a messenger to Worms where he distinguishes himself—especially with the ladies at court. The importance of a courtly-knightly ethos may explain why Dietrich's role is small in this poem. He appears in the role of an ally of Etzel and is in exile. Once again he initially displays a reluctance to fight Sifrit. This dual motif is also found in *Rosengarten zu Worms* and *Þiðrekssaga*. The poet of *Biterolf und Dietleip* pokes some fun at this motif by having Dietrich turn pale at the prospect of fighting Sifrit.

The fight before Worms occurs within a knightly context. Indeed, the greatest warriors in the Germanic heroic tradition are assembled. The battles reprise the familiar constellation of the Burgundians and their allies versus the Huns and Amelungs. The choice of a tournament ensures that the conflict will not end in a bloodbath (cf. *Nibelungenlied*); however, the ensuing fights do vacillate between sport and life and death. Another indication of some knightly-courtly influence is the more visible role of the female figures. Brünhild and Kriemhild are portrayed as the perfect social hostesses to the messenger,

Rüedeger. During the combat the ladies are present and seem to inspire the knights to greater deeds. The assembled ladies, however, are not the goals of the fighting, and the focus of the poem is undeniably on the fighting itself, not on *minne* (love). As in the *Rosengarten zu Worms* the climax of the many contests is the combat between Dietrich and Sifrit.

While the focus on knighthood enables the poet of *Biterolf und Dietleip* to achieve a peaceful resolution of the conflict, this depicted knighthood, for the most part, is superficial and arbitrary. For example, the motivation for the confrontation at Worms arises from the uncourtly conduct of Dietleip, who despite his victory over Hagen, Gernot, and Gunther refuses to accept the Burgundians' apology. It should be noted that during the Worms segment Dietleip and Biterolf essentially vanish from the narrative.

Within the narrative time frame of the Dietrich legend Biterolf und Dietleip appears to depict a time coinciding with the beginning of the *Nibelungenlied.* At the beginning of this poem Hagen is still at Etzel's court and thus knows Rüedeger. When Dietleip encounters the Burgundians, they are just returning from the successful Saxon wars. Emmerich as well as Witege and Heime are portrayed as allies of Etzel and thus appear as positive figures.

EDITIONS

Biterolf und Dietleip. Ed. André Schnyder. Bern: Haupt, 1980.

Biterolf und Dietleib. Ed. Oskar Jänicke. *Deutsches Heldenbuch.* 5 vols. Berlin: Weidmann, 1866. Vol. 1, 1–197. Reprinted 1963.

STUDIES

Firestone, Ruth H. "On the Similarity of *Biterolf und Dietleib* and *Dietrich und Wenzelan.*" *Comparative Research on Oral Traditions.* Ed. John Miles Foley. Columbus, OH: Slavica, 1987. 161–83.

Hagenmeyer, Alfred. *Die Quellen des Biterolf.* Heilbronn: Baier and Schneider, 1926.

Knapp, Fritz Peter. "Sagengeographie und europäischer Krieg in 'Biterolf und Dietleib.'" *2. Pöchlarner Heldenliedgespräch. Die historische Dietrichepik.* Ed. Klaus Zatloukal. Vienna: Fassbaender, 1992. 69–77.

Lunzer, Justus. "Die Entstehungszeit des Biterolf." *Festschrift für B. Seuffert.* Ergänzungshefte zum *Euphorion* 16, 1923. 8–24.

———. "Humor im Biterolf." *ZDA* 63 (1926): 25–43.

Rauff, Willy. *Untersuchungen zu Biterolf und Dietleip.* Bonn, 1907.

Williams, Jennifer. "Etzel: Auf den Spuren der deutschen Ordensritter? Biterolf und Dietleip 1388–1627." *ZDA* 110 (1981): 28–34.

Zimmermann, Günter. " 'Biterolf und Dietleip:' Gedanken zu Gattung, Sinnstruktur und Thema." *Die mittelalterliche Literatur in der Steiermark.* Eds. Alfred Ebenbauer, Fritz Peter Knapp, and Anton Schwob. Bern: Lang, 1988. 317–333.

LAURIN

This adventure poem is in rhymed couplets and was probably composed sometime around the middle of the thirteenth century.

In Bern Hildebrand recounts the strange tale of a rose garden surrounded by a thread, cultivated and guarded by the dwarf-king Laurin. The violation of this thread and the garden represents an assault on Laurin, who demands of any trespasser a right foot and left hand as compensation. Dietrich and Witege seek out the garden and then proceed to destroy it. Magnificently clad, Laurin appears angrily, demanding his compensation. Dietrich at first seems reluctant to fight the dwarf but is forced to when Laurin overcomes Witege. During the long battle Hildebrand offers valuable advice that allows Dietrich to be victorious in spite of Laurin's indestructible armor, *Tarnkappe* (cloak of invisibility), and magical belt. Initially Dietrich is unwilling to grant the dwarf his life. Laurin asks for Dietleip's intervention, saying that he holds Dietleip's sister prisoner in his kingdom. Dietleip then fights Dietrich, but the ever-wise Hildebrand brings about peace between the two combatants.

The warriors (Witege, Wolfhart, Hildebrand, Dietleip, and Dietrich) then return with Laurin to his mountain realm, where they are warmly received. Dietleip's sister, Künhilt, finally appears. Laurin, however, is still angry about the destruction of his rose garden, so he imprisons Dietleip and drugs and throws the other warriors into a dungeon. Künhilt is instrumental in rescuing the warriors. She has in her possession a magical ring that enables the wearer to see the invisible dwarfs. A great battle ensues, but, thanks to the magic, the warriors are able to overcome the dwarfs as well as their allies—five giants—who perish. The dwarfs, however, are allowed to live. Laurin decides to become a Christian, and only then is he truly reconciled with Dietrich.

While *Laurin* treats the Dietrich legend, it nonetheless has a number of motifs reminiscent of the Siegfried legend. For example, Laurin has a *Tarnkappe* (cloak of invisibility) and his armor has been dipped in dragon's blood. These two devices along with a magical belt make him an almost invincible opponent. In this poem the Dietrich figure is combined with an earlier, popular tale: the abduction of a lady or maiden by dwarfs (see *Goldemar*). The presence of Dietleip and his sister, Künhilt, two members of the royal family of Steiermark (Styria), lends the poem a local flavor. According to Müllenhoff (edition, xliv ff.), the story of the dwarf-king Laurin, his garden, and his kingdom of the underworld can be traced back to a Tyrolean tale.

What is important to our discussion is the depiction of Dietrich and his trusted warriors. While the subsequent fighting is precourtly, some courtly influence is reflected in the original cause of the narrative action: the desire for adventure, that is, to see this fabulous garden. Once again Hildebrand appears as the sage and competent elder warrior-advisor, who continually helps his lord, Dietrich. Dietleip is here given a sister who shows courage and resourcefulness in helping her brother and the other warriors overcome their enemies. While Dietrich is portrayed as a living legend, he again is shown to be reluctant to fight. Here Witege is depicted as a trusted member of the Dietrich circle.

The conclusion of *Laurin* offers a somewhat optimistic worldview. It is noteworthy that Christianity is somewhat more visible in this poem. While treated with dignity by Laurin and his people, Künhilt, nevertheless, has no desire to remain with them because they are heathens. Moreover, a true and lasting reconciliation between Laurin and Dietrich is shown to be only possible after Laurin has converted to Christianity.

Seventeen manuscripts and eleven printed copies survive.

This summary follows the manuscript L₁, but we should also point out that this version is one of many. Joachim Heinzle sees at least five distinct versions. Manuscript L₁ is of special interest since it anticipates its sequel, *Walberan.*

EDITIONS

Laurin und der kleine Rosengarten. Ed. Georg Holz. Halle: Niemeyer, 1897.

Laurin und Walberan. [Ed. Karl Müllenhoff.] *Deutsches Heldenbuch.* 5 vols. Berlin: Weidmann, 1866. Vol. 1, 201–257. Reprinted 1963 . Müllenhoff's name does not appear on the edition, but it is assumed that he edited the sections of the *Deutsches Heldenbuch* that bear no name.

STUDIES

Dahlberg, Torsten. *Zum dänischen Lavrin und niederdeutschen Lorin. Mit einem Neudruck des einzig erhaltenen niederdeutschen Exemplars.* Lund: Gleerup, 1950.

Flood, John L. "Das gedruckte Heldenbuch und die jüngere Überlieferung des Laurin D." *ZDP* 91 (1972): 29–48.

Halasz, Katalin. "The intermingling of Romance Models in a 13th Century Prose Romance: Roman de Laurin." *Forum for Modern Language Studies* 22 (1986): 273–283.

Heinzle, Joachim. *Mittelhochdeutsche Dietrichepik.* Munich: Artemis, 1978.

Klein, Klaus. "Eine wiedergefundene Handschrift mit Laurin und Rosengarten." *ZDA* 113 (1984): 214–228.

Schröer, K. J. "Ein Bruchstück des Gedichtes Luarin [sic] oder der Kleine Rosengarten." *Jahresprogramm der Presburger* [sic] *Oberrealschule* 7 (1857): 19–28.

Wessels, P. B. "König Laurin." *BGDSL* (T) 84 (1962): 245–265.

Zips, Manfred. "König Laurin und sein Rosengarten. Ein Beitrag zur Quellenforschung." *Tiroler Heimat* 35 (1972): 5–50.

WALBERAN

The opening lines of *Walberan* link it to the closing of *Laurin*. *Walberan* was probably written around the middle of the thirteenth century. Like its predecessor this poem is written in rhymed couplets.

Dietrich and his followers (including Laurin) are in Bern. Here Laurin himself is the impetus for the narrative action.

Word reaches Walberan in his castle Kanachas on the Euphrates about the uncertain fate of his kinsman Laurin. Walberan immediately sets about assembling an army of 60,000 to fight Dietrich of Bern. Before the battle he sends Schiltunc as a messenger to Dietrich. Meanwhile Laurin has become a friend and ally of Dietrich and is not in any danger. Walberan's mighty army has one great advantage—they can make themselves invisible—but Dietrich, Hildebrand, Dietleip, Witege, and Wolfhart still possess magical rings, presumably acquired in the earlier Laurin episode. When battle seems inevitable, Laurin himself acts as a messenger on Dietrich's behalf. He is able to bring about a peaceful resolution of the conflict. It is decided that Dietrich and Walberan will engage each other in combat. On the day of the fight Walberan's troops are so radiant that the people of Bern believe them to be from heaven. First Schiltunc and Wolfhart fight and then Dietrich and Walberan. After a long and inconclusive fight the wise Hildebrand intercedes and brings about peace. The two foes swear friendship and Walberan is welcomed into Bern, where a great celebration takes place.

The editor[2] of the edition in the *Deutsches Heldenbuch* was correct when he suggested that the chief aim of the poem was to depict Laurin in a positive light. The poem leaves no doubt whatsoever about Laurin's loyalty to Dietrich. Only by acting personally as a messenger for Dietrich is Laurin finally able to dissuade his kinsman Walberan from staging a massive attack. Inevitably Dietrich has to engage Walberan in combat. In the Dietrich cycle Dietrich's fight with a formidable foe is a recurring motif. Mirroring the upbeat mood of the poem, not a single life is lost. The positive worldview persists as the former foes are reconciled. Loyalty is a dominant theme, and Walberan equals Laurin's loyalty to Dietrich in his own loyalty to his kinsman.

---

[2] Karl Müllenhoff, whose name does not appear in the edition. It is common knowledge that Müllenhoff edited the portions of the *Deutsches Heldenbuch* that bear no editor's name, but we have been unable to locate documentation outside of scholarly oral tradition. Heinzle (*Dietrichepik*), who is generally careful about facts, assumes Müllenhoff to be editor of the *Laurin* and *Walberan*.

The depiction of the Orient in the poem is also noteworthy. While it appears as an exotic place, it is not portrayed negatively.

Walberan appears whole in one of the *Laurin* manuscripts, and a second contains only the beginning. There is no independent transmission of the poem.

EDITION

Laurin und Walberan. Deutsches Heldenbuch. 5 vols. Berlin: Weidmann, 1866. Vol. 1, 201–257. Reprinted 1963. No editor is named, but the two texts are assumed to have been edited by Karl Müllenhoff, see footnote 2.

DIETRICH UND WENZELAN

This poem in rhymed couplets stands between the fairy-tale poems and the historical poems. It does not fit clearly into the historical story of the *Buch von Bern/Rabenschlacht* sequence, but it does place Dietrich in exile at Etzel's court. The poem is usually dated in the middle of the thirteenth century and exists only in a fragmentary manuscript.

> After receiving a public challenge to fight Wenzelan, the prince of Bolan, Dietrich consults with Wolfhart. Dietrich's reluctance to fight is gradually overshadowed by the possibility of his loss of fame and honor. Etzel then expresses a desire to be present at the fight. The mood is festive as the two armies meet; ladies, too, are present. The joust between the prince of Bolan and Dietrich is long and intense. When Dietrich appears to be weakening, Wolfhart is able to rally and incite Dietrich, who fights with renewed vigor and determination.

This poem depicts two recurring and popular motifs of the Dietrich legend: 1) Dietrich is required to fight a formidable opponent and 2) Dietrich is at first reluctant to do so. For unexplained reasons Hildebrand and Wolfhart are hostages at Wenzelan's court. Rüedeger of Bechelaren, another figure associated with the Dietrich legend, makes a brief appearance as the marshal.

Etzel appears as Dietrich's lord, who, upon learning of the challenge, shows great loyalty to his vassal. Etzel thus rides out with Dietrich. The contest is fought in the presence of the ladies, who are essentially decorative, having no real function. The ensuing battle harks back to a precourtly era: it is long and bloody. The poem abruptly breaks off just as Dietrich is rallying against Wenzelan, a most capable opponent.

EDITION

Dietrich und Wenzelan. Ed. Julius Zupitza. *Deutsches Heldenbuch.* 5 vols. Berlin: Weidmann, 1870. Vol. 5, 267–274. Reprinted 1968.

STUDIES

Eis, Gerhard. "Zu Dietrichs Slawenkämpfen. 1. Dietrich und Wenezlan." *ZDA* 84 (1952–1953): 70–77.

Firestone, Ruth H. "On the Similarity of *Biterolf und Dietleib* and *Dietrich und Wenzelan.*" *Comparative Research on Oral Traditions.* Ed. John Miles Foley. Columbus, OH: Slavica, 1987. 161–183.

Lunzer, Justus. "Dietrich und Wenezlan." *ZDA* 55 (1917): 1–40.

Schröder, E. "Das Fragment Dietrich und Wenezlan." *ZDA* 70 (1933): 142–144.

DER WUNDERER

This curiosity is probably a product of the fifteenth century. It exists in two versions, both of which tell approximately the same story.

Etzel is holding a grand festival at which all of his tributary kings and nobles are present. The poem emphasizes the security of Etzel's rule, which allows him to leave the castle gates open. A young woman appears asking to speak to Etzel. She tells him that she is being pursued by a monster and asks for a champion to fight for her. Rüdiger and Etzel both refuse. Dietrich, who is so young that he is not even allowed to eat with the established heroes, offers to do so. She puts a spell on him that is supposed to protect him. He carries on a long fight with the monster and eventually defeats him. The woman identifies herself as Lady Fortune (Frau Saelde) before leaving the court.

The court situation is reminiscent of the Arthurian court, and, in fact, Etzel is compared favorably to Arthur in the opening strophes, so we can assume the "contamination" of Dietrich legend by Arthurian adventures was intended. The motif of a human hunted by a monster also occurs in the *Eckenlied*, but there is no necessity to assume direct influence. The situation imagined by the poem is not even provided for in the legendary "history" because Dietrich does not come to Etzel's court until he is a mature man. The poem exists in a strophic version and in a version in couplets. The couplet version survives only in fragments, while the strophic text is found in the *Dresdener Heldenbuch* and in two printed books of the early sixteenth century.

EDITIONS

Hagen, Friedrich Heinrich von der, and Alois Primisser, eds. *Der Helden Buch in der Ursprache.* 2 vols. Berlin, 1820–1825. Edition of the *Dresdener Heldenbuch.*

Zink, Georges, ed. *Le Wunderer. Fac-Simile de L'Edition de 1503.* Paris: Aubier, 1949. Facsimile reprint of the print of 1503 with introductory discussion of the versions of the poem.

ERMENRÎKES DÔT

An odd collection of motifs from heroic legend finds its way into the Low German ballad *Ermenrikes Dot* ("The Death of Ermanaric"). The poem survives only in printed broadsides and collections beginning in the late sixteenth century.

Dirick and his men ride out in search of the king of Armentrik. Hillebrand's wife tells him where to find him and advises taking along the twelve-year-old giant Bloedelinck. The twelve men set out to Freysack (Friesach in Carinthia?), where they see fresh gallows set up for them. The men appear with silk clothing over their armor and with flowers in their hair as if coming to a dance. They confront the king, and, when he refuses to say why he has set up the gallows, they behead him. The twelve warriors fight with the king's men and defeat them, killing all but the faithful gatekeeper Reinhold of Meilan. Dirick fears the young Bloedelink has been lost, but he is found in a dungeon, where he has wounded 350 warriors.

This odd concatenation of heroic motifs seems to echo the expedition of Hamðir and Sörli from the *Hamðismál*, but Dietrich appears here as the attacker and he is immediately successful. John Meier suggests that the poem is more closely related to *Dietrichs Flucht* and that the similarities to *Hamðismál* are accidental. Brady, on the other hand, expands the number of parallels by incorrectly reporting in her synopsis of the story that Bloedelinck is killed. She brings this nonexistent killing into a relationship with that of Erp, the half-brother of Hamðir and Sörli who is killed along the way to Jörmunrek's court.

Ermenrikes Dôt is typical of the hodgepodge of heroic motifs we find in later Scandinavian ballads, and an influence from Danish ballads on our text cannot be ruled out.

EDITION AND STUDIES

"Ermenrichs Tod." *Deutsche Volkslieder: Balladen.* Ed. John Meier. Berlin: de Gruyter, 1935. 21–27. Includes commentary and discussion of relationship to other Dietrich narratives.

Boer, R. C. *Die Sagen von Ermanarich und Dietrich von Bern.* Halle: Waisenhaus, 1910.

Brady, Caroline. *The Legends of Ermanaric.* Berkeley: University of California Press, 1943.

Haug, Walter. "Ermenrikes dot." *Deutsche Literatur des Mittelalters: Verfasserlexikon, Ed. Kurt Ruh et al.* 2d ed. Berlin: de Gruyter, 1977ff. Vol 2, 611–618.

In the course of the fifteenth century a collection of heroic legends became more or less standardized. This took place first in manuscripts produced in lay scriptoria,[3] but the collection was soon printed and the first printing formed the basis for a century of unauthorized reprints. The collection reached its final form in the *Heldenbuch* ("Book of Heroes") printed in Strasbourg in 1483. It contained the following texts: *Ortnit, Wolfdietrich, Rosengarten,* and *Laurin.* The text was prefaced by an extensive prose introduction in which the legendary past was retold. The printed book also included a general rhymed introduction that complained about the degradation of morals and customs and recommended the reading of books as a remedy. The prose matter was variously placed at the beginning and end of various printings so that it has sometimes been called the Preface (*Vorrede*) and sometimes the Appendix (*Anhang*) to the *Heldenbuch.* We have followed Heinzle's suggestion to call it simply *Heldenbuch*-Prose. Heinzle lists six printings of the collection in the period from 1483 to 1590.

The introduction sets out to tell where heroes come from and how their race had come to an end. It includes an extensive discussion of dwarfs in which the appearance of giants and heroes is also introduced. The giants were introduced to protect the dwarfs, from the monstrous creatures that roamed the earth, and the heroes were introduced to protect the dwarfs from the giants. There follows a list of heroes, sometimes with their lineage or their place of origin.

Then follow the stories of Ortnit and Wolfdietrich told in considerable detail, following the texts that appear later in the book. Here, as in *Wolfdietrich D,* Dietrich of Bern is the grandson of Wolfdietrich.

We are told that a spirit appeared to the mother of Dietrich during her pregnancy who foretold the son's strength and also said that he would be able to spew fire from his mouth when he became angry. The Devil (apparently the same spirit) built a castle in three days for Dietrich in Bern.

Then the story of the Rosengarten is inserted in which Seifrid (Siegfried) is killed by Dietrich. The story of the rape of Sibech's (Sifka's) wife by Ermanaric is told much as it is in the *Þiðrekssaga* and Sibech's

---

[3] Until about the beginning of the fifteenth century even secular books were produced by scriptoria in monasteries. As literacy began to spread quickly around 1400, the demand for books brought about the founding of several lay scriptoria in which books were copied wholesale for booksellers. It was this great demand for books that led to the invention of printing with movable type in the middle of the century.

revenge is much the same. He leads Ermanaric to kill his nephews and drive Dietrich from his lands. With the help of Markgraf Riediger (Rüdiger) Dietrich is able to find refuge with Etzel. Etzel has Dietrich marry his niece and helps him regain his lands.

Crimhilt marries Etzel in order to gain vengeance on Dietrich for the death of Seifrid. She attempts to get Hagen to start the fight, but he refuses because no harm has been done to him. She then twice sends out her son to strike Hagen. The first time Hagen sends him away with a warning, but the second time he beheads the boy and the fight is underway. All the heroes battle. Hildebrant is wounded and goes to inform his lord about the battle. Dietrich comes and takes the two brothers of Crimhilt captive and sends them bound to her. She strikes off their heads. Dietrich cuts her in two.

Dietrich and Hildebrant ride back to Bern, where a battle takes place. Hildebrant is killed by Guther, Crimhilt's brother, and the remaining heroes in the world are killed there with the exception of Dietrich. A dwarf appears and says to him: "You shall go with me. Your kingdom is no longer in this world." Dietrich goes with him and no one knows where he is, or whether he is alive or dead.

This compilation has not received much attention in research literature, but it is a fascinating glimpse into the understanding of the Dietrich legend available to a fifteenth-century writer. Since the collection contained the texts of *Ortnit, Wolfdietrich, Rosengarten*, and *Laurin*, these were the focus of much of the prose addendum, but the most interesting portion is contained in the material added to fill out the life of Dietrich. Here we find a mixture of motifs we know from such places as the *Þiðrekssaga* and the *Nibelungenlied*, but in a logical connection that defies both earlier sources. Here Dietrich is Siegfried's killer and Kriemhild marries Etzel to gain vengeance against him. It is hard to imagine that the author of this text knew the *Nibelungenlied*, but the echoes of details are too strong to be coincidental. Kriemhild's sending her son to strike Hagen (the version we know from the *Þiðrekssaga*) and Hildebrand's mission to inform Dietrich of the battle and Dietrich's binding of the "brothers" of Kriemhild are echoes of the version we know in the *Nibelungenlied*.

This confusion cannot be unraveled here, but it is typical of a retelling from oral transmission in which the motifs of different oral and written versions have become hopelessly muddled. We find a similar muddle in *Das Lied vom Hürnen Seyfrid* (see below, p. 129).

EDITIONS
Heldenbuch nach dem ältesten Druck in Abbildung. Ed. Joachim Heinzle. Göppingen: Kümmerle, 1981. 1–6. Facsimile of 1483 *Heldenbuch* printed in Strasbourg.

"Alte Vorrede des Heldenbuchs." *Heldenbuch*. Ed. Friedrich Heinrich von der Hagen. Leipzig: Scholze, 1855.

CHAPTER 8

The Nibelung Legend

The Nibelung legend consists generally of the story of Siegfried/Sigurð, his youth, bridewinning, and murder, and the story of the fall of the Burgundians, who in most Norse sources are simply called Niflunga. The Northern versions of the story place more emphasis on the family of Sigurð, the Völsungs, and on the deeds of Sigurð's relatives. This is expanded to the greatest extent in the Icelandic *Völsungasaga*, which traces Sigurð's ancestry back to the god Oðin (Wodan).

In Germany the *Nibelungenlied* seems to have satisfied the need for a literary version of the legend, since there are fewer competing versions of the story.

Berndt, Helmut. *Die Nibelungen: Auf Spuren eines sagenhaften Volkes.* Oldenburg: Stalling, 1978.

Beyschlag, Siegfried. "Überlieferung und Neuschöpfung: Erörtert an der Nibelungen-Dichtung." *WW* 8.205–213 (1957–1958).

Dinkelacker, Wolfgang. "Nibelungendichtung außerhalb des 'Nibelungenliedes.'" *Ja muz ich sunder riuwe sin. Festschrift für Karl Stackmann zum 15. Februar 1990.* Ed. Wolfgang Dinkelacker. Göttingen: Vandenhoeck and Ruprecht, 1990.

Heusler, Andreas. *Nibelungensage und Nibelungenlied.* Dortmund: Ruhfus, 1920.

Ploss, Emil. *Siegfried—Sigurd. Der Drachenkämpfer.* Cologne: Böhlau, 1966.

NIBELUNGENLIED

Uns ist in alten mæren   wunders vil geseit
von helden lobebæren,   von grôzer arebeit
von fröuden, hôchgezîten,   von weinen und von klagen,
von küener recken strîten,   muget ir nu wunder hören sagen.

("We have been told in ancient tales many marvels of famous heroes, of mighty toil, joys and high festivities, of weeping and wailing, and the fighting of bold warriors—of such things you can now hear wonders unending!" Hatto, 17)

With this powerful opening stanza the *Nibelungenlied* poet boldly broke with the chivalric-knightly literary tradition in vogue around 1200. Instead, to relate his magnificent tale of murder, treachery, and revenge, the poet chose the popular and ancient legends as his raw material.

The tragic mood is already established in the first few stanzas. Many warriors will die because of one woman, Kriemhild. The impending tragedy is immediately reinforced by the young Kriemhild's troubling dream. Kriemhild lives with her mother, Ute, and her brothers (the three kings) Gunther, Gernot, and Giselher in Worms.

The setting shifts to Xanten, home of the accomplished knight-prince Siegfried and his parents, Sigmund and Sigilind. Although he sets off for Worms to woo Kriemhild, Siegfried initially challenges Gunther's kingship. The matter, however, is peacefully resolved, and Siegfried becomes an important ally in the Saxon war against Liudeger and Liudegast. Siegfried is at court in Worms one year before he sees Kriemhild. At the banquet celebrating the victory over the Saxons Siegfried and Kriemhild instantly fall in love with each other.

Before Siegfried can marry Kriemhild he must help Gunther win the powerful and formidable queen Brünhild. He accomplishes this by using a magical *Tarnkappe* (a cloak that allows its wearer to become invisible and gives him the strength of twelve men). Later Siegfried is forced to subdue Brünhild so that Gunther can consummate the marriage. With her virginity taken Brünhild loses her extraordinary strength.

Siegfried and Kriemhild depart for Xanten, where Sigmund renounces the throne in favor of his son. Years pass, and Brünhild convinces Gunther to invite his vassal Siegfried to visit Worms. At a tournament the two queens argue over the importance of their respective husbands, which later leads to a confrontation outside of the cathedral. Here Kriemhild tells Brünhild that Siegfried, not Gunther, took her virginity. Brünhild's public humiliation prompts Hagen, the chief vassal of the Burgundian kings, to seek revenge.

After tricking Kriemhild into revealing Siegfried's one vulnerable spot, Hagen slays the famous warrior while out on a hunt. Kriemhild dissuades Sigmund and his men from taking revenge, and they depart. At the behest of her relatives Kriemhild decides to remain in Worms, and eventually she is reconciled with her brothers, but not with Hagen. Kriemhild's brothers eventually convince her to have Siegfried's treasure brought to Worms, but Hagen eventually takes it away from her and sinks it in the Rhine.

Years pass. Helche, the wife of Etzel, dies, and his advisors urge him to marry Kriemhild, who is reluctant until her kinspeople persuade her to accept Etzel's proposal. With Etzel's messenger, Rüedeger, Kriemhild journeys to Etzel. After a number of years Kriemhild convinces Etzel to invite her brothers and Hagen, to his court. Neither Ute's warning nor the sea nymphs' prophecy deters the Burgundians from their journey. Hagen now assumes a dominant role, singlehandedly transporting the vast army across the Danube. Only after destroying the raft does he finally inform them of their doom. A fight ensues when the Bavarians attempt to avenge the ferryman whom Hagen had slain.

Their stay with Rüedeger is the last happy occasion for the Burgundians. Giselher is betrothed to Rüedeger's daughter. At Etzel's court the tension becomes increasingly palpable until finally Kriemhild incites the Huns to attack. At a feast warfare breaks out, and Hagen beheads the son of Etzel and Kriemhild. Dietrich manages to save Kriemhild and Etzel, but all the other Huns in the hall perish. Rüedeger is forced to fight for his lord against his new kinsmen, the Burgundians, and is killed by Gernot. Both Hagen and Giselher refrain from fighting against Rüedeger.

Dietrich is finally drawn into the battle and takes the only two surviving Burgundians, Hagen and Gunther, prisoner. Kriemhild kills first her brother then Hagen. The slaying of such a great warrior as Hagen demands instant retribution: Kriemhild is slain by Hildebrand in front of Etzel and Dietrich, who mourn the great loss of life.

The *Nibelungenlied* poet's retelling of the well-known legends of Siegfried's murder and the fall of the Burgundians is dramatic, innovative, and above all modern. While the phrase, "in alten maeren" ("in ancient tales"), hearkens back to an earlier, precourtly era, the *Nibelungenlied* is actually a political poem that sets out to document the systematic breakdown of social (political) order. The *Nibelungenlied* poet, conservative in his social views, attributes the unfolding national tragedy to the irreconcilable clash between the chivalric-knightly and the heroic-aristocratic value systems. In the course of the *Nibelungenlied* the poet demonstrates that the new courtly ethos is actually dangerous to the aristocratic social (political) order.

The clash between these two value systems is highly visible in the *Nibelungenlied*'s depiction of kingship. While most of the discussion has focused on Gunther, both Siegfried and Etzel also represent weak kings. Siegfried, Gunther, and, to a lesser extent, Etzel all needlessly expose themselves to danger or possible loss of face in the pursuit of their respective brides. Siegfried's initial belligerence upon his arrival at Worms places him as well as his chosen opponent Gunther at unnecessary risk. Indeed, throughout his quest for Kriemhild, Siegfried puts himself at risk on no fewer than four separate occasions: 1) he volunteers to fight against the Saxons; 2) posing as Gunther's vassal, he overcomes the threatening Brünhild; 3) after this victory he journeys alone to his Nibelungen warriors, who at first fail to recognize him; and 4) he must once again overcome Brünhild so that Gunther can consummate the marriage. In all of these instances Siegfried's service to Gunther causes a blurring of his social status, which in turn later leads to his death.

A recurrent question is: What is Siegfried's political relationship to Gunther? The poet provides the audience with ample information that Siegfried is indeed superior to Gunther. For instance, while Brünhild and her court are familiar with the glorious deeds of Siegfried, Siegfried himself is compelled to introduce Gunther and then praise him. Here and elsewhere Siegfried and the others conspire to deceive Brünhild. Therefore Siegfried immediately establishes his "inferior" status by identifying himself as Gunther's "man": "wand' er ist mín herre" (420, 4), which his subsequent behavior confirms. Consequently, Brünhild is led to believe that Siegfried is actually Gunther's vassal. Siegfried's ambiguous political status undermines the political order, and therefore he must be killed in order to restore it (Gunther's and Brünhild's loss of face).

Gunther is typically viewed as a weak monarch. His weakened kingship is especially evident in the first part of the poem, where he not only relies heavily on Hagen for advice but also persistently seems to shun fighting. When Siegfried challenges him, he appears unwilling to fight. Later he seems to need Siegfried's assistance to defeat the troublesome Saxons. Gunther most seriously undermines his own kingship when he knowingly employs deceit to win Brünhild for his wife. This tactic affirms his unworthiness and, as we have seen, eventually destabilizes the political order. It should be noted, however, that Gunther undergoes a transformation. During the bloody and ferocious fighting at Etzel's court Gunther distinguishes himself as a capable and fierce warrior.

After the death of his wife, Helche, Etzel decides to seek Kriemhild's hand. He sends his most distinguished vassal and best negotiator, Rüedeger of Bechelaren, as his representative to Worms. Kriemhild's marriage to Etzel gives her the resources to achieve her revenge—the destruction of the Burgundians.

The bridewinning sequence here parallels the one involving Siegfried in the first half of the epic. Both men hear about Kriemhild's beauty and nobility and seek her hand in marriage without having seen her. In fact this example can be expanded textually to support Theodore Andersson's convincing argument that the first half of the *Nibelungenlied* was modeled after the second part. The downfall of the Burgundians is not only a result of the murder of Siegfried, it forms the structural parallel to it in the second half.

In the *Nibelungenlied* the "courtly" episodes function to strip the chivalric-knightly ethos of its idealism. At the beginning of the poem Ute's (the queen mother's) interpretation of Kriemhild's dream is reminiscent of the *Minnesang* tradition in which the knight is sometimes portrayed as a falcon. This dream foretells the disastrous consequences of the *minne* (love) relationship of Siegfried and Kriemhild. Thus it is not surprising that the language of Siegfried's courtship of Kriemhild is strikingly different—it is replete with *Minnesang* imagery. Kriemhild's marriage to Siegfried brings about a lessening of both Siegfried's and Gunther's kingship as well as leading finally to the great loss of life.

In his retelling of the two legends the *Nibelungenlied* poet enhanced the role of Kriemhild, who functions as the "bridge" binding the two parts of the poem. In the course of the poem she evolves from young maiden to haughty queen, to grieving widow, and finally to vengeful queen. Kriemhild has a pivotal role in both the death of Siegfried and the destruction of the Burgundians. The epithet "valandinne" (she-devil) applied to her both by Dietrich and by Hagen underscores her antiheroine role in the poem. This word would be used again by the poet of *Rosengarten* to vilify Kriemhild. Nonetheless, the very fact that the poem attributes the death of countless warriors to Kriemhild is a significant departure from the traditional depiction of female figures in our legends. Indeed, with the characterizations of Kriemhild and, to a lesser extent, Brünhild, the role of the female figure is expanded. At the same time, however, this increased focus on the female figures (or the effect of wooing them) itself reflects the irreconcilable clash between the courtly and aristocratic-feudal value system. Indeed, the more prominent roles of these two female figures points to an instability within the society depicted in the *Nibelungenlied*.

The winning of Brünhild is predicated on deceit, which in the course of the poem has disastrous consequences for most of the main figures. Brünhild's submission is brought about in two interrelated stages. First, she is bested by Siegfried, who uses magic in a series of physical contests. This defeat forces her to relinquish control of her kingdom. Second, Siegfried must again overcome her on her wedding night so that Gunther can consummate his marriage. The loss of her virginity brings about the loss of her supernatural powers and independence. After her quarrel with Kriemhild, Brünhild assumes a more typical female role in that she recedes into the background of events.

The *Nibelungenlied* poet reassembled only a few of the chief figures of the Dietrich circle. He does depict Dietrich accompanied by Hildebrand in exile at Etzel's court. Dietrich is an exemplary warrior who despite his rather late appearance in the poem immediately distinguishes himself. He is thus responsible for saving Etzel and Kriemhild when they are trapped in the hall. True to the Dietrich tradition, however, he refrains from fighting—at least initially. Once he decides to fight, he proves himself to be a capable warrior, quickly defeating Gunther and Hagen. This battle between Dietrich and the

Burgundians in the *Nibelungenlied* would become a popular and recurring motif in such Dietrich poems as *Rosengarten* and *Biterolf und Dietleip*.

Hildebrand, the ever wise and loyal advisor-warrior, shares a kinship with Hagen. Both figures embody and celebrate the warrior ethos or, in other words, the older, conservative order. As a vassal to Gunther (and his brothers) Hagen exemplifies feudal loyalty. Yet Hagen's fierce loyalty is shown to make him inflexible—he is unable to pursue the possibility of a peaceful resolution. In the *Nibelungenlied* Hildebrand's warrior role is emphasized more than his familiar role as sage counselor. Forced into a belligerent stance by his nephew Wolfhart, Hildebrand fights furiously against the Burgundians, leaving the battle as the last of Dietrich's men left alive only after he is wounded. Tellingly, the *Nibelungenlied* poet chooses Hildebrand to reestablish order by beheading Kriemhild, the instigator of the disorder and death.

A great deal of discussion has focused on Rüedeger, who experiences a terrible conflict of loyalties. With this characterization the *Nibelungenlied* poet artistically shows the tragic effects when aristocratic-feudal loyalties clash with blood-familial loyalties. While Rüedeger's sympathies are clearly stronger for his kinsmen the Burgundians (his daughter is betrothed to Giselher), he is ultimately forced to acknowledge his original allegiance to Kriemhild and Etzel and must fight the Burgundians.

Three of the above-mentioned figures of the Dietrich legend (Dietrich, Rüedeger, and Etzel) share another significant trait in the *Nibelungenlied*—they are all unsuccessful peacemakers. Each figure at some point of the conflict attempts to bring about a peaceful resolution, but each fails for different reasons. Rüedeger's bonds with both sides of the quarreling parties should have made him a strong candidate to mediate, but instead these conflicting loyalties destroy him. Etzel, too, at the beginning of the Burgundians' stay at his court has the potential for negotiating a peaceful settlement, but Hagen's murder of Etzel's and Kriemhild's son effectively destroys this possibility. Etzel must now become involved in the bloodletting. Dietrich attempts to bring a late reconciliation when he does not kill the last two surviving Burgundians, Gunther and Hagen. Dietrich, however, errs when he entrusts their safety to Kriemhild, who kills them.

These failed attempts at peacemaking also confirm the minor role that Christianity plays in this poem. The Christianity depicted in the epic is largely ritualistic and superficial. One glaring example of this tendency is the famous quarrel between Kriemhild and Brünhild outside the cathedral. While both figures attend the mass, it does not appear to have any mitigating influence on their rage, since afterward their argument dramatically escalates. While Christianity does not come under direct attack (as does the chivalric-knightly ethos), it is, by its very insignificance, shown to be largely irrelevant to the conservative and aristocratic feudal order.

The *Nibelungenlied* occupied a unique place in the contemporary literature around 1200. By seriously questioning the chivalric-knightly value system, this poem deals with the political and societal realities in thirteenth-century German society. While its treatment of these issues makes the *Nibelungenlied* quite modern, it nonetheless represents the culmination of the heroic literary tradition. Earlier and later works have reworked these two legends, but none has ever equaled the brilliance and mastery of the *Nibelungenlied*.

The numerous surviving manuscripts of the *Nibelungenlied* affirm its popularity. There seems to be no way, however, to construct a manuscript hierarchy. The usual dating of the chief manuscripts is C (c. 1220), B (c. 1250), and A (somewhat later). It is now commonly accepted that A is a version of B. Most critical editions and translations are based on the B manuscript.

The C manuscript represents an extensive revision of the poem designed to soften the vilification of Kriemhild and to cast greater blame on Hagen. This tendency is also present in *Diu Klage,* which is included in all but one of the complete manuscripts of the epic.

EDITIONS AND TRANSLATIONS

Das Nibelungenlied: Paralleldruck der Handschriften A, B und C nebst Lesarten der übrigen Handschriften. Ed. Michael S. Batts. Tübingen: Niemeyer, 1971.

Der Nibelunge Nôt. Ed. Karl Bartsch. Hildesheim: Olms, 1966. Reprint of 1876 edition. Based on MS B.

Das Nibelungenlied. Mittelhochdeutscher Text und Übertragung. Ed. and tr. Helmut Brackert. 2 vols. Frankfurt: Fischer, 1971.

Das Nibelungenlied. Ed. Helmut de Boor. 22d Edition by Roswitha Wisniewski. Wiesbaden: Brockhaus, 1988 (based on edition of Karl Bartsch).

Das Nibelungenlied: A Complete Transcription in Modern German Type of the Text of Manuscript C. Ed. Heinz Engels. New York: Praeger, 1969.

The Nibelungenlied. Tr. A.T. Hatto. Baltimore: Penguin Books, 1965. Numerous reprints.

The Song of the Nibelungs. Tr. Frank G. Ryder. Detroit: Wayne State University Press, 1962.

BIBLIOGRAPHIES

Abeling, Theodor. *Das Nibelungenlied und seine Literatur.* Leipzig, 1907. Reprint. New York: Franklin, 1970.

Krogmann, Willy, and Ulrich Pretzel. *Bibliographie zum Nibelungenlied.* Berlin: Schmidt, 1966.

Überschlag, Doris. "Nibelungen-Bibliographie seit 1980." *AGSN*, 293–350.

STUDIES

Anderson, Philip N. "Kriemhild's Quest." *Euphorion* 79 (1985): 3–12.

———. "The Hunting of the Schelch: A New Interpretation of Nibelungenlied 937,2." *Germanic Notes* 16 (1985): 25–26.

Andersson, Theodore M. "The Encounter Between Burgundians and Bavarians in Adventure 26 of the *Nibelungenlied*." *JEGP* 82 (1983): 365–373.

———. "The Epic Source of Niflunga saga and the Nibelungenlied." *Arkiv för nordisk filologi* 88 (1973): 1–54.

———. *A Preface to the Nibelungenlied*. Stanford: Stanford University Press, 1987.

Armstrong, Marianne Wahl. *Rolle und Charakter: Studien zur Menschendarstellung im Nibelungenlied*. Göppingen: Kummerle, 1979.

Bäuml, Franz H. "The Unmaking of the Hero: Some Critical Implications of the Transition from Oral to Written Epic." *The Epic in Medieval Society*. Ed. Harald Scholler. Tübingen: Niemeyer, 1977.

———, and Eva-Maria Fallone. *A Concordance to the Nibelungenlied*. Leeds: Maney, 1976.

———, and Edda Spielmann. "From Illiteracy to Literacy: Prolegomena to a Study of the Nibelungenlied." *Forum for Modern Language Studies* 10 (1974): 248–259.

———, and Donald J. Ward. "Zur mündlichen Überlieferung des Nibelungenliedes." *DVLG* 41 (1967): 351–390.

Bekker, Hugo. "The Nibelungenlied: Rüdeger von Bechlaren and Dietrich von Bern." *Monatshefte* 66 (1974): 239–253.

———. *The Nibelungenlied: A Literary Analysis*. Toronto: University of Toronto Press, 1971.

Bender, Ellen. *Nibelungenlied und Kudrun: Eine vergleichende Studie zur Zeitdarsellung und Geschichtsdeutung*. Frankfurt: Lang, 1987.

Benkert-Dodrill, Renate L. "The Role of the Dragon-Fighter and the Swan-Maiden in Early Germanic Literature." *Coranto: Journal of the Friends of the Libraries, University of Southern California* 13 (1985): 24–34.

Beyschlag, Siegfried. "Das Motiv der Macht bei Siegfrieds Tod." *Zur germanisch-deutschen Heldensage*. Ed. Karl Hauck. Darmstadt: Wissenschaftliche Buchgesellschaft, 1965. 195–213.

———. "Das Nibelungenlied als aktuelle Dichtung seiner Zeit." *Germanisch-Romanische Monatsschrift* 48 (1967): 225–230.

Boehringer, Michael. "Sex and Politics? Etzel's Role in the Nibelungenlied. A Narratological Approach." *AGSN*, 149–168.

Bostock, J. K. "The Message of the Nibelungenlied." *MLR* 55 (1960): 200–212.

Brackert, Helmut. "Nibelungenlied und Nationalgedanke. Zur Geschichte einer deutschen Ideologie." *Mediaevalia litteraria: Festschrift für Helmet de Boor zum 80. Geburtstag*. Eds. Ursula Hennig and Herbert Kolb. Munich: Beck, 1971. 343–364.

Classen, Albrecht. "The Defeat of the Matriarch Brünhild in the Nibelungenlied, with Some Thoughts on Matriarchy As Evinced in Literary Texts." *AGSN*, 89–110.

Curschmann, Michael. "Nibelungenlied und Nibelungenklage. Über Mündlichkeit und Schriftlichkeit im Prozeß der Episierung." *Deutsche Literatur im Mittelalter, Kontakte und Perspektiven*. Ed. Christoph Cormeau. Stuttgart: Metzler, 1979. 85–119.

Dickerson, Jr., Harold D. "Hagen: A Negative View." *Semasia* 2 (1975): 43–59.

Dürrenmatt, Nelly. *Das Nibelungenlied im Kreis der höfischen Dichtung.* Lungern: Burch, 1945. Bern

Ehrismann, Otfrid. "Archaisches und Modernes im Nibelungenlied. Pathos und Abwehr." *HS,* 164–174.

————. *Nibelungenlied. Epoche—Werk—Wirkung.* Munich: Beck, 1987.

Eifler, Günter. "Siegfried zwischen Xanten und Worms." *Sprache—Literatur—Kultur. Studien zu ihrer Geschichte im deutschen Süden und Westen.* Eds. Albrecht Greule and Uwe Ruberg. Stuttgart: Steiner, 1989. 277–290.

Falk, Walter. *Das Nibelungenlied in seiner Epoche: Revision eines romantischen Mythos.* Heidelberg: Winter, 1974.

Fenik, Bernard. *Homer and the Nibelungenlied: Comparative Studies in Epic Style.* Cambridge, MA: Published for Oberlin College by Harvard University Press, 1986.

Fleet, Mary. "The Recent Study of the Nibelungenlied." *JEGP* 52 (1953): 32–49.

Fromm, Hans. "Der oder die Dichter des Nibelungenliedes?" *I Nibelunghi,* 63–77.

Gentry, Francis G. "Hagen and the Problem of Individuality in the Nibelungenlied." *Monatshefte* 68 (1976): 5–12.

————. *Triuwe und Vriunt in the Nibelungenlied.* Amsterdam: Rodopi, 1975.

————. "Trends in Nibelungenlied Research Since 1949." *ABäG* 7 (1974): 125–139.

Göhler, Peter. *Das Nibelungenlied. Erzählweise, Figuren, Weltanschauung, literaturgeschichtliches Vorfeld.* Berlin: Akademie, 1989.

Haug, Walter. "Höfische Idealität und heroische Tradition im Nibelungenlied." *I Nibelunghi,* 35–50.

————. "Montage und Individualität im Nibelungenlied." *PN,* 277–293.

Haymes, Edward R. "Dietrich von Bern im Nibelungenlied." *ZDA* 114 (1985): 159–165.

————. *The Nibelungenlied: History and Interpretation.* Urbana: University of Illinois Press, 1986.

————. "A Rhetorical Reading of the 'Hortforderungsszene' in the Nibelungenlied." *ASGN,* 81–88.

Heinzle, Joachim. *Das Nibelungenlied: eine Einführung.* Munich: Artemis, 1987. Revised edition published under the same title, Frankfurt:Fischer, 1994.

————, and Anneliese Waldschmidt, eds. *Die Nibelungen. Ein deutscher Wahn, ein deutscher Alptraum.* Frankfurt: Suhrkamp, 1991.

Heusler, Andreas. *Nibelungensage und Nibelungenlied.* Dortmund: Ruhfus, 1920. (Many later reprints)

Hoffmann, Werner. *Das Nibelungenlied. Interpretation.* Munich: Oldenbourg, 1969.

————. *Das Nibelungenlied.* 7th. ed. Stuttgart: Metzler, 1992.

————. "Das Nibelungenlied in der Literaturgeschichtsschreibung von Gervinus bis Bertau." *HS,* 19–37.

Höfler, Otto. "Die Anonymität des Nibelungenliedes." *Zur germanisch-deutschen Heldensage.* Ed. Karl Hauck. Darmstadt: Wissenschaftliche Buchgesellschaft, 1965. 330–392.

Homann, Holger. "The Hagen Figure in the Nibelungenlied: Know Him by His Lies." *MLN* 97 (1982): 759–769.

Ihlenburg, Karl Heinz. *Das Nibelungenlied: Problem und Gehalt.* Berlin: Akademie, 1969.

Jaeger, C. Stephen. "The Nibelungen Poet and the Clerical Rebellion Against Courtesy." *Spectrum Medii Aevi: Essays in Early German Literature in Honor of George Fenwick Jones.* Göppingen: Kummerle, 1983. 177–205.

Kratz, Henry. "Inconsistencies in the Nibelungenlied." *AGSN*, 71–80.

Kuhn, Hugo. "Tristan, Nibelungenlied, Artusstruktur." *I Nibelunghi*, 7–21.

Martin, Bernhard R. *Nibelungen-Metamorphosen: Die Geschichte eines Mythos.* Munich: Iudicium, 1992.

Maurer, Friedrich. *Leid. Studien zur Bedeutungs- und Problemgeschichte besonders in den großen Epen der staufischen Zeit.* Bern: Francke, 1951

McConnell, Winder. "Marriage in the 'Nibelungenlied' and 'Kudrun.'" *Spectrum Medii Aevi: Essays in Early German Literature in Honor of George Fenwick Jones.* Göppingen: Kümmerle, 1983. 299–320.

———. *The Nibelungenlied.* Boston: Twayne, 1984.

McMahon, James V. "The Oddly Understated Marriage of Kriemhild and Etzel." *AGSN*, 131–48.

Mowatt, D. G. "Studies Towards an Interpretation of the Nibelungenlied." *German Life and Letters* 14 (1961): 257–270.

———, and Hugh Sacker. *The Nibelungenlied: An Interpetative Commentary.* Toronto: University of Toronto Press, 1967.

Mueller, Werner A. *The Nibelungenlied Today.* Chapel Hill: University of North Carolina Press, 1962.

Nagel, Bert. "Das Dietrichbild des Nibelungenliedes I. Teil." *ZDP* 78 (1959): 258–268.

———. "Das Dietrichbild des Nibelungenliedes II. Teil." *ZDP* 79 (1960): 28–57.

———. *Das Nibelungenlied: Stoff—Form—Ethos.* Frankfurt: Hirschgraben, 1965.

Nelson, Charles G. "Virginity (De)Valued: Kriemhild, Brünhild, and All That." *AGSN*, 111–130.

Neumann, Friedrich. *Das Nibelungenlied in seiner Zeit.* Göttingen: Vandenhoeck and Ruprecht, 1967.

Newmann, Gail. "The Two Brünhilds?" *ABäG* 16 (1981): 69–78.

Osselman, Dawn. "The Three Sins of Kriemhilt." *Western Folklore* 49 (1990): 226–332.

Panzer, Friedrich Wilhelm. *Nibelungische Problematik: Siegfried und Xanten.* Heidelberg: Winter, 1954.

———. *Das Nibelungenlied: Entstehung und Gestalt.* Stuttgart: Kohlhammer, 1955.

Price, Arnold H. "Characterization in the Nibelungenlied." *Monatshefte* 51 (1959): 341–350.

Ranke, Friedrich, and Helmut de Boor. "Der Dichter des Nibelungenliedes um 1200." *Die grossen Deutschen* 1 (1956): 87–100.

Reichert, Hermann. *Nibelungenlied und Nibelungensage.* Vienna: Böhlau, 1985.

Samples, Susann T. "Maternal Loyalty in the Nibelungenlied and Kudrun." *Von Otfried von Weißenburg bis zum 15. Jahrhundert.* Ed. Albrecht Classen. Göppingen: Kummerle, 1991. 103–112.

Schmidt, Gerhard. "Die Darstellung des Herrschers im Nibelungenlied." *Wissenschaftliche Zeitschrift der Karl-Marx Universität Leipzig* 4 (1954–1955): 485–499.

Schröder, Walter Johannes. *Das Nibelungenlied: Versuch einer Deutung.* Halle (Saale): Niemeyer, 1954.

Schröder, Werner *Nibelungenlied-Studien.* Stuttgart: Metzler, 1968.

———. *Wolfram von Eschenbach, das Nibelungenlied und die Klage.* Wiesbaden: Steiner, 1989.

Splett, Jochen. *Rüdiger von Bechelaren. Studien zum zweiten Teil des Nibelungenliedes.* Heidelberg: Winter, 1968.

Thelen, Lynn D. "The Internal Source and Function of King Gunther's Bridal Quest." *Monatshefte* 77 (1984): 143–155.

———. 'The Vassalage Deception, or Siegfried's Folly." *JEGP* 87 (1988): 471–491.

Wachinger, Burghart. *Studien zum Nibelungenlied. Vorausdeutungen, Aufbau, Motivierung.* Tübingen: Niemeyer, 1960.

Wailes, Stephen L. "The Nibelungenlied as Heroic Epic." *Heroic Epic and Saga: An Introduction to the World's Great Folk Epics.* Ed. Felix J. Oinas. Bloomington: Indiana University Press, 1978. 120–143.

Weber, Gottfried. *Das Nibelungenlied. Problem und Idee.* Stuttgart: Metzler, 1963.

Wenzel, Horst. "Szene und Gebärde: Zur visuellen Imagination im Nibelungenlied." *ZDP* 111 (1992): 321–343.

DIU KLAGE

The title *Diu Klage* ("the Lament") actually reflects the intention of the anonymous poet: "ditze liet heizt diu klage" ("this song is called the lament") (4322). The *Klage* was probably written around 1220.

This poem is appended to all but one of the extant complete *Nibelungenlied* manuscripts and, moreover, has the notable distinction of being a contemporaneous commentary on the *Nibelungenlied.* It does not appear independently.

The poem begins with a retelling of the events leading up to the tragedy in the second part of the *Nibelungenlied.* The siege of the Burgundian warriors is recounted from the Huns' perspective. Although Kriemhild is the instigator of the eventual carnage, she is continually shown to be acting out of loyalty to her slain husband, Siegfried. Conversely, Hagen as well as the Burgundians are shown to be culpable for the tragedy because of their arrogance and haughtiness. In spite of the

Burgundians' faults they are nonetheless portrayed as great and valiant fighters. As the grisly task of burying the dead proceeds, the chief slain warriors from both sides are sorely lamented by the surviving warriors. Etzel almost despairs over the loss of so many noble warriors, but Dietrich consoles him.

Messengers are sent to inform the bereaved parties of the tragedy. The circumstances leading up to Rüedeger's death are recounted to his wife, Gotelint, and his daughter, who grieve for him. The messengers journey to Pilgrim, the bishop of Passau and kinsman of the Burgundian royal family. They then travel to the Rhine, where Brünhild and Uote, the queen mother, receive the dire news. Here, however, the mood shifts from grief to a tentative optimism, since Gunther's son, Siegfried, will now assume the throne. Dual festivities occur at Worms (the coronation) and at Etzel's court, where Dietrich weds Herrat and then departs.

The poet of the *Klage* was reacting against the nihilism of the *Nibelungenlied*, which ends with the annihilation of the Burgundian and Hunnish warrior-class. In order to reassign blame for this great tragedy the poet consciously recasts the chief figures of Kriemhild and Hagen. Indeed, a kind of role reversal occurs. Kriemhild is depicted as a victim whose subsequent actions are shown to stem from her loyalty to her murdered husband, Siegfried. In his effort to rehabilitate Kriemhild the poet even rewards her loyalty with a place in heaven. On the other hand, Hagen now assumes the role of *vâlant* (devil), whose *superbia* is the blame for the ensuing catastrophe. Actually both the Burgundians and Siegfried appear in a less favorable light; their demise is attributed to their arrogance.

The tragic events are further emphasized by the great outpouring of grief on the part of the surviving figures. Most noteworthy is Etzel's uncontrolled mourning. The journey of the messengers, understandably, offers ample opportunities to depict this unrestrained mourning and to praise the fallen warriors.

Despite the unmistakable doleful tenor of the *Klage* its ultimate goal is to reestablish the order destroyed at the end of the *Nibelungenlied*. Consequently, after all the wanton death and intense grieving, life is affirmed and celebrated. The dire and pessimistic ending of the *Nibelungenlied* is now replaced by the festive and upbeat mood generated by the crowning of Gunther's son, Siegfried, and the wedding of Dietrich and Herrat.

EDITIONS AND TRANSLATION

Die Klage. Ed. Karl Bartsch. Darmstadt: Wissenschaftliche Buchgesellschaft, 1964.

Die Klage. Ed. Anton Edzardi. Hannover: Rumpler, 1875.

The Lament of the Nibelungen (Div Chlage). Tr. Winder McConnell. Columbia, S.C.: Camden House, 1994.

Die Nibelunge Noth und die Klage. Ed. Karl Lachmann. 6th ed. Berlin: de Gruyter, 1960.

Das Nibelunge Liet und Diu Klage. Ed. Werner Schröder. Cologne: Böhlau, 1969.

STUDIES

Curschmann, Michael. "Nibelungenlied und Nibelungenklage: Über Mündlichkeit und Schriftlichkeit im Prozess der Episierung." *Deutsche Literatur im Mittelalter: Kontakte und Perspektiven. Hugo Kuhn zum Gedenken.* Ed. Christoph Cormeau. Stuttgart: Metzler, 1979. 85–119.

Fourquet, Jean. "Probleme der relativen Chronologie: Nibelungenlied, Parzival, Klage" *Festschrift für Werner Schröder zum 75. Geburtstag.* Eds. Kurt Gartner and Joachim Heinzle. Tübingen: Niemeyer, 1989. 243–256.

Kaiser, Gert. "Deutsche Heldenepik." *Europäisches Hochmittelalter.* Ed. Hennig Krauss. Wiesbaden: Athenaion, 1981. 181–216.

Körner, Josef. *Die Klage und das Nibelungenlied.* Leipzig: Reisland, 1920.

Günzburger, Angelika. *Studien zur Nibelungenklage: Forschungsbericht, Bauform der Klage, Personendarstellung.* Frankfurt: Lang, 1983.

Leicher, Richard. *Die Totenklage in der deutschen Epik von der ältesten Zeit bis zur Nibelungen-Klage.* Breslau: Marcus, 1927.

McConnell, Winder. "The Problem of Continuity in Diu Klage." *Neophilologus* 70 (1986): 248–255.

Scholler, Harald. *A Word Index to the Nibelungenklage.* Ann Arbor: University of Michigan Press, 1966.

Vogt, Friedrich Hermann Traugott. *Zur Geschichte der Nibelungenklage.* Marburg: Koch, 1913.

Voorwinden, Norbert. "Nibelungenklage und Nibelungenlied." *HS*, 102–113.

Wachinger, Burghart. "Die 'Klage' und das Nibelungenlied." *HS*, 90–101.

SIGURÐ'S YOUTH AND MURDER IN THE *ÞIÐREKSSAGA*

The stories of Sigurð's youth follow the Norse version of the story more closely, but there are considerable differences in all directions.

Sigurð's father, Sigmund, wins his wife, Sisibe, through a relatively unproblematic bridewinning sequence. Not knowing she is pregnant, he leaves her behind to go war. When he returns, a member of his court accuses her of unfaithfulness, and Sigmund banishes her without seeing her or hearing her side of the story. The child is born in the wild and placed in a glass container, in which it floats to an island where it is nourished by a hind. The smith Mimir finds the child, recognizes his special qualities, and raises him as his apprentice. Sigurð tyrannizes the other apprentices, so Mimir decides to get rid of him. He sends him to the forest to cut wood. There Sigurð encounters a dragon (actually

Mimir's brother Regin), which he proceeds to kill and eat. After tasting the dragon's blood he understands the language of the birds, who advise him to kill Mimir as well. He returns to the smithy and is given excellent armor and a sword by Mimir, whom he then kills. He then goes to Brynhild's castle, where he is given the horse Grani.

Later in the saga the story of Sigurð's betrayal of Brynhild is woven into the story of Gunnar's bridewinning. Sigurð sleeps with Brynhild in Gunnar's shape to overcome her supernatural strength.

When Brynhild is brought back to Niflungaland, she argues with Grimhild over precedence in the hall, and, when Grimhild tells her that Sigurð had taken her virginity, Brynhild seeks revenge. She forces Gunnar and his brothers to kill Sigurð. Högni (Hagen) kills him in the forest in a scene very similar to that in the *Nibelungenlied*.

The treatment of Young-Sigurð (Sigurðr-Sveinn, as he is invariably called) in the *Þiðrekssaga* combines elements we know from the North (see the summary of the *Völsungasaga* below) and from the southern traditions behind the *Nibelungenlied*. The story of Sigmund and Sisibe and the birth of Sigurð is different from any other source, but it contains so many elements that are typical of "hero births" that we could assume it to have arisen independently of other versions. The fight between the queens and the murder by Högni/Hagen in the forest are identical in their main points with the treatment in the *Nibelungenlied*. This is consonant with the German (rather than Norse) versions of the legend we find elsewhere in the saga.

VÖLSUNGASAGA

The *Völsungasaga* was written in Iceland sometime in the thirteenth century. It is a relatively pedestrian retelling of the story of the Völsung family from its origins to its final end in the story of Svanhild.

The saga begins with a genealogy leading from the god Óðin to King Völsung, the father of Sigmund. Völsung's twin children, Sigmund and Signy, are featured in the first real story. Signy is forced to marry a king named Siggeir, who shows his gratitude to the Völsung family by killing the king and all of his sons. Sigmund manages to escape to the forest, where he lives in a cave. Signy sends her sons by Siggeir to Sigmund, but they fail a test of courage and he kills them at their mother's behest. Signy then arranges to exchange shapes with a sorceress and spends three nights with Sigmund. The child of this union is Sinfjötli, who aids his father in avenging Völsung's killing by burning Siggeir and his men in their hall. Signy comes out of the burning hall to tell Sigmund he is Sinfjötli's father and then returns to die beside her hated husband. After a number of adventures involving Sigmund's second son, Helgi Hundingsbani, Sinfjötli is poisoned by his stepmother. Sigmund is killed in battle when his sword is shattered by contact with Óðin's spear.

Sigmund's second wife, Hjordis, bears Sigurð after Sigmund's death. Sigurð is raised by a smith named Regin, who tells the story of his own family. He had had a brother named Ottr, who was in the habit of spending his time in the shape of an otter. Óðin and Loki killed the otter and afterward sought shelter with Ottr's father Hreiðmar. The father demanded compensation for his son. The gods were forced to cover completely the flayed skin of the otter with gold. Loki then went to a waterfall, where a pike named Andvari had a great horde of gold. Loki took all the gold including a ring, which would have allowed Andvari to build up his treasure again. Andvari cursed the ring when Loki took it away. When Hreiðmar had been compensated, his son Fáfnir killed him and took the gold, leaving Regin fatherless and destitute. Fáfnir then turned himself into a dragon to guard the gold, and Regin now wants Sigurð to kill him so Regin can be avenged for his father's death and receive his just portion of the settlement for his other brother. Sigurð agrees to do so, but only after he has avenged his own father.

After killing all those involved in the battle against his father Sigurð goes and kills the dragon. After tasting the dragon's blood he understands the language of the birds, who warn him about Regin's treacherous intentions. Sigurð kills Regin and rides away with all the treasure.

Attracted by a bright glow, he comes to a rampart of shining shields inside of which is a sleeping warrior. He cuts open the armor and discovers that it is a woman, Brynhild. The saga attempts to combine several different versions of the story, but they all end with Brynhild and Sigurð exchanging vows to marry no one else.

Sigurð goes to live at the court of King Gjuki, his sons Gunnar, Guttorm, and Högni, and his daughter, Guðrún. Gjuki's wife, Grimhild, brews an "ale of forgetfulness," and Sigurð forgets his oaths to Brynhild and marries Guðrún. Sigurð agrees to help Gunnar win Brynhild (who is now depicted as the daughter of Buðli and sister of Atli). Gunnar is unable to pass through the flame barrier around her hall, so Sigurð exchanges shapes with him. Sigurð spends three nights disguised as Gunnar with Brynhild with a drawn sword between them. Later, while bathing in the river, Guðrún and Brynhild quarrel about their husbands. Guðrún shows Brynhild the ring Sigurð had taken from her while disguised as Gunnar, making the deception public. Brynhild claims that Sigurð had betrayed Gunnar's trust while disguised and urges that he be killed. Guttorm kills Sigurð in his bed, but the victim is able to throw the sword back at his killer and avenge himself. Brynhild laughs when she hears Guðrún's cry, tells Gunnar she had lied about Sigurð's betrayal, and kills herself, joining Sigurð on his funeral pyre.

Guðrún is married against her will to Atli, who desires the treasure that had belonged to Sigurð. He invites the surviving brothers Gunnar and Högni to a feast, where they are attacked and killed. (The narration here attempts to follow both the *Atlakviða* and the *Atlamál* from the *Poetic Edda*, see below). Guðrún avenges her brothers by killing her sons by Atil and serving them to their father at his victory feast. When Atli is asleep, she kills him and burns down the hall.

Guðrún attempts to kill herself by wading into the sea, but she is buoyed up and washes ashore in the realm of a king named Jonák, who marries her. Her daughter by Sigurð, Svanhild, is married to King Jörmunrek (Ermanaric), who has her trampled by horses following trumped-up charges of adultery. Guðrún goads her three sons to go and kill Jörmunrek, but they quarrel along the way and the half-brother is killed. When they attack the king, they are able to hack off his arms and legs, but are kept from killing him by the king's retainers. They lament that the king would now be dead if they had not killed their brother. They are killed by stoning since weapons cannot cut them.

The saga draws most of its material from the poems collected in the *Poetic Edda* and must be considered a secondary source for the legends except in those areas in which the *Poetic Edda* is lacking. It provides us with a clear view of the way the Nibelung story as a whole was understood in thirteenth-century Iceland and thus allows us to see the poems of the *Poetic Edda* as they related to the central story.[1] The writing of the *Völsungasaga* may well have proceeded from the same antiquarian interest that apparently drove the collection of poems in the *Poetic Edda*, the retelling of heathen mythology in *Snorri's Edda*, and the composition of the great historical sagas.

The *Völsungasaga* is the only source for many specifically Norse aspects of the legend, particularly the mythological connection between the human heroes and the gods. Although many Anglo-Saxon and Old Norse genealogies of kings begin with Óðin, this is not a feature of any of the other versions of the Nibelung legend. Without additional sources it is impossible to determine whether the divine origin of Sigurð has any basis in the legendary tradition.

The saga appears with *Ragnars saga Loðbrókar* in the only surviving medieval manuscript of both works. The stories are connected by having Ragnar, from whom the kings of Norway are descended, marry Aslaug, the daughter of Sigurð and Brynhild. This linking is clearly an attempt to bring together all the known

---

[1] Dietrich is absent from all Icelandic versions of the legendary material except for the brief mention in the *Poetic Edda*, see below, p. 119.

legendary stories in one grand synthesis (and to have the Norwegian kings descended from mythological ancestors). We can see the same endeavor in the *Þiðrekssaga,* using virtually all the German sources known in Norway.

EDITIONS AND TRANSLATIONS

The Saga of the Volsungs: Together with Excerpts from the Nornageststhattr and Three Chapters from the Prose Edda. Tr. George K. Anderson. Newark: University of Delaware Press, 1982.

The Saga of the Volsungs: The Norse Epic of Sigurd the Dragon Slayer. Tr. Jesse L. Byock. Berkeley: University of California Press, 1990.

Völsunga Saga. Ed. Uwe Ebel. Frankfurt: Haag and Herchen, 1983.

Völsunga Saga. Ed. and tr. R.G.Finch. London: Nelson, 1965. Facing page translation with original text.

"Die Geschichte von den Völsungen." *Isländische Heldenromane.* Tr. Paul Herrmann. Jena: Diederichs, 1923. 37–136. German translation often cited in secondary literature.

STUDIES

Andersson, Theodore M. *The Legend of Brynhild.* Ithaca: Cornell University Press, 1980.

Finch, R. G. "Atlakviða, Atlamál, and Volsunga Saga: A Study in Combination and Integration." *Speculum Norroenum: Norse Studies in Memory of Gabriel Turville-Petre.* Eds. Ursula Dronke et al. Odense: Odense University Press, 1981. 123–138.

Heinrichs, Anne. "Brynhild als Typ der präpatriarchalen Frau." *Arbeiten zur Skandinavistik.* Ed. Heinrich Beck.. Frankfurt: Lang, 1985. 45–66.

NORNAGESTS ÞÁTTR

The story of Nornagest ("Guest of the Norns") is found in two manuscripts of a saga of King Óláf Tryggvason (r. in Norway 995–1000) written early in the fourteenth century in Iceland.

A mysterious stranger appears at the court of Oláf Tryggvason in the year 998. He asks for hospitality and promises to earn his keep by telling stories and playing the harp. He tells of his past adventures stretching over a supernatural lifetime of three hundred years. He summarizes the story of Sigurð's youth with Regin, the smith. He claims to have been present at the battle against the sons of Hunding which he narrates in great detail, and follows it with a summary of the story of Sigurð's death, including both versions (being killed in bed and being killed in the forest) and even referring to a third version in which Gunnar and Högni take Sigurð with them to an assembly and kill him there. He is understandably unsure about Sigurð's death, since he only heard about it from others. Nornagest also spent time with Ragnar loðbrók and other heroes. His final story concerns his own infancy, when two female seers prophesied a long and happy life for him. The third seer was incensed at being excluded and prophesied that he would live only until the candle at his head burned down. The first seer extinguished the candle and gave it to Gest's mother, who passed it on to him. At the end of the story Gest accepts baptism, lights his candle, and dies when it burns down and goes out.

This odd little story cannot be seen as an independent source for the legend of Sigurð, since virtually everything in it is also contained in the *Völsungasaga,* but it does show something about the attitudes of medieval Icelanders toward these old stories. The passage in which Gest tells three different versions of Sigurð's death is particularly interesting, because it shows a restraint in changing oral versions of a story, even if one or more of them is manifestly incorrect. The frame story of Gest's long life, conversion, and death ties in well with the theme of the saga as a whole, which presents Óláf as the first Christian missionary king of Norway.

A translation of portions of this short text is included in Anderson's translation of the *Völsungasaga* cited above.

EDITION
Nornagests Þáttr. Fornaldar Sögur Norðurlanda. Ed. Guðni Jónsson. 3 vols. Reykjavík: Islendingasagnaútgáfan, 1954. Vol. 1, 305–335.

NIFLUNGA SAGA IN THE *ÞIÐREKSSAGA*

As was indicated in the section on the *Þiðrekssaga,* most of the Nibelung legend is included within the story of Dietrich. The longest independent section of the saga is the story of the fall of the Nibelungs, called here *Niflunga saga.*

The story follows the *Nibelungenlied* so closely that it is necessary only to point out the discrepancies to get a fairly complete version of the story. The first of these lies in the motivation for the invitation. Here the motive of avarice on Attila's part is added to Grimhild's desire for revenge. After the Niflungs arrive, Grimhild sends out her child to strike Högni in order to get the fighting started. (In the *Nibelungenlied* it is the news of the killing of the squires that starts the battle—Hagen then strikes off the boy's head.) In the saga Þiðrek enters the fray to avenge the killing of Roðingeir (Rüedeger), not to bring the fighting to an end. He fights a very long battle with Högni that ends when he loses his composure and breathes fire at his opponent. Högni surrenders and is allowed to spend his last night alive with a woman with whom an heir is conceived who will avenge him. Upon seeing Kriemhild thrusting a firebrand into the mouth of her brother Gisler to see whether he was still alive (he died as a result), Þiðrek, with Attila's permission, kills her.

The close similarity of this portion of the *Þiðrekssaga* is the most persuasive evidence for a written epic source for both this saga and the second half of the *Nibelungenlied*. The major disagreement among scholars has been the localization of this epic version. Heusler assumed it to be Austrian without any real evidence, but the widespread acceptance of his family tree of the *Nibelungenlied* has swept most competing ideas away. Just as plausible is the idea of a version from the Rhineland suggested by Heinrich Hempel and others.

POETIC EDDA

The *Poetic Edda* is a manuscript collection of mythological and heroic poetry in Old Norse that was written down in Iceland sometime around 1270. The collectors of the poems were aware of the distinction between mythological and heroic poetry and marked the beginning the section devoted to heroic poetry with a large initial. The preponderance of the heroic poetry is devoted to the Nibelung legend, while Dietrich is only mentioned in two of the prose bridges and in one of the poems (*The Third Lay of Guðrún*). The combination of Nibelung and Dietrich legends we know from German sources (including the *Þiðrekssaga*) seems to be almost unknown in these purely Norse versions.

The manuscript is missing at least one gathering in the midst of the Sigurð poems. This gap has occasioned a vast amount of speculation about the contents of the missing poems.

None of the poems can be dated with certainty before the beginning of the thirteenth century, but the antiquity of the materials has led many scholars to date some of the poems to a very early time. If our reconstruction of the origin of Eddic poetry is correct, then the oldest poems can be no older than the ninth or tenth centuries, i.e. after the establishment of skaldic verse in Iceland and the Scandinavian courts. The latest poems are almost certainly products of the twelfth or thirteenth century. Most scholars would date the poems into this three- to four-hundred-year period, but few would agree on the criteria we can use to date them more precisely.

A characteristic of the collection is the inclusion of several parallel poems on each of the most important legends. There are thus at least two poems each on Helgi Hundigsbana, Sigurð, Atli, and Guðrún. It will be easier to discuss these if we group them under their topics.

EDITIONS AND TRANSLATIONS

Edda. Lieder des Codex Regius nebst verwandten Denkmälern. Ed. Gustav Neckel. 4th ed. by Hans Kuhn. Heidelberg: Winter, 1962. Standard edition.

Poems of the Elder Edda. Tr. Patricia Terry. Philadelphia: University of Pennsylvania Press, 1990.

The Poetic Edda. Ed. and tr. Ursula Dronke. Vol. 1. Oxford: Clarendon, 1969. Exemplary edition and translation of a small portion of the whole text.

STUDIES

Andersson, Theodore M. "The Lays in the Lacuna of Codex Regius." *Speculum Norroenum: Norse Studies in Memory of Gabriel Turville-Petre.* Eds. Ursula Dronke et al. Odense: Odense University Press, 1981. 6–26.

Beck, Heinrich. "Eddaliedforschung heute: Bemerkungen zur Heldenlied-Diskussion." *Helden und Heldensage: Otto Gschwantler zum 60. Geburtstag.* Eds. Hermann Reichert and Günter Zimmermann. Vienna: Fassbaender, 1990. 1–24.

Harris, Joseph. "Eddic Poetry." *Old Norse–Icelandic Literature: A Critical Guide.* Eds. Carol J. Clover and John Lindow. Ithaca: Cornell University Press, 1985. 68–156.

———. "Eddic Poetry as Oral Poetry: The Evidence of Parallel Passages in the Helgi Poems for Questions of Composition and Performance." *Edda: A Collection of Essays.* Eds. Robert J. Glendinning and Haraldur Bessason. Winnipeg: University of Manitoba Press, 1983. 210–242.

Kellogg, Robert L. "The Prehistory of Eddic Poetry." *PSMA*, 187–99.

Kuhn, Hans. "Heldensage vor und außerhalb der Dichtung." *Zur germanisch-deutschen Heldensage.* Ed. Karl Hauck. Darmstadt: Wissenschaftliche Buchgesellschaft, 1965. 173–194.

Neckel, Gustav. *Beiträge zur Eddaforschung, mit Exkursen zur Heldensage.* Dortmund: Ruhfus, 1908.

Sigurðsson, Gisli. "On the Classification of Eddic Heroic Poetry in View of the Oral Theory." *PSMA*, 245–255.

Helgi Hundingsbani

Two lays from the *Poetic Edda* concern themselves with Helgi, a half-brother to Sigurð and Sinfjötli. He defeats a king named Hunding and falls in love with Sigrun, a Valkyrie. She tells him she cannot marry him unless he defeats another suitor, a king named Höðbrodd. He does this and marries Sigrun. The first of the two lays ends at this point, but the second includes a grisly continuation in which Helgi is killed and returns to Sigrun as a ghost. She goes to meet him at his grave mound and soon dies. Both poems seem to be defective. The story of Helgi does not seem to spill over into the rest of the Völsung legend. There is no mention of Helgi in other versions of the story (except for the *Völsungasaga*, which is dependent on these poems).

STUDIES

Harris, Joseph. "Eddic Poetry as Oral Poetry: The Evidence of Parallel Passages in the Helgi Poems for Questions of Composition and Performance." *Edda: A Collection of Essays.* Eds. Robert J. Glendinning and Haraldur Bessason. Winnipeg: University of Manitoba Press, 1983. 210–242.

—————. "Satire and the Heroic Life, Two Studies: (Helgakviða Hundingsbana I, 18, and Björn Hítdœlakappi's Grámagaflím)." *Oral Traditional Literature: A Festschrift for Albert Bates Lord.* Ed. John Miles Foley. Columbus, OH: Slavica, 1981. 322–340.

Sigurð and Brynhild

The lays regarding Sigurð and Brynhild make up a considerable portion of the *Poetic Edda,* and it is clear that this complex was of great importance to the collector. The stories follow generally the pattern we find in the *Völsungasaga,* which seems to have used the narrative poems on Sigurð's life and career as its major source.

The section involving Sigurð begins with what is almost certainly one of the younger poems of the collection, the *Grípispá* ("Prophecy of Gripir"). It is a prophecy concerning Sigurð's career placed in the mouth of the hero's maternal uncle, Gripir. The poem jumps from high point to high point in Sigurð's career as the young man forces his uncle onward through the future events, including eventually the stories of treachery and death that form the central events of his story. A dream and its interpretation or a prophecy regarding the hero's future are fairly standard features of Norse narrative in general and the *fornáldarsögur* in particular.

Reginsmál ("The Story of Regin") tells the same story of the killing of Ottr, the robbing of Andvari, and the killing of Hreiðmar we find in the *Völsungasaga,* word for word in some parts. A version of this poem was clearly the source for the story in the saga. This section of the *Edda* concludes with the battle with the sons of Hunding that is told in such detail in the tale of Nornagest (see above).

Fáfnismál continues the story of the young Sigurð with a passage in prose that tells of Regin's urging Sigurð to kill the dragon Fáfnir. The mortally wounded dragon addresses his killer in verses. He warns him that the treasure he has won will bring him an early death. Along with specific prophecies having to do with Sigurð there are a number of strophes that seem to come from wisdom poems having nothing to do with Sigurð. After Fáfnir's death Regin reappears and clearly expects to share the spoils of Sigurð's victory. Sigurð roasts the dragon's heart and, upon tasting the blood, is able to understand the language of the birds. They warn him that Regin plans to kill him and advise him to kill the dwarf instead, which Sigurð does. They then tell him of a maiden who awaits him at Gjuki's court and of a sleeping warrior maiden.

The manuscript continues without a break into a new section that is called *Sigrdrífamál* in the editions. Sigurð sees a bright light on top of a hill and finds "a man" asleep in full armor. He removes the helmet and discovers that it is a woman. He frees her from the armor, and, after finding out who had awakened her, she greets the day and the world. She says that she is called Sigrdrífa, which means "victory driver," and that she was a valkyrie who had been punished by Óðin for disobedience. Most of the text is occupied first with general advice concerning magic runes and later with proper and wise behavior. In the middle of all this is a short passage that suggests that Sigurð and the valkyrie swear to marry. There is no suggestion that Sigrdrífa is Brynhild, but the author of the *Völsungasaga* clearly thought she was.

The missing part of the manuscript interrupts the text at this point. Following the lacuna is the *Brot af Sigurðarkviða* ("Fragment of a Sigurð Lay"), which was once probably the longer of the two Sigurð poems. It begins with the murder plans of Gunnar and Högni. Högni opposes the murder, but Guttorm is given the flesh of a wolf, a serpent, and a vulture to make him savage enough to carry out the deed. Sigurð is killed in the forest, and birds prophesy the death of Gunnar and Högni in Atli's court. In the night after the murder Brynhild enters the hall and tells Gunnar and the others that they have done a dreadful deed and that she had lied about Sigurð's having betrayed them. A short prose passage at the end discusses the different versions of Sigurð's death.

After the *First Lay of Gúðrun* (see below) we find the *Sigurðarkviða inn skammi* ("Shorter Lay of Sigurð"), a second telling of the story of Sigurð at the court of the Gjukungs. Unfortunately this version is also very brief in its treatment of the winning of Brynhild. There does not seem to have been any betrothal between Sigurð and Brynhild, and the narration here is only at pains to tell that Sigurð had laid the sword between them on the nights when they lay together. We are not told why Sigurð spends three nights with Brynhild. Here the murder is driven only by Brynhild's desire for Sigurð. Guttorm is also the killer here, but the version is the one told in the *Völsungasaga,* in which Sigurð is killed in his bed and is able to avenge himself by throwing his sword at his attacker. Most of the poem is taken up by Brynhild's long speech in which she foretells the future of Gunnar and Guðrún.

The section devoted to Sigurð and Brynhild concludes with the *Helreið Brynhildar* ("Brynhild's Ride to Hel"), a fantasy on the question of Brynhild's guilt in the catastrophes that have been inflicted or will be inflicted on Gunnar and his clan. Here Brynhild identifies herself with the Sigrdrífa of the *Sigrdrífamál* by citing the events in the valkyrie's career as events in her own life. The poem is considered to be late and not to be useful as a separate source for the legends.

STUDIES

Andersson, Theodore M. "Beyond Epic and Romance: *Sigurðarkviða in Meiri.*" *Sagnaskemmtun: Studies in Honor of Hermann Pálsson on His 65th birthday, 26th May 1986.* Eds. Rudolf Simek, Jónas Kristjánsson, and Hans Bekker-Nielsen. Cologne: Böhlau, 1986. 1–12.

————. *The Legend of Brynhild.* Ithaca: Cornell University Press, 1980.

Bumke, Joachim. "Die Quellen der Brünhildfabel im Nibelungenlied." *Euphorion* 54 (1960): 1–38.

Classen, Albrecht. "The Defeat of the Matriarch Brünhild in the Nibelungenlied, with Some Thoughts on Matriarchy As Evinced in Literary Texts." *AGSN*, 89–110.

Ehrismann, Otfrid. "Die Fremde am Hof. Brünhild und die Philosophie der Geschichte." *Begegnung mit dem 'Fremden.' Grenzen—Traditionen—Vergleiche. Akten des VIII Internationarlen Germanisten-Kongresses.* Ed. Ejiro Iwasaki. Tokyo, 1990. Munich: Iudicium, 1991. 320–331.

Haimerl, Edgar. "Sigurd—ein Held des Mittelalters. Eine textimmanente Interpretation der Jungsigurddichtung." *Alvíssmál* 2 (1993): 81–104.

Nelson, Charles G. "Virginity (De)Valued: Kriemhild, Brünhild, and All That." *AGSN*, 111–130.

Newmann, Gail. "The Two Brünhilds?" *ABäG* 16 (1981): 69–78.

Ploss, Emil. *Siegfried—Sigurd. Der Drachenkämpfer.* Cologne: Böhlau, 1966.

Reichert, Hermann. "Die Brynhild-Lieder der Edda im europäischen Kontext." *PSMA*, 71–95.

Toman, Lore. "Der Aufstand der Frauen. Ein strukturalistischer Blick auf die Brünhild-Sage." *Literatur und Kritik* 131 (1979): 25–32.

Guðrún

There are four poems that are identified with Guðrún. The first of these (*Guðrúnarkviða in fyrsta*) is something of a fantasy on Guðrún's grief after Sigurð's death. Guðrún sits over Sigurð's body, unable to weep. The other women at the court tell of their sorrows until Guðrún is finally able to pour out her tears. She complains of her sorrow and accuses her brothers of having killed Sigurð for Fáfnir's gold. The poem concludes with a condemnation of Brynhild followed by a short prose passage in which we are told that Guðrún fled the court seeking solitude and spent three and a half years with Þora, the daughter of the Danish king. The same passages tells that Brynhild killed herself in order to be burned with Sigurð.

The second *Guðrúnarkviða* is perhaps more interesting. It assumes a version of Sigurð's death that is otherwise mentioned only in *Nornagests Þáttr.* Sigurð had ridden with Gunnar and his brothers to a Thing (assembly) and was killed there. Guðrún wanders through the woods in search of his body. She eventually arrives at the Danish court, where she spends three and a half years with Þora, the daughter of the Danish king. Grimhild, her mother, comes and prepares a draught of forgetfulness so that she will accept compensation and marry Atli. She resists remarriage, particularly to Brynhild's brother, Apparently under the influence of the draught she relents and is returned home to marry Atli. The poem concludes with a strange sequence of strophes in which the death of Gunnar and Högni and the dreadful events that followed are foretold.

The third *Guðrúnarkviða* involves an event at Atli's court. Atli's former mistress Herkja accuses Guðrún of having had improper relations with Þiðrek (who appears in the *Edda* only here and in the prose section of the second *Guðrúnarkviða*). Guðrún undergoes the ordeal of boiling water and proves her innocence. Her accuser fails the ordeal and is banished. The events of this poem do not fit into the Atli story as it is told elsewhere because they take place after the death of Högni and Gunnar and before Atli's death. Both Atli poems have Guðrún's revenge follow immediately after the death of her brothers.

The fourth Guðrún poem is discussed below in connection with the *Hamðismál*, p. 126.

STUDIES

Glendinning, Robert J. "*Guðrúnaqviða forna*. A Reconstruction and Interpretation." *Edda: A Collection of Essays*. Eds. Robert J. Glendinning and Haraldur Bessason. Winnipeg: University of Manitoba Press, 1983. 258-282.

Vestergaard, Elisabeth. "Gudrun/Kriemhild—soster eller husfru?" *Arkiv för nordisk filologi* (1984): 63–78.

Oddrun

Oddrun does not seem to be a figure in the traditional legend, but she is mentioned in the *Short Lay of Sigurð* and in one of the prose bridges, and there is a lament (*Oddrúnargrátr*) associated with her in the *Edda*. This poem follows the third *Guðrúnarkviða* in the manuscript. Oddrun is the sister of Atli and Brynhild. After Brynhild's death Gunnar seeks her hand but is refused by Atli. Gunnar and Oddrun meet secretly but are discovered by Atli's men. When Högni is killed and Gunnar put in the snake pit, Oddrun sets out to save him, but Atli's mother in the form of a serpent has already killed him. The poem is clearly an attempt to tell the story of the fall of the Nibelungs from a different point of view.

Atli

The two poems that tell of Atli's invitation to his brothers-in-law, their treacherous murder, and Guðrún's revenge follow the same story quite closely, but their emphases and narrative styles are quite distinct from one another.

There is general agreement among most scholars that the *Atlakviða* is among the older poems in the collection. It seems to reflect the earliest known version of the story and to contain the most linguistic and stylistic indicators of early composition. The poem is marked "the Greenlandic" in the manuscript, but most scholars feel that this label is simply a contamination from the *Atlamál*, which is also so indicated and may actually come from Greenland.

The poem is one of the broadest of the Eddic narratives, but it is still highly economical in comparison with any of the older materials from England or the Continent. Ursula Dronke (13ff.) divides the narration into three "acts." The first consists of the invitation with its secret warning to the brothers (a wolf's hair wrapped around the rings sent as a token), the farewell celebration, and the voyage to Atli's land.

The second act begins as the brothers are fettered and the gold is demanded of them. Gunnar refuses as long as Högni is still alive. The trembling heart of the coward Hjalli is brought before Gunnar, who recognizes the trick, and the Huns go back and bring Högni's heart. Gunnar triumphantly announces that the Rhine will keep the "inheritance of the Niflungs" as he is taken to the snake pit, where he plays the harp as he awaits death.

The third act is devoted to Guðrún's vengeance. She invites the Huns to partake of a festival meal. When they are suitably satiated and drunk, she tells Atli that he has been eating the flesh of his sons. She then stabs him in his bed and burns the hall down around them all.

The *Atlamál* is less economical in its structure. The warning wolf's hair has been replaced by runes subtly altered by the treacherous messenger. Högni's and Gunnar's wives have dreams foretelling the catastrophe, but their husbands interpret the dreams harmlessly. When they arrive at Atli's farm (the events seem to be in Iceland or Greenland rather than in the rich courts of Europe), the messenger breaks down and reveals his treachery. He is summarily killed by Högni and Gunnar. The two are joined by their sister in the battle that takes place in the hall. This time there is no mention of treasure as a reason for the strife. The killing of Högni concentrates on the cowardice of Hjalli (who is spared at Högni's request), and Gunnar ends up in the snakepit playing the harp, this time with his toes because his hands are bound.

Guðrún's vengeance gains an almost tender scene with her sons before they are killed, and the widespread motif of drinking vessels made out of skulls is used here very effectively to link the death of the boys to Atli's drunkenness. The poem closes with a long dialogue between Guðrún and the dying Atli.

The *Atlamál* seems almost to point toward the ballad style, with its extensive dialogues, dream visions, and brief treatment of the narrative itself. The style and language point to a relatively late composition for the poem and most scholars have leaned toward the eleventh or twelfth century.

STUDIES

Andersson, Theodore M. "Did the Poet of Atlamál Know Atlaqviða?" *Edda: A Collection of Essays.* Eds. Robert J. Glendinning and Haraldur Bessason. Winnipeg: University of Manitoba Press, 1983. 234–257.

Finch, R. G. "Atlakviða, Atlamál, and Volsunga Saga: A Study in Combination and Integration." *Speculum Norroenum: Norse Studies in Memory of Gabriel Turville-Petre.* Eds. Ursula Dronke et al. Odense: Odense University Press, 1981. 123–138.

Kroesen, Riti. "More than Just Human: Some Stylistic Remarks on the Old Atli Lay." *Neophilologus* 76 (1992): 409–424.

Hamðismál

After the death of Atli Guðrún sets out to drown herself, but the waves carry her to the kingdom of Jonák, who marries her and fathers at least two sons, Hamðir and Sörli, with her. A third son of Jonák, Erp, seems to be a half-brother. Sigurð's daughter Svanhild is married to King Jörmunrek. She is accused of adultery with her stepson Randvér, and Jörmunrek has her trampled by horses. Guðrún learns of this and goads her sons to seek vengeance in the poem called *Guðrúnarhvöt* ("Guðrún's Goading"). This poem also includes her remembrance of the sufferings she has endured. It concludes when she is laid out to be burned and calls on Sigurð to come from Hel to fetch her.

The *Hamðismál* proper tells of the journey of Hamðir, Sörli, and Erp to avenge Svanhild. On the way Hamðir and Sörli quarrel with Erp. He is asked how he will help them. He says that he will help them like one foot the other or one hand the other. They interpret this as mockery and kill him. When they attack Jörmunrek in his hall, they manage to hack off the king's feet and his hands but are unable to reach his head to finish the job. They realize that the head would be off if Erp had been there. The men in the hall stone the two because they are protected by magic from cutting blades. This story is probably the oldest element in this book, since it goes back to the death of Ermanaric in 375 (see Ermanaric above, p. 18), but it is also one of the most recent additions to the Nibelung legend, since the combination of the Svanhild story with Sigurð and Guðrún is found only in relatively late texts from Iceland.

STUDIES

Andersson, Theodore M. "Cassiodorus and the Gothic Legend of Ermanaric." *Euphorion* (1963): 28–43.

Boer, R. C. *Die Sagen von Ermanarich und Dietrich von Bern.* Halle: Waisenhaus, 1910.

Brady, Caroline. *The Legends of Ermanaric.* Berkeley: University of California Press, 1943.

SNORRA EDDA

The name "Edda" was not originally attached to the collection of poems we most often associate with it. The name was the invention of Snorri Sturluson (1179–1241), the one writer of heroic narrative about whom we know more than just a name. He was a prominent political figure at a time of great turmoil in Iceland. In spite of his many political and business activities he was able to write some of the most important works of Icelandic literature. Among these is the handbook for poets we call *Snorra Edda* (Snorri's Edda) or the *Prose Edda*. Much of the book is concerned with providing a narrative framework for the surviving poems about pagan gods, but several heroic matters are told here as well. The story of Sigurð is told very briefly in a few pages. It does not differ materially (except in brevity) from the presentation of the same story in the *Völsungasaga*.

EDITION AND TRANSLATION

Edda Snorra Sturlusonar. Ed. Finnur Jónsson. Copenhagen, 1931.

Snorri Sturluson. *Edda*. Tr. Anthony Faulkes. London: Dent, 1987. Only available translation of entire work; Nibelung legend 101–106.

ROSENGARTEN ZU WORMS

Rosengarten zu Worms was written down in the mid-thirteenth century. The poem is composed in four-line strophes similar to the Nibelungenstrophe.

The setting is the kingdom of Worms along the Rhine. Kriemhild possesses a magnificent rose garden that is guarded by twelve warriors, among whom are her father, Gibech, her brothers, Gernot and Gunther, the warrior Hagen, and Siegfried, the celebrated hero.

Kriemhild wishes to challenge Dietrich and his warriors and employs one of her ladies-in-waiting, Bersâbe, as a bribe in order to have Sabin, the duke of Brâbant, to act as her messenger. Sabin rides out with five hundred men. At Dietrich's court a hostage from Worms, a lady, identifies Sabin and escorts him to Dietrich. Kriemhild challenges Dietrich to assemble twelve men to fight the twelve guardians of the rose garden. The winner(s) will receive a rose wreath and a kiss from Kriemhild. This message is not well received. Dietrich reacts angrily and the guests are in danger, but Hildebrand intercedes and they are treated well. After the guests depart, Dietrich seeks Hildebrand's counsel in choosing his warriors. The twelfth man is the monk Ilsân, who is Hildebrand's brother. The warriors visit the monastery where Ilsân receives permission to fight.

Sixty thousand of Dietrich's men ride toward the Rhine. Gibech rides out with five hundred men to welcome them. Dietrich still does not want to fight over the rose garden. For eight days a truce is declared, and Dietrich and his men are honored guests.

Twelve battles occur involving the following matched opponents: 1) Pusôlt-Wolfhart; 2) Ortwîn-Sigestap; 3) Schrûtan-Heime; 4) Aspirân-Witege; 5) Stûdenvuhs-Ilsân; 6) Walther-Dietleip; 7) Volker-Ortwîn; 8) Hagen-Eckehart; 9) Gernot-Helmschrôt; 10) Gunther-Amelolt; 11) Gibech-Hildebrand; 12) Siegfried-Dietrich.

Dietrich's men all overcome their opponents, but Dietrich once again shows a reluctance to fight. Ilsân returns to the rose garden to defeat an additional fifty-two foes in order to receive fifty-two rose wreaths and kisses from Kriemhild for his fellow monks. Gibech is forced to become a vassal of Dietrich. Dietrich and his warriors return home to a celebration, and then they go their separate ways.

This poem reunites the chief figures from Worms with those from Bern. The main motifs are the rose garden and the battle between Siegfried and Dietrich. The motif of the rose garden surrounded by a thread also occurs in *Laurin*, where the rose garden is also the site of a battle.

Rosengarten zu Worms seems to have been heavily influenced by the *Nibelungenlied*. One striking example is its vilification of Kriemhild. Like its literary predecessor it blames Kriemhild for the death of many warriors (see opening lines). Further she is portrayed as a haughty and arrogant woman. The poet even employs the infamous *Nibelungenlied* word *vâlandinne* (she-devil) to describe Kriemhild. This antifemale attitude is reinforced by Dietrich's negative reaction to Kriemhild's public challenge. Dietrich's stance is also a rejection of the courtly-knightly concept of adventure. It is worth noting that Kriemhild alone owns the rose garden, which places its twelve guardians under her control. The vilification of Kriemhild, then, could be a reaction to a woman exercising power and independence. At one point Kriemhild is portrayed taking delight in the suffering of the battling warriors. The poet makes it clear that Kriemhild is responsible for the pain and suffering. One major discrepancy between the two poems is that Siegfried is portrayed as Kriemhild's fiancé in the *Rosengarten*, a role he never plays in the *Nibelungenlied*.

The assembling of the two mighty groups of warriors and the subsequent twelve battles are the focus of this poem. The Siegfried-Dietrich battle is the climax of the series. These battles are formulaic; each is told in essentially the same words. Siegfried appears here as an ally of Gibech, not as Kriemhild's husband. After cajoling (and in one case bribing) his eleven chosen warriors Dietrich balks when he himself must fight. Only Hildebrand's deception (allowing Wolfhart to report him dead to Dietrich) prompts Dietrich to face Siegfried. The poem shows vestiges of courtliness, but the battles themselves depict a more precourtly ethic. While the giants are summarily slain, the warrior-knights are spared, revealing a double standard. The poet appears to poking fun at the notion of the "love reward" when he has the monk Ilsân fight fifty-two opponents in order to demand fifty-two kisses from Kriemhild, who must endure having her cheek rubbed raw because of his stubbly face. Absent from the Nibelungen side are Giselher, the youngest brother, and Uote, the queen-mother.

Within the context of the narrative time frame of the Dietrich cycle, *Rosengarten zu Worms* occurs before Dietrich's forced exile, since Heime and Witege are portrayed as loyal followers of Dietrich. At least eighteen manuscripts, many fragmentary, show the popularity of the poem in the Middle Ages. Some of the versions differ greatly from one another.

EDITIONS

Die Gedichte vom Rosengarten zu Worms. Ed. Georg Holz. Halle: Niemeyer, 1893.

Der Rosengarte. Ed. Wilhelm Grimm. Göttingen: Dietrich, 1836.

Spottlied, Märchen und Heldenlied vom Rosengarten. Ed. Henrik Becker. Halle: Niemeyer, 1955.

STUDIES

Benedikt, Erich. *Untersuchungen zu den Epen vom Wormser Rosengarten.* Unpublished dissertation, Vienna, 1951.

Boer, R. C. "Die Dichtungen von dem Kampfe im Rosengarten." *Arkiv* 24 (1908): 103–155, 260–291.

Boor, Helmut de. "Die literarische Stellung des Gedichtes vom Rosengarten in Worms." *BGDSL (T)* 81 (1959): 371–391.

Brestowsky, Carl *Der Rosengarten zu Worms. Versuch einer Wiederherstellung der Urgestalt.* Stuttgart: Kohlhammer, 1920.

Grimm, Wilhelm. "Bruchstücke aus einem unbekannten Gedicht vom Rosengarten." *Abhandlungen der phil.-hist. Kl. der königlichen Akademie der Wissenschaften zu Berlin 1859.* Berlin, 1860. 483–500.

Klein, Klaus. "Eine wiedergefundene Handschrift mit Laurin und Rosengarten." *ZDA* 113 (1984): 214–228.

Lunzer, Justus. "Rosengartenmotive." *BGDSL* 50 (1927): 161–213.

Nadler, Josef. "Goldhort/Rosengarten/Gral." *Festschrift für Dietrich Kralik.* Horn: Berger, 1954. 111–129.

DAS LIED VOM HÜRNEN SEYFRID

The latest version of the Nibelung legend that can be considered in any way medieval is this poem in strophes ("The Song of Horn-skinned Seyfrid") that is transmitted only in printed popular books of the sixteenth century and later. The text is garbled and occasionally unintelligible. There seems to have been an attempt to meld several different versions to produce a new text, but the "editor" of the surviving text seems to have had little luck in his endeavor to provide a coherent narrative.

Seyfrid, the son of Sigmund, is a prince, but he is so badly behaved that his parents send him away to be raised by a smith at the edge of the woods. He wreaks so much havoc in the smithy that he is sent off to the forest in the expectation that a dragon there would make an end of him.

He kills the dragon and then attacks a vast number of dragons and other monsters by piling up trees, which he then sets afire. The monsters melt in the fire, and Seyfrid applies the molten dragon skin to his own to produce the horny covering that would protect him from all weapons everywhere on his body but his back, where he cannot reach.

He then sets out for Worms, where he serves King Gybech and wins his daughter.

The story flashes back to the moment when a great dragon steals Krimhilt from her family's castle in Worms. The dragon turns into a man briefly and tells her that he will wed her when he next assumes human form in five years and that she will accompany him to Hell. Seyfrid is introduced anew, and he sets out to rescue the maiden from her captor.

He follows his dogs into the forest, where he encounters a dwarf named Euglein, who tells him who his father and mother are and that a beautiful maiden named Krimhilt is being held captive by the dragon on the mountain.

On the way he encounters a giant named Kuprian, who has the key to the dragon's lair. Most of the poem is devoted to the battles between Seyfrid and Kuprian. Seyfrid eventually kills the giant and turns to face the dragon, whom he also dispatches.

The dwarf tells him of his future, that he will be killed and that his wife will avenge him. The poem concludes with the return to Worms and the beginnings of a conspiracy against Seyfrid. We are told to read about that story in a poem referred to as "Seyfrid's Wedding."

We can see all kinds of different versions of the Siegfried story thrown together here. We can also see the tendency to tell stereotyped giant- and dragon-killing stories about heroes, even if they do not fit into the hero's biography as the audience may have known it from other sources.

Since it is unlikely that the Norse versions of Siegfried's story could have become known in Germany, the presence in the *Hürnen Seyfrid* of many elements from the version of Siegfried's youth told there suggests that they were also current in some form in Germany until this poem was written down. Being raised in the forest by a smith, killing dragons, deriving invulnerability from the dragon in some way, gaining a great treasure—all of these motifs are well documented in the Norse versions, while they are given short shrift in the *Nibelungenlied*. A lost late manuscript of the *Nibelungenlied*, known to us only through a table of contents (the *Darmstädter Aventiurenverzeichnis*), seems to have incorporated these stories into the literary epic.

Hans Sachs, the prolific sixteenth-century adapter of medieval stories to the taste of his time, wrote a tragedy based on the printed version of the poem and an anonymous prose retelling in chapbook form kept the story in print until the nineteenth century.

EDITIONS

Das Lied vom Hürnen Seyfrid. Ed. Wolfgang Golther. Halle: Niemeyer, 1889. Includes the 1726 *Volksbuch vom gehörnten Siegfried.* 2d ed. 1911.

Das Lied vom Hürnen Seyfrid. Critical Edition with Introduction and Notes. Ed. K.C. King. Manchester: Manchester University Press, 1958. Includes extensive introduction and bibliography.

STUDIES

Brunner, Horst, "Hürnen Seyfrid," *Die deutsche Literatur des Mittelalters: Verfasserlexikon.* Ed. Kurt Ruh et al. 2d ed. Berlin: de Gruyter, 1977ff. Vol. 4, cols. 317–326.

Kreyher, Volker-Jeske. *Der Hürnen Seyfrid: Die Deutung der Siegfriedgestalt im Spätmittelalter.* Frankfurt: Lang, 1986.

Weigand, Karl. "Zu den Nibelungen." *ZDA* 10 (1856): 142-146. Text of the *Damstädter Aventiurenverzeichnis.*

CHAPTER 9

Related Legends

WOLFDIETRICH-ORTNIT

This small, relatively close-knit group of texts is not directly related to either of our major legendary cycles. The appearance of the name Dietrich, which occurs in the poems as part of two compound names—Hugdietrich, the father, and Wolfdietrich, the son—led the author of one version of the story (*D*) to identify Wolfdietrich as the grandfather of Dietrich of Bern. On the basis of name evidence some scholars have identified Wolfdietrich with the Frankish king Dietrich, grandson of Clovis.

The story of Wolfdietrich generally occurs in manuscripts together with the bridewinning romance *Ortnit*. The two legends are connected through Wolfdietrich's later vengeance for Ortnit, leading to Wolfdietrich's marriage with Ortnit's widow. It would be a mistake, however, to look upon the two poems as two parts of the same legend. It is much more likely that they were entirely separate until they found their way into the medieval literary versions we know.

Both texts display the same strophic form in all their versions.

Ortnit

Ortnit combines a typical bridewinning story with an unusual dragon adventure.

The emperor Ortnit is urged by his advisors to seek a bride, but the only one of appropriate rank and attractiveness is the daughter of a heathen king, who has vowed that he will never allow his daughter to marry, since he intends to marry her himself when his wife dies. This evil design only serves to spur Ortnit on in his desire to win the princess. Before departing on the expedition he rides out in the countryside, where he encounters a dwarf named Alberich, who is Ortnit's father. The dwarf is invisible to all except Ortnit and is able to help his son win the heathen bride. After his daughter has been kidnapped, the heathen king sends dragon eggs to Ortnit's kingdom of Lombardy, and the dragon that hatches is soon devastating Ortnit's lands.

Ortnit is one of the very few unsuccessful dragon fighters in medieval literature. He sets out to fight the dragon but on the way falls asleep under a magic tree so that the monster is able to carry him back as food for her children. The dragon is unable to open Ortnit's armor, so she sucks the hapless knight out through the openings, leaving the armor and Ortnit's sword to the warrior who can eventually vanquish the dragon.

Ortnit appears as Hertnit in the *Þiðrekssaga*.

Wolfdietrich D(B)

The common version of *Wolfdietrich* also begins with a bridewinning adventure, but this one leads up to the hero's birth and not to his wedding.

Hugdietrich, being young and beardless, disguises himself as a princess and goes to live with the unattainable princess as a companion. Their companionship is so close that the princess finds herself pregnant. After the child is born, the princess hides him in a basket that is lowered from the tower window with a rope, allowing a wolf to steal the child. The child is rescued by some of his grandfather's hunters, and the ruse is exposed. The child is named Wolfdietrich in honor of his having almost become a wolf's breakfast. The infant's baptism coincides with Hugdietrich's return. The general relief paves the way for a reconciliation between Hugdietrich and his new father-in-law.

After his father's death Wolfdietrich is driven from his rightful throne by his younger brothers, who claim that he is illegitimate. The brothers imprison Wolfdietrich's loyal vassals, the sons of his foster-father, Berchtung. Wolfdietrich spends years going through many adventures, all the time hoping to be able to win his land back..

The story of Ortnit is repeated at this point, and Wolfdietrich assumes the responsibility of avenging his old friend. He kills the dragon and marries Ortnit's widow. (Dietrich von Bern plays this role in the version of the same story in the *Þiðrekssaga*.)

He uses the forces from Lombardy to reconquer his land and free his vassals from their imprisonment.

The *D* version concludes with an episode in which the aged Wolfdietrich withdraws from his kingdom and becomes a monk. Shortly before his death he spends a night dreaming that he is battling all of the men he had killed. He is then able to die in peace.

Wolfdietrich A

The *A* version of *Wolfdietrich* is found only in the *Ambraser Heldenbuch* of the early sixteenth century and in a condensed version in the *Dresdener Heldenbuch* of the 1480s. In this version Wolfdietrich is the youngest of Hugdietrich's sons and not the oldest. He is born while his father is absent at war and the evil counselor Sabene casts doubt on his legitimacy. He is put out in his baptismal garment and is miraculously saved by wolves, from whom he takes his name. He is later raised by Berhtung, the faithful vassal. The older brothers force him out of the kingdom and take Berhtung and his sons captive. The adventures that follow do not differ in kind from those in the other Wolfdietrich versions. The Ambras text is incomplete and the Dresden text is heavily condensed, so that we have no authoritative conclusion to the text.

Wolfdietrich C

The *C* version of *Wolfdietrich* exists only in tiny fragments salvaged from parchment used in book binding. There is enough material here to show that the version was probably more different from either of the surviving versions than they are from each other.

EDITION AND TRANSLATION

Ortnit and Wolfdietrich: Two Medieval Romances. Tr. J. W. Thomas. Columbia, SC: Camden House, 1986.

Ortnit und die Wolfdietriche. Eds. Oskar Jänicke and Arthur Amelung. *Deutsches Heldenbuch.* 5 vols. Berlin: Weidmann, 1871–1973. Vols. 3–4. Reprinted 1968.

STUDIES

Baecker, Linde. *Grundlagen der Geschichte des Wolfdietrichstoffes.* Unpublished dissertation, Mainz, 1961.

Dinkelacker, Wolfgang. *Ortnit-Studien.* Berlin: Schmidt, 1972.

Firestone, Ruth H. "A New Look at the Transmission of 'Ortnit.'" *ABäG* 18 (1982): 129–142.

Gehrts, Heino. "Der Schlaf des Drachenkämpfers Ortnit." *Euphorion* 77 (1983): 342–344.

Gottzmann, Carola. *Heldendichtung des 13. Jahrhunderts. Siegfried—Dietrich—Ortnit.* Frankfurt: Lang, 1987.

Kratz, Bernd. "Gawein und Wolfdietrich: Zur Verwandschaft der Crone mit der jüngeren Heldendichtung." *Euphorion* 66 (1972): 396–404.

———. "Von Werwölfen, Glückshauben und Wolfdietrichs Taufhemd." *Archiv für das Studium der neueren Sprachen und Literaturen* 211 (1974): 18–30.

Lecouteux, Claude. "Des König Ortnits Schlaf." *Euphorion* 73 (1979): 347–355.

Meyer, Elard H. "Quellenstudien zur mittelhochdeutschen Spielmannsdichtung II." *ZDA* 38 (1894): 65–95.

Rupp, Heinz. "Der 'Ortnit'—Heldendichtung oder ?" *Deutsche Heldenepik in Tirol, König Laurin und Dietrich von Bern in der Dichtung des Mittelalters. Beiträge der Neustifter Tagung 1977 des Südtiroler Kulturinstituts*. Ed. Egon Kühebacher. Bolzano: Athesia, 1979. 231–252.

Schmid-Cadalbert, Christian. *Der 'Ortnit AW' als Brautwerbungsdichtung. Ein Beitrag zum Verständnis mittelhochdeutscher Schemaliteratur*. Bern: Francke, 1985.

Schneider, Hermann. *Die Gedichte und die Sage von Wolfdietrich*. Munich: Beck, 1913.

Seemüller, Joseph. "Die Zwergensage im Ortnit." *ZDA* 26 (1882): 201–211.

Voorwinden, Norbert. "Zur Überlieferung des Ortnit." *ABäG* (1974): 183–194.

KUDRUN

Kudrun was probably written between 1230 and 1240 in Southern Germany. The author of this poem is unknown. The dating of *Kudrun* is largely based on a reconstruction of the history of the *Kudrun* strophe, a four-line end-rhymed stanza, which is similar to and almost certainly derived from the *Nibelungenlied* strophe.

Hagen, the son of Sigebant and Ute, is abducted by a griffin. He escapes and is raised by three princesses, who later accompany him on his journey home. When a rival of his father attempts to take him hostage, Hagen throws thirty of the duke's men overboard and forces him to sail to his parents in Ireland. Hagen marries one of the princesses, Hilde of India, and they have a daughter, Hilde, whom Hagen jealously guards.

King Hetel of the Hegelings sends three messengers (Wate, Horant, and Morung) disguised as merchants to court the younger Hilde. Wate's appearance is so warrior-like that he attracts Hagen's attention. The two men eventually engage in combat. Meanwhile the princess Hilde is approached by Horant, accepts Hetel's proposal, and departs for Hetel's kingdom. Hagen discovers the plan and pursues his daughter by ship. A battle ensues in which Hagen wounds Hetel but in turn is wounded by Wate. Hilde finally intercedes and peace is declared. Hagen stays twelve days and returns to report to his wife that their daughter is happily married.

Hetel and Hilde have a daughter named Kudrun and a son named Ortwin. Kudrun's beauty attracts many suitors, whom Hetel rejects. Hartmut, son of Ludwig and Gerlint, has his proposal spurned because of his low status (his father, Ludwig, is a vassal of Hetel). Years pass, and Herwig and Hartmut separately journey to Hetel's court to woo Kudrun. After being rejected Herwig returns with 30,000 men. Impressed by Herwig's ferocity, Kudrun accepts his marriage proposal, but the wedding is delayed for one year. Another rejected suitor, Siegfried, attacks Herwig, who then asks Hetel for help. With Hetel's land unprotected Hartmut and Ludwig attack and carry off Kudrun and her ladies-in-waiting.

Hetel, Herwig, and Siegfried, their new ally, battle Hartmut's and Ludwig's forces at Wülpensand, where Hetel is killed by Ludwig. The men of Normandy escape. Only Wate dares to inform Hilde of the disaster. Hilde secures a promise from the surviving warriors that they will participate in the next invasion, which will have to wait for the next generation and for a rebuilt fleet.

Kudrun is left in the care of Gerlint, Hartmut's mother, who attempts to break Kudrun's strong will by forcing her to do increasingly more difficult menial labor. During the last five and a half years of her captivity Kudrun does laundry by the shore.

After thirteen years Hilde finally rebuilds her fleet. The reconstituted invasion fleet lands quietly at Normandy. Ortwin and Herwig set out alone and encounter Kudrun and her faithful lady, Hildeburg, washing. Kudrun recognizes them first. Plans are made. As a ruse Kudrun consents to become Hartmut's wife and is finally treated with the respect due her station.

Hilde's forces attack. Against Gerlint's advice the warriors do not remain within the fortress. Herwig slays Ludwig. Hartmut rescues Kudrun from one of his mother's assassins. Wate takes Hartmut prisoner but beheads Gerlint.

Reunited with her mother, Kudrun almost immediately assumes the role of peacemaker. Four royal weddings take place, bonding all the families. Kudrun finally bids farewell to her mother, but not before pledging her and Herwig's loyalty to Hilde.

Kudrun has three main divisions. The first two sections are devoted to the exploits of Kudrun's maternal ancestors, concentrating on her grandfather Hagen and her parents, Hilde and Hetel. The extension of the family history of Kudrun backward through two generations is common to several medieval German narratives. Both *Parzival* and *Tristan* tell the life stories of the heroes' parents, and this pattern is also evident in *Wolfdietrich* and the *Buch von Bern*. The third section, comprising some two thirds of the poem, focuses alternatively on Kudrun and her mother, Hilde. *Kudrun* thus is a family saga encompassing three generations.

With its emphasis on the sea, which is reflected in its vocabulary, story-line, action in Denmark, the building of ships, and the invading fleets, *Kudrun* celebrates the Age of the Vikings. Indeed, it can be argued that the depicted Danish kingdom refers to the historical realm of Valdemar II (1202–1241). The geography of *Kudrun* is noteworthy: while a number of places and names are identifiable, their locations are not always accurate and others are pure fantasy.

Kudrun and the *Nibelungenlied* seem to share a close bond. At the very least the names of such figures as Siegfried, Ortwin, and Hagen indicate a Nibelung and Dietrich influence. Thornton has tried to show that the two works are linguistically related. These two poems, however, also signal two distinct stages of development and evolution. This difference is most evident in the manner by which they treat alliances and revenge. The alliances in *Kudrun*, though strong, tend to be more flexible. Revenge figures prominently in *Kudrun*, but in stark contrast to the *Nibelungenlied* it is more of an impetus, not a single overriding force. While in *Kudrun* there is a clash between the courtly and feudal demands, there is also a more concerted effort to cooperate.

Unlike the *Nibelungenlied*, *Kudrun* has a "happy ending": the warring families are reconciled. It should be pointed out, however, that this reconciliation occurs only after the slaughter of men, women, and children in Normandy. This positive outcome as well as the portrayal of certain figures has prompted some critics to view *Kudrun* as an anti-*Nibelungenlied* (Hoffmann, Bender).

There has been a tendency to view this reconciliation along generational lines. Wate and Ludwig certainly embody the fierce warrior ethos, in which loyalty and revenge figure prominently, whereas the younger generation of warriors (Ortwin, Herwig, and Hartmut) appears to be more open to cooperation.

This cooperative tendency of the poem may be attributed to its unmistakable focus on female heroes. While the male figures continue to have the action roles, a great deal of attention is directed at the two chief female protagonists, Hilde and Kudrun. Like the men these two women represent the two competing generational views. While Hilde exploits her warriors' desire for revenge to rebuild her fleet in order to rescue her daughter, Kudrun becomes the peacemaker who orchestrates four royal weddings to forge alliances between the quarreling families. The portrayal of Kudrun's suffering is replete with Christian imagery. Indeed, the concept of cooperation or reconciliation reflects a courtly and Christian influence. Yet this poem also reflects and affirms feudal order; Kudrun remains steadfastly loyal to her clan.

In stark contrast to the *Nibelungenlied* there is only one extant manuscript, the *Ambraser Heldenbuch*, a sixteenth-century collection made for Emperor Maximilian I. Further, the Kudrun story probably has no traditional sources and may indeed be the invention of the author.

EDITIONS AND TRANSLATIONS

Kudrun. Ed. Karl Bartsch. 5th ed. Wiesbaden: Brockhaus, 1980.

Kudrun. Die Handschrift. Ed. Franz H. Bäuml. Berlin: de Gruyter, 1969.

Das Nibelungenlied. Kudrun. Ed. Werner Hoffmann. Darmstadt: Wissenschaftliche Buchgesellschaft, 1972.

Kudrun. Tr. Sidney Johnson and Marion Gibbs. New York: Garland, 1992.

Kudrun. Tr. Winder McConnell. Columbia, SC: Camden House, 1992.

Kudrun. Tr. Brian Murdoch. London: Dent, 1987.

Kudrun. Ed. B. Symons. Tübingen: Niemeyer, 1964.

Unterkircher, Franz, ed. *Vollständige Faksimile-Ausgabe im Originalformat des Codex Vindobonesis. Seria nov 2663 der Österreichsichen Nationalbibliothek.* Graz: Akademische Druck- und Verlaganstalt, 1973.

STUDIES

Beck, Adolf. "Die Rache als Motiv und Problem in der 'Kudrun': Interpretation und sagengeschichtlicher Ausblick." *Germanisch-Romanische Monatschrift* 37 (1957): 305–330.

Bender, Ellen. *Nibelungenlied und Kudrun: Eine vergeleichende Studie zur Zeitdarstellung und Geschichtdeutung.* Frankfurt: Lang, 1967.

Blamires, David. "The Geography of Kudrun." *MLR* 61 (1966): 436–445.

Boesch, Bruno. "Zur Frage der literarischen Schichten in der Kudrundichtung." *Festschrift für Siegfried Gutenbrunner.* Eds. Oscar Bandle, Heinz Klingenberg, and Friedrich Maurer. Heidelberg: Winter, 1972. 15–31.

Campbell, Ian R. *Kudrun: A Critical Appreciation.* Cambridge: Cambridge University Press, 1978.

————. "Kudrun's wilder Hagen, Vâlant aller Künige." *Seminar* 6 (1970): 1–14.

Grimm, Gunter. "Die Eheschließung in der Kudrun. Zur Frage der Verlobten- oder Gattentreue Kudruns." *ZDP* 90 (1971): 48–70.

Hoffmann, Werner. "Die Hauptprobleme der neueren 'Kudrun'-Forschung." *WW* 14 (1964): 183–196, 233–243.

————. *Kudrun: Ein Beitrag zur Deutung der nachnibelungischen Heldendichtung.* Stuttgart: Metzler, 1967.

Huber, Eduard. "Die Kudrun um 1300: Eine Untersuchung." *ZDP* 100 (1981): 357–380.

Jungbluth, Günther. "Einige 'Kudrun' episoden: Ein Beitrag zum Textverständnis." *Neophilologus* 42 (1958): 289–299.

Kettner, Emil. "Der Einfluß des Nibelungenliedes auf die Gudrun." *ZDP* 23 (1891): 145–217.

Loerzer, Eckart. *Eheschließung und Werbung in der "Kudrun."* Munich: Beck, 1971.

McConnell, Winder. "Death in Kudrun." *Fifteenth Century Studies* 17 (1990): 229–243.

————. *The Epic of Kudrun: A Critical Commentary.* Göppingen: Kummerle Verlag, 1986.

————." Wate and Wada." *MLN* (1977): 572–576.

Nolte, Theodor. *Das Kudrunepos: Ein Frauenroman?* Tübingen: Niemeyer, 1985.

Panzer, Friedrich. *Hilde-Gudrun. Eine sagen- und literargeschichtliche Untersuchung.* Halle: Niemeyer, 1901.

Pearson, Mark. "Sigeband's Courtship of Ute in the Kudrun." *Colloquia Germanica* 25.2 (1992): 101–111.

Rosenfeld, Hellmut. "Die Kudrun: Nordseedichtung oder Donaudichtung?" *ZDP* 81 (1962): 289–314.

Rupp, Heinz, ed. *Nibelungenlied und Kudrun*. Darmstadt: Wissenschaftliche Buchgesellschaft, 1976.

Samples, Susann T. "Maternal Loyalty in the Nibelungenlied and Kudrun." *Von Otfried von Weißenburg bis zum 15. Jahrhundert*. Ed. Albrecht Classen. Göppingen: Kummerle, 1991. 103–112.

Schulze, Ursula. "Nibelungen und Kudrun." *Epische Stoffe des Mittelalters*. Eds. Volker Mertens and Ulrich Müller. Stuttgart: Kröner, 1984. 111–140.

Siefken, Hinrich. *Überindividuelle Formen und der Aufbau des Kudrunepos*. Munich: Fink, 1967.

Ten Venne, Ingmar. "Einige Überlegungen zu Handlungsstrukturen mittelhochdeutscher Heldenepen am Beispiel des Kudrun-Epos." *Jahrbuch der Reineke Gesellschaft* 2 (1992): 241–254.

Thomas Perry Thorton. "Die Nibelungenstrophen in der Gudrun." *MLN* 67 (1952): 304–309.

Wailes, Stephen L. "The Romance of Kudrun." *Speculum* 58 (1983): 347–367.

Ward, Donald J., and Franz H. Bäuml. "Zur Kudrun-Problematik: Ballade und Epos." *ZDP* 88 (1969): 19–27.

Wisniewski, Roswitha, *Kudrun. Heldendichtung III*. 2d ed. Stuttgart: Metzler, 1969.

Wild, Inga. *Zur Überlieferung und Rezeption des "Kudrun"*. Göppingen: Kummerle, 1979.

ROTHER

This poem in rhymed couplets was written down sometime after the middle of the twelfth century. Its author is unknown.

The story of the Western emperor Rother has been included in our book because of its kinship with the Dietrich legend. Some of the common characteristics are easily recognizable. For instance, like Dietrich, Rother is portrayed as the emperor of Rome and as such embodies the ideal ruler, being gracious, brave, and generous. Both Rother and Dietrich demonstrate a fierce and strong loyalty to their men that sets them apart from their chief antagonists, Constantine and Ermanich, respectively. Rother's selection of the alias Dietrich while he is in feigned exile at Constantine's court calls forth associations with the literary Dietrich. The close affinity of Rother to the Dietrich legend can also be evidenced by its *Brautwerbung* ("bridewinning") episode, which shares a number of unusual motifs with one portrayed in the *Þiðrekssaga*.

Rother is the Western emperor who is persuaded by his loyal subjects to woo the daughter of Constantine, the Eastern emperor. Twelve messengers under the leadership of Luppold depart for Constantinople on a ship laden with fabulous riches.

Upon learning of the messengers' intentions, Constantine has them thrown into prison, where they suffer great deprivation. Constantine then impounds the ship and its riches.

The long absence of his messengers causes Rother to be concerned and prompts him to take action. In his deliberations Rother consults with Berchter, a faithful counselor-warrior, as well as his other knights. Instead of amassing an army it is decided that Rother will visit Constantine's court as a wealthy and powerful exiled knight to determine the fate of his messengers. Rother's alias in Constantinople is Dietrich.

Among his companions are giants who frighten and intimidate Constantine's court. At Berchter's suggestion Dietrich-Rother leaves Constantine's court and establishes his own court. He is quickly widely known and esteemed for his great generosity and soon has a large following.

Constantine's daughter, curious to see this famed knight, persuades her father to hold a festival. A quarrel breaks out between kinsmen of Constantine and Dietrich-Rother's giants. Constantine refuses to become involved.

The young queen sends Herlind, her lady-in-waiting, to Dietrich-Rother with request that he visit her. After a carefully planned diversion and a *Schuhprobe* ("shoe test") he finally reveals his true identity to her and enlists her aid to free his imprisoned messengers.

Ymelot, a ruler from the East, is about to attack Constantinople. Rother is the de facto leader of the defending army. Thanks to the efforts of his men, especially his fierce giants, Rother is able to vanquish the invading army. As a reward for such loyal service Rother is allowed to act as messenger to Constantine's wife and daughter. Rother, however, has other plans and departs with Constantine's daughter to Rome.

Rother's wife is then kidnapped at the behest of her father and brought back to Constantinople. Rother amasses a mighty army and sails to Constantinople.

Meanwhile Ymelot, who has escaped earlier, has conquered Constantinople and has forced Constantine to give his daughter (who is with child by Rother) to his son. Rother and two trusted men pose as pilgrims to spy on Constantine's court but are forced to reveal themselves. Their execution is thwarted by a loyal knight Arnold, his men, and Rother's forces. The heathen army is vanquished. Rother spares both Constantinople and Constantine's life. He is reunited with his wife, who bears a son, Pippin, who will be an ancestor of the great ruler Charlemagne.

After Pippin is knighted, Rother and some of his trusted men withdraw into a monastery. Rother's wife likewise retires to a convent.

Rother offers a fascinating and idealized portrait of trends and events of twelfth-century German society. The bridewinning sequence may indeed reflect a historical event that occurred in 1143–1144, when Roger II of Sicily courted the daughter of a Byzantine emperor. The work also reveals a Crusade influence. Rother's residence, Bari, was an important pilgrim-crusade port. The battles against the heathen Ymelot exude a crusading fervor.

In contrast to many of our poems *Rother* focuses more on the court than on battles. The scenes depicting court life are much more descriptive and vibrant than those depicting warfare. The two courts and their respective rulers underscore the inherent differences between the East (Byzantium) and the West (Rome). Some humor is interjected by the presence and antics of the uncouth and muscle-bound giants, who appear as Rother's faithful allies.

While the other poems may occasionally hint at a historical event or personage, at *Rother's* conclusion its unknown author attempts to place it firmly within a historical context. Rother is shown to be an illustrious ancestor of the Carolingian line; he is the father of Pippin, the grandfather of Charlemagne. This tendency could also reflect the poet's desire to extol the Staufen dynasty by linking it with Charlemagne, thereby affirming its legitimacy and enhancing its glory.

EDITIONS AND TRANSLATIONS

King Rother. Tr. Robert Lichtenstein. Chapel Hill: University of North Carolina Press, 1962.

König Rother. Editor. Günter Kramer. Berlin: Verlag der Nation, 1961.

König Rother. Eds. Theodor Frings, Joachim Kuhnt, and Ingeborg Köppe-Benath. Halle: Niemeyer, 1968.

STUDIES

Bäuml, Franz H. "A Note to König Rother." *MLN* 71 (1956): 351–353.

Curschmann, Michael. *"Spielmannsepik." Wege und Ergebnisse der Forschung 1907–1965. Mit Ergänzungen und Nachträgen bis 1967. Überlieferung und mündliche Kompositionsform.* Stuttgart: Metzler, 1968.

Frings, Theodor. "Rothari—Roger—Rothere." *BGDSL* 67 (1945): 368–370.

Fromm, Hans. "Die Erzählkunst des Rother-Epikers." *Euphorion* 54 (1960): 347–379.

Gellinek, Christian. *König Rother. Studie zur literarischen Deutung.* Bern: Francke, 1968.

Hünnerkopf, Richard. "Die Rothersage in der Thidrekssaga." *BGDSL* 45 (1921): 291–297.

Krogmann, Willy. "Ein verkümmertes Motiv im König Rother." *ZDP* 62 (1937): 244–248.

Neuendorff, Dagmar. "Kaiser und Könige, Grafen und Herzöge im Epos von König Rother." *Neuphilologische Mitteilungen* 85 (1984): 45–58.

Ortmann, Christa, and Hedda Ragotzky. "Brautwerbung, Reichsherrschaft und staufische Politik: Zur politischen Bezeichnungsfähigkeit literarischer Strukturmuster am Beispiel des 'König Rother.'" *ZDP* 112 (1993): 321–343.

Pogatscher, Franz. *Zur Entstehungsgeschichte des mhd. Gedichtes vom König Rother.* Halle: Niemeyer, 1913.

Schröder, Walter Johannes. "König Rother. Gehalt und Figur." *DVLG* 29 (1955): 301–322.

———. "Zu König Rother v. 45–133." *BGDSL (T)* 80 (1958): 67–72.

Glossary of Names

The following list attempts to provide something of a cross index to the names of figures that occur throughout the legends. The individual entries are designed to provide a quick overview of the appearances of the figure in the literary works described above, not to provide an independent treatment of the figures. For a more detailed list see George T. Gillespie, *A Catalogue of Persons Named in German Heroic Literature (700–1600): Including Named Animals and Objects and Ethnic Names* (Oxford: Clarendon, 1973). Except for secondary literature devoted exclusively or largely to the figure in question, there has been no attempt to repeat the bibliographical materials covered under the literary works in the previous chapter.

ALBERICH: Dwarf name applied to two figures in the literary texts we are examining. In the *Nibelungenlied* Alberich is the keeper of Sifrit's treasure. Sifrit approaches his castles in disguise and is involved in a mighty wrestling match with Alberich before he identifies himself. In the *Ortnit* Alberich is the hero's father. He appears to be a small child, but his strength is that of several men and he is visible only to the wearer of a special ring. Alberich helps his son win his bride from her heathen father.

ALDRIAN: Name that appears to have been among those floating about for general use. In the *Nibelungenlied* it is the name of Hagen's father. In the *Þiðrekssaga* Aldrian is the father of Gunnar, Gisler, and Gernoz.

ALPHART: Young kinsman of Hildebrand in *Alpharts Tod* who embodies both the strengths and weakness of the knightly ethos. While he is not usually present as a member of the Dietrich circle, he resurfaces in *Buch von Bern,* where he dies twice at the hands of two different opponents.

AMELUNG: Name derived from the clan name of Theoderic the Great, Amal. The names ending in -ung originally indicated the descendants of someone, so that the Amelungen would have been the descendants of Amal. Jordanes mentions a king named Amal (ch. 14) in his description of the lineage of the Amali. In the *Þiðrekssaga* the Amelungs are Þiðrek's own men as opposed to those he rules for Erminrek. It is also used there and elsewhere as a personal name. There is, however, no legendary story attached to a person of that name.

BERHTUNG: Faithful vassal of Hugdietrich and Wolfdietrich in the *Wolfdietrich* poems. He and his ten sons are the "eleven vassals" Wolfdietrich makes into a kind of battle cry throughout the poem. The name may be derived from *Rother*, where a similar figure appears with the name Berhter.

BIKKI: See SIBECHE.

BITEROLF: Father of Dietleip. In *Biterolf und Dietleip* Biterolf abandons his wife, Dietlint, his son, and his kingdom in Toledo to seek out Etzel's famous court. Years later father and son engage in combat, but a tragic outcome is averted (cf. *Hildebrandslied*). Etzel eventually gives Biterolf and Dietleip Styria as a reward for their loyal service. In the *Rosengarten zu Worms* he is critical of Dietrich's acceptance of Kriemhild's challenge. In *Virginal* he and his son fight side by side as Dietrich's allies in order to free the young warrior from Nitger. In the *Þiðrekssaga* Biterolf also appears as the father of Þetleif, but the story is entirely different.

BRÜNHILD (PRÜNHILT, BRYNHILD): Her extraordinary and almost supernatural powers hark back to an earlier, perhaps mythic tradition. The *Völsungasaga* identifies her with the valkyrie Sigrdrífa, whom Sigurð had awakened in the *Sigrdrífamál* of the *Poetic Edda*. There may be an echo of this in the supernatural powers she displays in the *Nibelungenlied*. where she is the queen of Isenstein/Iceland in her own right and later the wife of Gunther. The most complete account of her life is told in the *Völsungasaga*, where she and Sigurð promise to marry each other. (There she also appears as the sister of Atli/Attila.) In the *Nibelungenlied*, however, no such vow occurs. In both narratives Sigurð-Siegfried is only able to overcome Brünhild by a combination of magic and treachery. Her loss of virginity signals her loss of power. She figures prominently in the murder of Sigurð-Siegfried. While she essentially recedes into the background after his murder in the *Nibelungenlied*, she defiantly stabs herself and throws herself onto Sigurð's funeral pyre in the *Völsungasaga*. In *Biterolf und Dietleip* she appears as the gracious hostess of a kingdom free of internecine strife.

Andersson, Theodore M. *The Legend of Brynhild.* Ithaca: Cornell University Press, 1980.

Classen, Albrecht. "The Defeat of the Matriarch Brünhild in the Nibelungenlied, with Some Thoughts on Matriarchy As Evinced in Literary Texts." *AGSN*, 89–110.

Ehrismann, Otfrid. "Die Fremde am Hof. Brünhild und die Philosophie der Geschichte." *Begegnung mit dem "Fremden." Grenzen—Traditionen—Vergleiche. Akten des VIII Internationarlen Germanisten-Kongresses.* Ed. Ejiro Iwasaki. Munich: Iudicium, 1991. 320–331.

Newmann, Gail. "The Two Brünhilds?" *ABäG* 16 (1981): 69–78.

See, Klaus von. "Die Werbung um Brünhild." *ZDA* 88 (1957): 1–20.

DANCRAT: See GIBECH.

DIETLEIP (ÞETLEIF): Son of Biterolf. See *Biterolf and Dietleip* for his story.

Þetleif the Dane in the *Þiðrekssaga* has a very different story, although he is also given a father named Biterolf, who plays an important part. Þetleif is a layabout as a boy and no one expects anything of him. Suddenly he rides out and distinguishes himself in a battle alongside his father against a band of robbers. He undergoes a number of unique adventures on the way to Rome, where he eventually proves himself worthy of joining Þiðrek's court. Gillespie suggests in his *Catalogue* that a confusion of the names Skane/Spanje led to Þetleif's being moved to Denmark, Skane having been a province of Denmark for most of the Middle Ages.

DIETMAR: Father of Dietrich of Bern in almost all versions. His name appears as Thiudimer in ancient sources and as Þetmar in the *Þiðrekssaga.*

DIETRICH: Legendary figure based loosely on the historical Ostrogothic king Theoderic, who ruled in Northern Italy from 493 to 526. For his legendary biography see above p. 6.

ECKE: Giant who sets out to test his mettle against Dietrich in *Eckenlied.* When faced with the choice of life or dishonor in the eyes of the three queens he serves, Ecke chooses death. Essentially the same story is told about Ekka in the *Þiðrekssaga.* In one Middle High German version of the *Eckenliet* Ecke appears as a totally negative figure, who terrorizes the queens.

EGIL: Brother of Weland in several version of the smith's story. In the *Völundarkviða* Egil is married to a Valkyrie named Ölrún, and he goes to search for her when she flies away.

Egil's name also appears in runes on the Franks casket.[1]

---

[1] See the description of the casket and its runes in Ralph W.V. Elliott, *Runes: An Introduction.* 2d ed. (New York: St. Martin, 1989). 123-139.

ERMENRICH (EMMERICH, JÖRMUNREK): Nemesis of Dietrich in the *Þiðrekssaga* and in the Middle High German "historical" Dietrich narratives. He seems to have taken over the role originally occupied by the historical Odoacer (see above, p. 20). His name comes from the Gothic king Ermanaric, who lived a century before Dietrich. The *Hamðismál* from the *Poetic Edda* and the *Völsungasaga* seem to preserve versions of a story of the historical Ermanaric. (See p. 18, above.) Because of his insertion in place of Odoacer, he seems to play his major role at the beginning of the German (and thus also the *Þiðrekssaga*) version of the legend, while the attempted murder story occurring at the end of the *Poetic Edda* and *Völsungasaga* accounts places him in a later generation. The two stories appear in a confused form in *Ermenríkes Dôt*.

ETZEL (ATTILA, ATLI): Dignified and powerful king of the Huns in the various versions of both the Nibelung and Dietrich legends. In stark contrast to the church-influenced chronicles most of the literary works treated here depict a flattering image of this figure. In most German narratives he appears as a gracious and loyal lord to the exiled Dietrich, while in the Scandinavian versions of the stories he is often depicted as avaricious and occasionally cowardly. His first wife is named Helche, and she appears as the supporter of Dietrich in the "historical" Dietrich poems. After Helche's death he marries Kriemhild (Grimhild, Guðrún), bringing him into the Nibelung legend. In *Rabenschlacht* and the *Þiðrekssaga* Etzel is the father of two sons who perish while in the care of Dietrich.

FÁFNIR: Dragon killed by Sigurð in the *Völsungasaga* and in the songs of the *Poetic Edda*. The saga identifies him as the brother of the smith Regin, who raises Sigurð in the wild. The dying Fáfnir tells Sigurð about his future in the Eddic *Fáfnisnmál*.

FITELA: See SINFJÖTLI.

GERNOT (GERNOZ): Middle brother and co-king of the Burgundians. Throughout most of the *Nibelungenlied* he is in the background. Nonetheless, he shows himself initially to be sympathetic and loyal to his sister, Kriemhild. Both he and his younger brother, Giselher, argue against Siegfried's murder and later are identified as her trusted relations. During the siege by the Huns Gernot demonstrates great courage and is the slayer of Rüedeger. Gernot also appears as a proven warrior in *Rosengarten zu Worms* and *Biterolf und Dietleip*.

In the *Edda* and the *Völsungasaga* Gernot is replaced by Guttorm, whose role is quite different but whose name seems to reflect the Godomar of the *Lex Burgondionum*.

GIBECH (GJUKI): Father of Kriemhild, Gernot, and Gunther in *Rosengarten zu Worms*, the *Þiðrekssaga*, the *Hürnen Seyfrid,* and the *Heldenbuch-Prose.* Gibech's importance as a warrior is indicated when he is matched with stalwart Hildebrant in the *Rosengarten.* After the defeat of all the guardians of the rose garden by the challengers Gibech is forced to become a vassal of Dietrich. In the Icelandic tradition the name appears as Gjuki. Both of these forms are clearly derived from the early name Gibica that appears in the *Lex Burgondium.* In the *Nibelungenlied* the father of the Burgundian kings is Dancrat.

GISELHER: Youngest brother and co-king of the Burgundians in the *Nibelungenlied* and the *Þiðrekssaga*, where his name is spelled Gisler. Of the three brothers Giselher is the closest to his sister, Kriemhild. Consequently, when Etzel proposes to Kriemhild, she seeks out both her mother's and her youngest brother's advice. When the Burgundians journey to Etzel's court, he becomes engaged to Rüedeger's daughter. When the warfare breaks out at Etzel's court, Giselher pointedly refrains from fighting Rüedeger. His valiant death is also lamented in the *Klage.* This figure does not appear in the northern retellings of the legends outside of the German-influenced *Þiðrekssaga.* The name is related to the Gislaharius of the *Lex Burgundionum.*

GOTELINT: Wife of Rüedeger who appears in the *Nibelungenlied* and the *Klage.* In the former poem she is the gracious hostess and happy mother whose daughter is betrothed to Giselher, the Burgundian co-regent. By contrast she appears as the grieving widow in the *Klage.* In the *Þiðrekssaga* her name appears as Guðilinda.

GRIMHILD: See UOTE and KRIEMHILD.

GUNTHER (GUNNAR): Son of Uote and Dancrat and the brother of Gernot, Giselher, and Kriemhild in the *Nibelungenlied.* With his two younger brothers he is co-king of the Burgundians in Worms, although he is clearly the ruling monarch. Before Siegfried's murder he appears as a somewhat ineffective ruler and lackadaisical warrior. Later in the epic he demonstrates repeatedly that he is indeed a valiant warrior. His loyalty to Hagen never wavers. He also appears in the same role in *Rosengarten zu Worms* and *Biterolf und Dietleip.*

In the North Gunnar is given the featured role in the confrontation with Atli (Etzel/Attila), while he plays a secondary role in the parallel scene in the *Nibelungenlied* (and its reflex in the *Þiðrekssaga*). The name appears already as Gundaharius in the *Lex Burgondionum.*

He also appears in the *Waltharius* (and other versions of the Walther story) as the avaricious king who, together with his brother Hagano, attempts to take a treasure away from the refugees Waltharius and Hiltgunt.

GUTTORM: See GERNOT.

GUÐRÚN: See KRIEMHILT.

HAGEN (HÖGNI, HAGANO): Loyal vassal and kinsman to the Burgundian kings in the *Nibelungenlied*. In his role as royal advisor Hagen exerts great power. Indeed, he at times overshadows his lords. He is the slayer of Siegfried and the destroyer of the *Hort* (Siegfried's treasure) and thus Kriemhild's arch-antagonist. Their enmity eventually leads to the deaths of countless warriors. He is slain by Kriemhild. Hagen also appears in *Rosengarten zu Worms* and *Biterolf und Dietleip*, where he acquits himself well as a warrior.

As Hagano this figure also plays a major role in the *Waltharius* and the other versions of the Walther legend.

In the North Högni is a brother to Gunnar and the second most important personage in the confrontation with Atli (Etzel). In the *Þiðrekssaga* he is only a half-brother, his father being a supernatural being who appeared to his mother during the king's absence.

A warrior-king of the same name appears in *Kudrun*.

Backenköhler, Gerd. *Untersuchungen zur Gestalt Hagens von Tronje in den mittelalterlichen Nibelungendichtungen*. Bonn: Universität, 1961.

Dickerson, Jr., Harold D. "Hagen: A Negative View." *Semasia* 2 (1975): 43–59.

Gentry, Francis G. "Hagen and the Problem of Individuality in the Nibelungenlied." *Monatshefte* 68 (1976): 5–12.

Haymes, Edward R. "A Rhetorical Reading of the 'Hortforderungsszene' in the Nibelungenlied." *AGSN*, 81–88.

———. "Hagen the Hero." *Southern Folklore Quarterly* 43 (1979): 149–155.

Homann, Holger. "The Hagen Figure in the Nibelungenlied: Know Him by His Lies." *MLN* 97 (1982): 759–769.

Stout, Jacob. *Und ouch Hagene*. Groningen: Walters, 1963.

Wapnewski, Peter. "Hagen: ein Gegenspieler?" *Gegenspieler*. Eds. Thomas Cramer and Werner Dahlheim. Munich: Hanser, 1993. 62–73.

HARLUNGEN: The story of the Harlungs is frequently mentioned in the background of other stories, but only in the *Þiðrekssaga* is it told in any extent. The name of the brothers is sometimes derived from a father named Harlung. In the saga, however, Egarð and Áki, the sons of Áki Aurlungatrausti, which preserves the name Harlung, are falsely accused of threatening the queen's virtue and are hanged by Erminrek. The father's name also appears as Áki Ömlungatrausti, associating him with the Amelungs. The names of the sons appear as Emerca and Fridla in *Widsiþ* and as Embrica and Fritla in the *Quedlinburg Annals.*

HEIME (HEIMIR, HAMA): Comrade in arms to Witege, whom he rescues from Alphart in *Alpharts Tod*. Although an able warrior, he is treacherous and thus frequently allied with Emmerich. In the *Þiðrekssaga* he shares these characteristics and spends some of his last years in a monastery, an experiment that eventually fails as Þiðrek appears to call him back to a warrior life.

HELCHE: The Christian wife of the pagan Etzel in the Dietrich legends. In the *Buch von Bern* and *Rabenschlacht* she demonstrates a strong loyalty to the exiled Dietrich. Refined and cultured, she is an active participant who provides Dietrich with men, goods, and a wife. Her loyalty, however, is sorely tested in *Rabenschlacht* (and the parallel passage in the *Þiðrekssaga*) when her two sons are killed while under the protection of Dietrich. She is a natural complement to Rüedeger, and both figures have harmonious relations with each other in the aforementioned poems as well as in *Biterolf und Dietleip*. In the *Nibelungenlied* Helche's death prompts Etzel to seek out Kriemhild for his wife.

HELGI HUNDINGSBANI: The second son of Sigmund in the *Völsungasaga* and the *Poetic Edda*. He is thus half-brother to both Sinfjötli and Sigurð. He avenges his father and goes on to win the love of a Valkyrie.

HERBORT: Nephew of Þiðrek in the *Þiðrekssaga*, he woos the beautiful Hild for his uncle but falls in love with her himself. He escapes with her after fighting off the pursuing army. The story has connections both to the Tristan legend (of which it seems to be a parody) and the Walther story. Herbort also appears with a version of a similar story in *Biterolf und Dietleip* without the Tristan echoes.

Frings, Theodor. "Herbort: Studien zur Thidrekssaga I." *Berichte über die Verhandlungen der Sächsischen Akademie der Wissenschaften, Philosophisch-historische Klasse* 95/5 (1943): 1–37.

HERRAT (HERAÐ): The wife or intended of Dietrich in many of the Dietrich legends. She is a member of Helche's entourage at Etzel's court. It is due to Helche's efforts that she is betrothed to Dietrich in *Buch von Bern* (*Dietrichs Flucht*). Their wedding preparations are interrupted in *Rabenschlacht* when Emmerich attacks Dietrich's lands. At the end of the *Klage* her marriage to Dietrich produces a more optimistic outcome than in the *Nibelungenlied*. In the *Þiðrekssaga* she accompanies Þiðrek back to Bern where she later dies.

HERTNIÐ: Name attached to at least two figures in the *Þiðrekssaga*, one of whom is an unlucky king married to a witch. The other figure is clearly a version of the Ortnit story, in which the role of Wolfdietrich is taken over by Þiðrek himself.

The two kings may be identical, but it is not clear from the narrative or the place-names.

HILDE: Name applied to two figures in the *Kudrun*. The elder of the two is Hilde of India, the wife of the fierce warrior Hagen. The younger Hilde is their daughter. She and her husband, Hetel, have two children, Kudrun and Ortwin. After Hetel is slain in battle, Hilde becomes the ruler even though their son is of age. While her gender ultimately restricts her from taking an active role in the battle to rescue her daughter, Hilde is shown to be the driving force behind the endeavor. With this act Hilde exhibits her strong loyalty to her daughter. Initially driven by revenge, Hilde eventually is reconciled with her foes.

HILDEBRAND: Dietrich's weapons-master who in the German poems and the *Þiðrekssaga* is invariably called Master Hildebrand. He makes his first appearance in the Old High German *Hildebrandslied*, where he engages in battle with his son. In the high medieval narratives Hildebrand and Dietrich are virtually inseparable companions. Hildebrand appears as the ageless-aged advisor-warrior who understandably often functions as a kind of surrogate father to Dietrich.

HILDEGUNT: Beloved and later wife of Walther in *Waltharius, Waldere, Walther und Hildegunt*, and the *Þiðrekssaga*. Like Walther she is a noble hostage at Attila's court. Having fallen in love with Walther, she agrees to run away with him.

HUGDIETRICH: Father of Wolfdietrich in the Middle High German poems about the latter. In the *D*-version, Hugdietrich has an adventure of his own in which he, while still young enough to get away with it, disguises himself as a young princess in exile. He manages to become the companion of his intended and eventually even shares the same bed with her. The result of all this is Wolfdietrich, whose premarital birth later allows his brothers to question his legitimacy. Hugdietrich appears in the versions *A*, *B*, and *D* of the *Wolfdietrich*.

KRIEMHILD (GRIMHILD, GUÐRÚN): Best-known female figure in medieval Germanic literature. In the famous opening lines of the *Nibelungenlied* she is shown to be responsible for the deaths of countless warriors. It can be argued that the *Nibelungenlied* is a kind of *Entwicklungsroman* (development novel) in terms of her characterization: she appears as a young maiden, happy wife, grieving widow, and vengeful queen. Her loyalty to her murdered husband, Siegfried, causes her to seek vengeance on her brothers and their chief advisor, Hagen. While *Rosengarten zu Worms* continues the negative portrayal of the *Nibelungenlied*, the *Klage* attempts to rehabilitate her.

Her name appears as Grimhild in the *Þiðrekssaga*. In the Norse versions of the legends found in the *Völsungasaga*, and the *Eddas*, she appears as Guðrún.

There are three late poems dealing with her in the *Edda*. In all these versions she survives Atli to marry a third time and become the mother of Hamðir and Sörli. The northern Guðrún seems to have no connection to the heroine of the South German epic *Kudrun*.

Anderson, Philip N. "Kriemhild's Quest." *Euphorion* 79 (1985): 3–12.

Frakes, Jerold C. "Kriemhild's Three Dreams: A Structural Interpretation." *ZDA* 113 (1984): 173–187.

Nelson, Charles G. "Virginity (De)Valued: Kriemhild, Brünhild, and All That." *AGSN*, 111–130.

Osselman, Dawn. "The Three Sins of Kriemhilt." *Western Folklore* 49 (1990): 226–232.

Schmidt-Wiegand, Ruth. "Kriemhilds Rache. Zu Funktion und Wertung des Rechts im Nibelungenlied." *Tradition als historische Kraft*. Eds. Norbert Kamp and Joachim Wollasch. Berlin: de Gruyter, 1982. 372–387.

Schröder, Werner. "Die Tragödie Kriemhilts im Nibelungenlied." *ZDA* 90 (1960–1961): 41–80, 123–160.

Vestergaard, Elisabeth. "Gudrun/Kriemhild–soster eller husfru?" *Arkiv för nordisk filologi* (1984): 63–78.

KUDRUN: Granddaughter of the fierce warrior Hagen and Hilde of India and daughter of Hilde and Hetel of the Hegelings. She is the major figure of the epic poem that bears her name. "Kudrun" is a reconstructed form. The name appears as "Chaudraun" in the late manuscript of the poem. The figure in the Middle High German epic has no connection with the Norse Guðrún.

LAURIN: In the poem bearing his name a dwarf king who rules over a subterranean kingdom inside a mountain, where he is the guardian of a rose garden protected only by a silken thread.

MIMIR: In the *Þiðrekssaga* Mimir replaces Regin as the dwarf who raises Sigurð. In this text the name Regin is transferred to the dragon-brother killed by Sigurð.

NIBELUNG (NIFLUNGAR): One of the most puzzling names in the history of German heroic legend. Most scholars associate the root with modern German *Nebel* ("fog"), but its use as a designation for a people seems enveloped in the same fog. The name appears in Norse both as Niflungar and Hniflungar. The latter spelling calls the derivation from Nebel/Nifl into question.

In the *Þiðrekssaga* the people in Worms on the Rhine who are ruled over by Gunnar and his brothers are referred to throughout as Niflungar.

In the *Nibelungenlied* this designation initially refers to a dynasty that Siegfried conquers and whose men later appear as his allies during the bridal quest of Brünhild (ch. 8). After the Burgundians have crossed the Danube, they are given this appellation. Some critics have suggested that the name is applied to the owners of the Nibelung treasure and is thus transferred from Siegfried to the Burgundians along with the treasure.

ORTNIT (OTNIT): The story of Ortnit is almost always attached to *Wolfdietrich* in the medieval manuscripts. Ortnit sets out to woo a heathen princess with the help of his dwarf father Alberich. He gains the princess, but his father-in-law seeks revenge by sending dragon eggs into his kingdom. Ortnit sets out alone to fight the dragon that hatches from them but falls asleep under a magic tree. This allows the dragon to capture and devour him. The name appears in the *Þiðrekssaga* as Hertnið.

OTACHER: The historical Odoacer (see above, p. 20) appears in the *Hildebrandslied* under this name. Elsewhere he is replaced in the Dietrich stories by Ermanaric.

ROTHER: The ruler of the Western Empire, with his capital in Italy in *König Rother*. In his story he bears a strong resemblance to Dietrich in his behavior (in fact he even uses Dietrich as an alias).

In the *Þiðrekssaga* his bridewinning story is attached to a northern king named Osantrix.

RÜEDEGER (ROÐINGEIR): Vassal of Etzel. He is best known for his role in the *Nibelungenlied,* where he experiences an acute conflict of loyalties resulting from his bonds both with Etzel and Kriemhild and with the Burgundians. In the end, the demands of state win out, and Rüedeger is forced to fight the Burgundians and is killed by Gernot. He plays essentially the same role in the *Þiðrekssaga*. As a vassal of Etzel, Rüedeger appears in number of the Dietrich poems, most notably *Buch von Bern (Dietrichs Flucht)* and *Rabenschlacht*.

SIBECHE (SIFKA, BIKKI?): Ally and advisor to Ermanrich/Emmerich In a number of the Dietrich poems . His treachery is well known; typically he falsely advises Emmerich in order to destroy this clan. In the *Þiðrekssaga* he appears as Sifka whose treachery is justified by Erminrek's seduction of Sifka's wife, Odila. The same story is told in the *Heldenbuch-Prose*. He is probably identical to the evil counselor Bikki in the *Hamðismál*.

SIEGFRIED (SIGURÐ, SÍFRIT, SEYFRID): In some ways the central figure of this book and in other ways almost marginal. The *Þiðrekssaga* concludes its telling of Sigurð's death with the words "everyone said that no man now lived or ever after would be born who would be like him in strength, courage, and in all sorts of courtesy, as well as in boldness and generosity that he had above all other men, and that his name will never perish in the German tongue, and the same was true with the Norsemen." (ch. 348) This impression is widespread in the literature, but Siegfried remains a frustrating hero. He never establishes himself as a king (except in the *Nibelungenlied*) and his main achievement is the killing of at least one dragon. He is always described as promising, but his early death prevents his fulfilling that promise.

Siegfried is certainly the most important figure for whom no historical model seems to exist. This frustrating situation has led scholars to attempt to associate him with the first-century Germanic leader Arminius (Höfler) and with various members of the Merovingian royal house. Except among the members of the relatively small group of Arminius supporters there is general agreement that the hero's name is Frankish, probably Merovingian, where Sigi- names abound.

In all sources but the *Nibelungenlied*, where he is given a proper courtly upbringing, Siegfried is raised by a smith in the wild. The smith sends him off to fight a dragon, and he returns after the successful fight with a great hoard of treasure. In the Norse sources Sigurð meets Brünhild, who provides him his horse, Grani. and promises to wed the Valkyrie/princess/amazon (see above under BRÜNHILD). He arrives as a wanderer at the court of the sons of Gjuki/Gibech and successfully woos their sister, Kriemhild/Guðrún. He helps Gunther/Gunnar win Brünhild through some form of trickery. He is later killed by Hagen/Högni or Guttorm.

This story is told in the songs of the *Poetic Edda*, in the *Snorra Edda*, in the *Völsungasaga, Nornagests Þáttr*, the *Þiðrekssaga*, the *Nibelungenlied* (with considerable weakening of the youth in the wilderness motif), and the *Hürnen Seyfrid*.

Andersson, Theodore M. "Why Does Siegfried Die?" *Germanic Studies in Honor of Otto Springer*. Ed. Stephen J. Kaplowitt. Pittsburgh: K & S, 1979. 29–39.

Bäuml, Franz H. "The Unmaking of the Hero: Some Critical Implications of the Transition from Oral to Written Epic." *The Epic in Medieval Society*. Ed. Harald Scholler. Tübingen: Niemeyer, 1977. 86–99.

Beck, Heinrich. "Zu Otto Höflers Siegfried Arminius Untersuchungen." *BGDSL* 107 (1985): 91–107.

Boor, Helmut de. "Hat Siegfried gelebt?" *Zur germanisch-deutschen Heldensage*. Ed Karl Hauck. Wege der Forschung 14. Darmstadt: Wissenschaftliche Buchgesellschaft, 1965. 31–51.

Byock, Jesse L. "Sigurðr Fáfnisbani: An Eddic Hero Carved on Norwegian Stave Churches." *PSMA*, 620–628.

Eifler, Günter. "Siegfried zwischen Xanten und Worms: Wolfgang Kleiber zu seinem 60. Geburtstag." *Sprache—Literatur—Kultur. Studien zu ihrer Geschichte im deutschen Süden und Westen*. Eds Albrecht Greule and Uwe Ruberg. Stuttgart: Steiner, 1989. 277–290.

Fechter, Werner. *Siegfrieds Schuld und das Weltbild des Nibelungenliedes*. Hamburg: Toth, 1948.

Fleet, Mary. "Siegfried as Gunther's Vassal." *Oxford German Studies* 14 (1983): 1–7.

Haimerl, Edgar. "Sigurd—Ein Held des Mittelalters. Eine textimmanente Interpretation der Jungsigurddichtung." *Alvíssmál* 2 (1993): 81–104.

Haustein, Jens. "Siegfrieds Schuld." *ZDA* 122 (1993): 373–387.

Hoffmann, Werner *Das Siegfriedbild in der Forschung.* Darmstadt: Wissenschaftliche Buchgesellschaft, 1979.

Höfler, Otto. *Siegfried, Arminius und der Nibelungenhort.* Vienna: Österreichische Akademie der Wissenschaft, 1978.

————. *Siegfried, Arminius und die Symbolik.* Heidelberg: Winter, 1961.

Kralik, Dietrich von *Die Sigfridtrilogie im Nibelungenlied und in der Thidrekssaga I.* Halle: Niemeyer, 1941.

Peeters, Joachim. "Siegfried von Niderlant und die Wikinger am Niederrhein." *ZDA* 115 (1986): 1–21.

Ploss, Emil. *Siegfried—Sigurd. Der Drachenkämpfer.* Cologne: Böhlau, 1966.

Quak, Arend. "Siegfried und die niederländischen Wikinger." *ZDA* 116 (1987): 280–283.

SIGELIND: Mother of Siegfried in the *Nibelungenlied.*

SIGMUND: In the Old English *Beowulf* Sigmund is the dragon slayer and the wanderer in the woods with his son Fitela (Old Norse Sinfjötli). Elsewhere Sigmund appears always as the father of Siegfried/Sigurð, although different stories are attached to him. In the *Poetic Edda* he is mentioned as the father of Helgi, Sinfjötli, and Sigurð, and on one occasion we are told of the death of his killer, but no stories are told about him. There is an extensive section of the *Völsungasaga* devoted to him. In the *Þiðrekssaga* he appears as a king in Tarlungaland (perhaps originally Karlungaland, i.e. the land of the Carolingians) who woos the princess Sisibe in Spain. He is successful, but evil counselors libel her while he is away fighting and she is exiled and bears her child in the wild. In the *Nibelungenlied* and the *Hürnen Seyfrid* Sigmund is a very ordinary king about whom no heroic stories are told.

SIGNY: Twin sister of Sigmund in the *Völsungasaga.* In order to produce a son able to help her brother avenge her father, she changes shape with a sorceress, sleeps three nights with her brother, and bears him a son, Sinfjötli.

SINFJÖTLI (FITELA): Son of Sigmund and his twin sister Signy in the *Völsungasaga.* Sinfjötli helps his father avenge his grandfather. Sinfjötli wanders for several years through the forest with his father in the shape of wolves.

There seems to be something of the werewolf adventure in the reference in *Beowulf* to his wandering through the world on adventures with his father.

UOTE (ODA): Queen-mother of Kriemhild, Gunther, Gernot, and Giselher and widow of Dancrat in the *Nibelungenlied.* She is an important member of

Kriemhild's trusted relations during her stay in Worms after Siegfried's murder. She is best remembered for her interpretation of the young Kriemhild's dream and her own futile attempt to warn her sons and their men of their impending doom as they set off for Etzel's kingdom. In the *Klage* she dies upon learning of the deaths of her children at Etzel's court. Uote also appears in the *Þiðrekssaga* as Oda, but the northern tradition generally has the name Grimhild for the wife of Gjuki.

VOLKER: Minstrel-warrior and stalwart companion to Hagen in the *Nibelungenlied*. He is a vassal of the Burgundian court. In the battle with the Huns at Etzel's court he distinguishes himself as a competent warrior. In the *Þiðrekssaga* his name appears as Folkher.

VÖLSUNG: Name of Sigurð's clan in the Eddic and *Völsungasaga* tradition in Scandinavia. In *Beowulf* Sigmund is referred to as the son of Wæls, based on the same root. The *Völsungasaga* uses the name Völsung to refer to Sigmund's father as well as to the clan as a whole.

WALTHER: Hostage at Attila's court who escapes with his beloved Hildegunt and engages in battle with Gunther and Hagen in the Vosges forest. He appears in *Waltharius*, *Waldere*, *Walther und Hildegunt*, *Biterolf und Dietleip*, and the *Þiðrekssaga*. See section above on Walther and Hildegunt (p. 59)

WATE: Fierce warrior who demonstrates an intense loyalty first to his lord, Hetel, and then to Hetel's widow, Hilde, in *Kudrun*. He has the distinction of besting Hilde's "imposing" father, Hagen. His warrior's stance and conduct appear to hark back to an earlier, precourtly time, but in the end, he too (after much bloodletting during the invasion) grudgingly accepts Kudrun's efforts at peacemaking.

The same name in its Norse form, Vadi, is attached in the *Þiðrekssaga* to the father of Velent (Wieland). There he is the giant offspring of King Vilkinus and a nameless mermaid.

McConnell, Winder. "Wate and Wada." *MLN* (1977): 572–576.

WIELAND (WAYLAND, VÖLUND): The legend of Wieland (Weland, Weland, Völund, Velent) the Smith was apparently known throughout the period when the legends flourished. The only more or less complete versions of the story are the *Völundarkviða* in the *Poetic Edda* and the story of Velent in the *Þiðrekssaga*. Velent is important in the heroic world because he is the son of the giant Vadi (Wate) and the father of the hero Viðga (Witege). Wieland's story is also referred to in the Old English *Deor*. There are numerous references to special armor and weapons as having been his work.

WITEGE (VIÐGA): Usually typecast as the disloyal warrior who betrays his lord, Dietrich, for Ermanrich. In this villainous role he not only slays the idealistic Alphart (*Alpharts Tod*) but also Dietrich's brother Diether and Etzel's two young sons (*Rabenschlacht*). In *Laurin* and *Rosengarten zu Worms* Witege appears as a trusted warrior of the Dietrich circle. In the *Þiðrekssaga* he is the son of Velent (Wieland) and plays the same role he does in *Rabenschlacht*. After killing the sons of Attila and Þiðrek's brother Þether Viðga escapes into the sea, where he is presumably protected by his grandmother, a sea-nymph.

He is often paired with Heime/Heimir, who has a similarly checkered career. The pairing goes back to Old English, where we find Widia and Hama mentioned together in *Widsiþ*.

WOLFDIETRICH: Figure unknown outside of the poems that bear his name. The wolf element of his name probably refers to his long period of exile, a condition that was often associated with wolves in German legend. The etiological stories associating him with real wolves are probably a late invention. In all versions of the story Wolfdietrich is driven from his rightful throne by his brothers who also imprison his loyal vassals. After many years of adventures he is able to return, free his vassals and assume his rightful position. See the discussion of the *Wolfdietrich* poems (p. 133) for his story.

Index

—A—

Abeling, Theodor, 107
Adacarus, 30
Aëtius, 18, 19, 30, 32
Aki Ömlungatrausti, 69, 150
Alberich, 133, 145, 154
Aldrian, 145
Alexander, Michael, 60, 63
alliterative verse, 12, 39, 41, 75
Alphart, 81, 145, 151, 158
Alpharts Tod, 42, 81, 82, 145, 151, 158
Amelung, 68, 146
Amelung, Arthur, 135
Anastasius, 30
Anderson, George K., 117
Anderson, Philip N., 107, 153
Andersson, Theodore M., Jr., 35, 37, 41, 47, 60, 71, 73, 104, 108, 117, 120, 122, 125, 126, 147, 155
Andvari, 115, 121
Apollonius of Tira, 69, 70
Arian Heresy, 16
Armstrong, Marianne Wahl, 108
Arthur, 3, 11, 14, 33, 70, 90, 96
    Artus, 69, 70, 87
Aslaug, 116
Atlakviða, 44, 116, 117, 124, 125
Atlamál, 4, 116, 117, 124, 125
Attila, 3, 4, 6, 10, 11, 17, 19, 20, 23, 30, 31, 32, 47, 58, 60, 61, 68, 69, 70, 72, 116, 119, 123, 124, 125, 126, 148, 149, 150, 152, 153, 158
Atli, 116, 119, 123, 124, 125, 126, 148, 149, 150, 153
Etzel, 6, 32, 63, 77, 78, 79, 80, 81, 89, 90, 91, 95, 96, 99, 103, 104, 105, 106, 108, 110, 112, 116, 119, 123, 124, 125, 126, 146, 148, 149, 150, 151, 153, 154, 157
Avars, 28

—B—

Backenköhler, Gerd, 150
Baecker, Linde, 135
ballad, 36, 42, 76, 97, 125
Bamberg, 31
barditus, 10
Bartsch, Karl, 107, 112, 138
Batts, Michael S., 107
Bäuml, Franz H., 47, 108, 142, 155
Bavaria, 13, 46
Beck, Heinrich, 47, 48, 73, 74, 87, 108, 109, 117, 120, 136, 139, 155
Becker, Henrik, 129

Bede, 29
Behr, Hans-Joachim, 82
Bekker, Hugo, 108
Bender, Ellen, 108, 139
Benedikt, Erich, 73, 129
Benerton, 82
Benkert-Dodrill, Renate L, 108
Benson, Larry D., 60
Benzing, Josef, 88
Beowulf, 12, 39, 40, 41, 53, 54, 59, 60, 62, 156, 157
Berchtung, 135, 146
Bernreuther, Marie Luise, 86
Bertangaland, 69
Bertelsen, Henrik, 72
Bessason, Haraldur, 48, 64, 120, 121, 125
Beyschlag, Siegfried, 101, 108
Biblical narrative, 40
Bibung, 83
Bindheim, Dietlind, 78
Birkhilt, 85
Biterolf, 83, 89, 90, 91, 96, 106, 146, 147, 148, 150, 151
Biterolf und Dietleip, 89, 90
Blamires, David, 139
Bleda, 30
Bloedelinck, 97
Boehringer, Michael, 108
Boer, R. C., 67, 86, 97, 126, 129
Boesch, Bruno, 139
Boethius, 21, 32
Boor, Helmut de, 67, 86, 87, 107, 108, 110, 129, 155
Boos, G., 86
Bornholm, 10
Bostock, J. K., 108
Bowra, Cecil Maurice, 47
Brackert, Helmut, 107, 108
Brady, Caroline, 22, 73, 97, 126
Braune, Wilhelm, 76
Bremen, 71

Brestowsky, Carl, 129
Brévart, Francis B., 86
Brosings, 60
Brot af Sigurðarkviða, 122
Brünhild, 3, 6, 21, 22, 27, 46, 69, 90, 102, 104, 105, 106, 108, 110, 112, 123, 146, 147, 153, 155
Brynhild, 69, 73, 114, 115, 116, 117, 121, 122, 123, 124, 146, 147
Brunichildis, 22, 46
Brunner, Horst, 131
Buch von Bern, 77, 78, 79, 80, 81, 95, 97, 137, 145, 151, 154
Buckmann, Ludwig, 80
Burgundians, 6, 9, 10, 14, 16, 18, 19, 20, 25, 46, 61, 62, 90, 91, 101, 103, 104, 105, 106, 108, 111, 112, 148, 149, 153, 154
Burns, Thomas S., 22
Byock, Jesse L., 117, 155

—C—

Campbell, Ian R., 139
Campbell, Joseph, 8, 14
Carolingian, 16, 17, 39, 142
Cassiodorus, 25, 126
Catalaunian Fields, 19
Châlon, 19
Chambers, R.W., 59
Charlemagne, 3, 16, 17, 33, 71, 141, 142
Chase, Colin, 60
Chilperic, 21, 22, 26
Chlothar, 21
Classen, Albrecht, 108, 111, 123, 140, 147
Clover, Carol J., 54, 120
Clovis, 11, 15, 17, 21, 28, 58, 133
Codex Regius, 45, 119, 120
Cologne Kings' Chronicle (Kölner Königschronik), 33

comitatus, 12
Constantine, 71, 140, 141
Constantinople, 15, 20, 25, 28, 140, 141
Cormeau, Christoph, 108, 113
Curschmann, Michael, 47, 67, 73, 108, 113
Custer, Legend of, 7, 8

—D—

Dahlberg, Torsten, 93
D'Alquen, Richard, 76
Dancrat, 19, 156
Deor, 57, 58, 59, 63
Dickerson, Jr. Harold D., 108, 150
Diether, 69, 79, 158
Dietleip, 68, 79, 83, 89, 90, 91, 92, 93, 94, 106, 127, 146, 147, 148, 150, 151
Dietmar, 32, 77, 147
Dietrich, 3, 4, 5, 6, 7, 8, 9, 11, 12, 21, 22, 31, 32, 33, 34, 40, 44, 53, 54, 60, 67, 68, 71, 73, 74, 77, 78, 79, 80, 81, 82, 83, 84, 85, 86, 87, 88, 89, 90, 91, 92, 93, 94, 95, 96, 97, 98, 99, 103, 105, 106, 108, 109, 112, 118, 119, 126, 127, 128, 129, 133, 134, 135, 136, 138, 140, 141, 145, 146, 147, 148, 149, 151, 152, 154, 156, 158
Dirick, 97
Þeodric, 57, 58, 62
Dietrich und Wenzelan, 95
Dietrichs erste Ausfahrt. *See* Virginal
Dinkelacker, Wolfgang, 101, 135
Dobbie, Elliott Van Kirk, 59
dráp Niflunga, 45
Drekanflis, 87
Dresdener Heldenbuch, 85, 86, 96, 97, 135

Droege, Karl, 73
Dronke, Ursula, 117, 120, 125
Dunlap, Thomas J., 14, 23
Dürrenmatt, Nelly, 109

—E—

Ebbinghaus, Ernst A., 76
Ebel, Uwe, 73, 76, 117
Ebenbauer, Alfred, 34, 37, 47, 91
Ebenrot, 84
Ecke, 68, 84, 85, 86, 88, 147
   Ekka, 68, 87, 147
Eckenlied, 82, 84
Eckerth, W., 63
Edda, 5, 13, 14, 18, 36, 37, 41, 44, 45, 48, 60, 63, 64, 73, 74, 116, 117, 119, 120, 121, 123, 124, 125, 148, 151, 153, 155, 156, 157
Eddic poetry, 45, 119
Edzardi, Anton, 112
Eggerich, 88
Egil (Brother of Wieland), 63, 64, 65, 147
Egil Skallagrimsson, 36, 43
Egilssaga Skallabrimssonar, 43
Ehrismann, Otfrid, 109, 123, 147
Eifler, Günter, 109, 155
Eis, Gerhard, 88, 96
Ekkehard of St. Gall, 61
Elbe, 30
Engels, Heinz, 107
epic, 8, 10, 12, 13, 21, 35, 36, 37, 38, 39, 40, 41, 42, 44, 47, 63, 74, 104, 106, 107, 119, 130, 149, 153
Erichsen, Fine, 72
Ermanaric, 10, 11, 18, 19, 21, 22, 26, 30, 31, 46, 58, 69, 73, 97, 98, 116, 126, 148, 154
   Armentrik, King of, 97

Emmerich, 77, 78, 79, 80, 81, 91, 140, 148, 151, 154, 158
Eormanric, 58, 60
Ermanrich, 6
Erminrek, 68, 69, 70, 72, 146, 150
Ermenríkes Dôt, 42, 97, 148
Erp, 97, 126
Euglein, 130

—F—

Fáfnir, 45, 115, 121, 148
Fáfnismál, 121
Falk, Walter, 109
Fallone, Eva-Maria, 108
Fechter, Werner, 155
Fenik, Bernard, 109
Fight at Finnsburh, 60
Finch, R. G., 117, 125
Finnegan, Ruth, 39
Firestone, Ruth H., 67, 91, 96, 135
Fleet, Mary, 109, 155
Flood, John L., 86, 88, 93
Foley, John Miles, 14, 48, 77, 91, 96, 121
Foote, Peter, 74
formula, 13, 14, 37, 38, 39, 40, 41, 42, 43, 47, 48, 49, 128
formulas, 38, 41
Forster, Leonard, 73
Fourquet, Jean, 113
Frá dauða Sinfjötla, 45
Frakes, Jerold C., 153
Franks, 9, 10, 11, 14, 16, 17, 21, 23, 26, 34, 46, 58, 61, 147
Frantzen, J.J.A.A., 73
Fredegar, 27
Fredegund, 21, 22, 27
Frederick I "Barbarossa," German Emperor, 33
Freiberg, Otto, 86
Friese, Hans, 73

Frings, Theodor, 73, 142, 151
Fromm, Hans, 109, 142
Frutolf von Michelsberg, 31, 32, 33, 34, 58
Fulda, 75

—G—

Galsuintha, 22
Gaul, 18, 20, 26, 30
Gehrts, Heino, 135
Geiserich, 29
Gellinek, Christian, 142
Genesis, 41
Gentry, Francis G., 109, 150
Gepids, 16
Gerald, Brother, 61
Gerlint, 136, 137
Gernot, 3, 6, 79, 90, 91, 102, 103, 127, 148, 149, 154, 156
Gesta Theoderici, 27
Getica, 21, 26
Gibbs, Marion, 138
Gibica, 18, 25, 58
Gibech, 19, 25, 127, 128, 149, 155
Gjuki, 19, 115, 149, 155, 157
Gybech, 130
Gillespie, George T., 145
Giselher, 3, 6, 18, 25, 102, 103, 106, 128, 148, 149, 156
Gisler, 18, 25, 149
Gisler, 119, 145, 149
Glendinning, Robert J., 48, 64, 120, 121, 125
Godden, Malcolm, 54
Godomar, 18, 25
Goffart, Walter, 23, 34
Göhler, Peter, 109
Goldemar, 82, 89, 92
Goossens, Jan, 74
Gordon, C. D., 23
Gotelint, 112, 149

Gothic, 10, 11, 16, 20, 21, 26, 28, 30, 34, 46, 126, 148
Goths, 9, 10, 11, 14, 16, 17, 18, 21, 23, 25, 27, 28, 30, 45, 46, 47, 58
Gottzmann, Carola, 67, 135
Gregory of Tours, 22, 23, 26, 34
Gregory the Great, Pope, 26, 32
Grendel, 59, 60
Grim, 87, 88
Grimhild, 69, 70, 114, 115, 118, 123, 124, 148, 157
Grimm, Gunter., 139
Grimm, Wilhelm, 34, 42, 129
Grimstad, Kaaren, 64
Gripir, 121
Gripispá, 121
Gronvik, Ottar, 76
Guðrúnarkviða, 123, 124
Gúðrún, 115, 116, 119, 123, 124, 125, 150, 155
Gundobad, 25
Gunther, 3, 6, 11, 18, 20, 25, 60, 61, 62, 69, 79, 90, 91, 102, 103, 104, 105, 106, 111, 112, 127, 146, 149, 155, 156
  Gundaharius, 11, 18, 25
  Gunnar, 18, 63, 69, 73, 114, 115, 116, 117, 122, 123, 124, 125, 145, 149, 150, 153, 155
Guntram, 26
Günzburger, Angelika, 113
Guttorm, 19, 25, 115, 122, 148, 150, 155

—H—

Hadubrand, 59, 75, 76
Hagen, 6, 7, 11, 58, 61, 63, 70, 79, 90, 91, 99, 102, 103, 104, 105, 106, 107, 108, 109, 110, 111, 112, 114, 118, 127, 136, 137, 138, 139, 149, 150, 152, 153, 155, 157

Högni, 63, 70, 114, 115, 116, 117, 118, 122, 124, 125, 150, 155
Hagen, Friedrich Heinrich von der, 97, 100
Hagenmeyer, Alfred, 91
Haimerl, Edgar, 123, 156
Hákon the Old (Norwegian King), 68
Halasz, Katalin, 93
Hamðir, 97, 126, 153
  Ammius, 18
  Hamidus, 30
Hamðismál, 18, 97, 126, 148
Harlungen, 150
Harris, Joseph, 48, 59, 76, 120, 121, 124
Hartmut, 136, 137, 138
Hatto, A.T., 14, 107
Hauck, Karl, 77, 108, 109, 120, 155
Haug, Walter, 97, 109
Haupt, M., 89
Haupt, Waldemar, 74
Haustein, Jens, 156
Hávamál, 44
Haymes, Edward R., 14, 40, 48, 72, 74, 109, 150
Heime, 58, 60, 68, 78, 79, 81, 82, 83, 91, 127, 128, 151
  Heimir, 68, 70, 151, 158
Heinrichs, Anne, 117
Heinzle, Joachim, 54, 67, 93, 98, 99, 109, 113
Helche, 77, 78, 79, 80, 103, 104, 148, 151
Heldenbuch, 78, 80, 82, 84, 85, 86, 88, 89, 91, 93, 95, 96, 97, 98, 99, 100, 135, 138, 149, 154
Heldenbuch Prose, 86, 98
Heldenlied, 37, 40, 41, 47, 48, 49, 120, 129
Helferich, 83

Helgi Hundingsbani, 48, 115, 119, 120, 121, 151, 156
Heliand, 40, 41
Helreið Brynhildar, 44, 122
Hempel, Heinrich, 74, 119
Hennig, Ursula, 87, 108, 113
Henry VI, German Emperor, 33
Herbort, 69, 73, 151
Herburt, 69
heroic epic, 21, 36, 40, 42
heroic legend, 5, 17, 18, 22, 29, 31, 33, 34, 35, 43, 45, 46, 97, 153
Herrad, 70, 79, 112, 151
Herrmann, Paul, 117
Hertnit, 134, 151
Herwig, 23, 136, 137, 138
Hetel, 58, 136, 137, 152, 153, 157
Heusler, Andreas, 36, 37, 40, 41, 42, 43, 48, 74, 101, 109, 119
Hilde, 136, 137, 138, 139, 152, 153, 157
Hildebrand, 3, 6, 59, 75, 76, 77, 79, 81, 83, 84, 88, 92, 93, 94, 95, 103, 105, 106, 127, 128, 145, 152
Hildibrand, 68, 70
Hillebrand, 97
Hildebrandslied, 4, 21, 37, 40, 41, 42, 46, 47, 48, 58, 75, 76, 77, 146, 154
Hildebrandslied, "Younger", 42, 76
Hildegund, 60, 61, 63, 69, 152
Hildigunn, 69, 72
History of the Franks, 26, 34
Hoffmann, Werner, 14, 54, 80, 89, 109, 138, 139, 156
Höfler, Otto, 109, 156
Hofmann, Dietrich, 74
Holz, Georg, 93, 129
Homann, Holger, 110, 150
Horant, 136
Hreiðmar, 115, 121

Huber, Eduard, 139
Hugdietrich, 133, 134, 146, 152
Hugus, Frank, 74
Hunding, 117, 120, 121
Hünnerkopf, Richard, 74, 142
Huns, 10, 17, 18, 19, 20, 28, 30, 46, 58, 61, 90, 103, 111, 125, 148, 157
Hürnen Seyfrid, 42, 99, 130, 131, 149
Hyltén-Cavallius, Olof, 73

—I—

Ibelin, 83
Iceland, 5, 9, 43, 44, 45, 46, 54, 71, 72, 74, 114, 117, 119, 120, 125, 126, 146
Ihlenburg, Karl Heinz, 110
Ildico, 20
Ilsân, 127, 128
Irminfrid, 30
Iron, 69

—J—

Jaeger, C. Stephen, 110
Jakob Twinger von Königshofen, 31
James, Edward, 14, 23
Jänicke, Oskar, 34, 91, 92, 135
Jeraspunt, 83
Jiriczek, Otto, 67, 82
John I, Pope, 21, 26, 29, 30, 32
Johnson, Sidney, 138
Jones, George Fenwick, 67
Jónsson, Guðni, 72, 118
Jordanes, 18, 19, 20, 21, 23, 25, 29, 31, 34, 146
Jörmunrek, 116, 126, 148
Julius Caesar, 32
Jung, Carl Gustav, 38
Jungbluth, Günther, 139
Justinus, Emperor, 30

—K—

Kaiser, Gert, 113
Kaiserchronik, 32, 33, 34
Kalevala, 36
Kellogg, Robert L., 48, 120
Kemenaten, Albrecht von, 82, 89
Kemp Malone, 58, 59, 60
kenning, 45
Kettner, Emil, 82, 139
Kiernan, Kevin S., 60
King, K.C., 131
Klaeber, Friedrich, 60, 62
Klage, Diu, 90, 107, 111, 112, 113, 149, 151, 157
Klare, Andreas, 76
Klein, Klaus, 93, 129
Knapp, Fritz Peter, 91
knighthood, 32, 80, 85, 90, 91
Kolb, Herbert, 87
Kölbigk, Tanzlied von, 42
Köppe-Benath, Ingeborg, 142
Körner, Josef, 113
Kralik, Dietrich von, 74
Kramer, Günter, 142
Kratz, Bernd, 135
Kratz, Dennis M., 62
Kratz, Henry, 86, 110
Kraus, Carl von, 84
Kreyher, Volker-Jeske, 131
Kriemhild, 3, 4, 6, 69, 90, 99, 102, 103, 104, 105, 106, 107, 110, 111, 112, 118, 123, 124, 127, 128, 130, 146, 148, 149, 150, 151, 152, 153, 154, 155, 156
Kristjánsson, Jónas, 74, 122
Kroesen, Riti, 126
Krogmann, Willy, 46, 48, 74, 76, 107, 142
Kudrun, 42, 58, 63, 108, 110, 111, 136, 137, 138, 139, 140, 150, 152, 153, 157
Kuhn, Hans, 119, 120
Kuhn, Hugo, 84, 110
Kuhnt, Joachim, 142
Künhilt, 92, 93
Kuprian, 130

—L—

Lachmann, Karl, 36, 37, 40, 113
Lapidge, Michael, 54
Lassbiegler, H., 86
Laurien, Hanna-Renate, 68
Laurin, 88, 89, 92, 93, 94, 95, 98, 99, 128, 129, 136, 153, 158
Lecouteux, Claude, 135
Lehmann, Winfred P., 48
Leicher, Richard, 113
Leitzmann, Albert, 78, 80
Leo, Emperor, 27, 28
Lex Burgundionum, 25, 149
Leyen, Friedrich von der, 48
Lichtenstein, Robert, 142
Liedertheorie, 36
Lindow, John, 54, 73, 120
Liudegast, 102
Liudeger, 102
Loerzer, Eckart, 139
Lohse, Gerhart, 74
Loki, 115
Lombard, 16, 46
Lombards, 17, 46
Lönnrot, Elias, 36
Lönnroth, Lars, 73
Lord, Albert Bates, 13, 14, 37, 38, 39, 41, 42, 43, 48, 121
Lunzer, Justus, 84, 91, 96, 129
Lutz, Hans Dieter, 48

—M—

Magoun, Jr., Francis Peabody, 59, 62, 63
Marold, Edith, 74
Martin, Bernhard R, 110

Martin, Ernst, 78, 80, 82
Maurer, Friedrich, 110
McConnell, Winder, 74, 110, 113, 139, 157
McDonald, William C., 77
McMahon, James V., 110
McTurk, Rory, 74
Meier, Hans-Heinrich, 77
Meier, John, 76, 97
Merovingian, 21, 22, 26, 155
Mertens, Volker, 67
Metzner, Ernst Erich, 42, 48
Meyer, Elard H., 135
Meyer, Matthias, 87
Middle High German, 14, 42, 53, 54, 58, 63, 67, 70, 87, 147, 148
Mime, 153
Mimir, 113, 153
minne, 89, 91, 105
Mohr, Wolfgang, 68
Moselle, 33
Mowatt, D. G., 110
Mueller, Werner, 110
Müllenhoff, Karl, 34
Müller, Ulrich, 67
Mundt, Marina, 74
Münster, 71
Murko, Matija, 37
Musset, Lucien, 23
Muter, 83

—N—

Nadler, Josef, 129
Nagel, Bert., 110
Neckel, Gustav, 119, 120
Nelson, Charles G., 110, 123, 153
Neo-Heuslerians, 41, 42
Neuendorff, Dagmar, 142
Neumann, Friedrich, 110
Newmann, Gail, 110, 123, 147
Nibelung, 3, 4, 5, 8, 9, 10, 12, 18, 21, 25, 36, 44, 46, 60, 75, 101, 116, 118, 119, 126, 129, 138, 148, 153, 154
Niflunga, 45, 69, 71, 73, 74, 101, 108, 118, 125
Nibelungenlied, 4, 5, 6, 7, 13, 14, 19, 35, 36, 42, 46, 47, 48, 54, 61, 63, 69, 73, 74, 75, 79, 80, 90, 91, 99, 101, 102, 103, 104, 105, 106, 107, 108, 109, 110, 111, 112, 113, 114, 118, 119, 123, 128, 130, 136, 138, 139, 140, 145, 146, 147, 148, 149, 150, 151, 152, 153, 154, 155, 156, 157
Niflunga saga, 71, 73, 108, 118
Nitger, 83, 146
Nolte, Theodor, 139
Nornagest, 117, 121

—O—

Oddrun, 124
Oddrúnargráttr, 124
Óðin, 64, 114, 115, 122
Odoacer, 10, 11, 17, 20, 21, 22, 27, 28, 29, 30, 31, 32, 46, 59, 148, 154
Ofen, 32
Old English, 39, 40, 41, 42, 43, 45, 46, 47, 54, 57, 59, 62, 63, 156, 158
Old High German, 21, 39, 40, 42, 43, 45, 46, 47, 75, 77
Old Norse, 36, 39, 40, 43, 54, 63, 71, 73, 76, 116, 119, 120
Old Saxon, 39, 40, 41, 42, 43, 45
Ömlung, 68
oral poetry, 12, 35, 37, 38, 40, 43
oral tradition, 4, 7, 12, 13, 21, 25, 29, 30, 31, 35, 37, 38, 40, 42, 45, 47, 71
Ortmann, Christa, 143
Ortnit, 42, 67, 98, 99, 133, 134, 135, 136, 145, 151, 154

Ortwin, 136, 137, 138, 152
Osantrix, 69, 72, 154
Osselman, Dawn, 110, 153
Ostrogoths, 17, 18, 19, 20, 22
Otfrid von Weissenburg, 41, 42

—P—

Paff, William J., 74
Pálsson, Hermann, 48, 74, 122
Panzer, Friedrich, 74, 110, 139
Parry, Milman, 37, 38, 41, 48
Patzig, Hermann, 68, 74
Pearson, Mark, 139
Peeters, Joachim, 156
Péttursson, Einar G., 74
Pilgrim, 112
Ploss, Emil, 101, 123, 156
Plötzeneder, Gisela, 68
Pogatscher, Franz, 143
Premerstein, Richard von, 79, 80
Pretzel, Ulrich, 107
Price, Arnold H., 110
Primisser, Alois, 97
Priscus, 19
Prose Edda, 45, 117
Ptolomaeus, 27, 28
Pütz, Horst P., 68, 75

—Q—

Quak, Arend, 156
Quedlinburg Annals, 29, 31, 151

—R—

Rabenschlacht, 42, 78, 79, 80, 81, 95, 148, 151, 154, 158
Ragnar loðbrók, 116, 117
Ragotzky, Hedda, 143
Ranke, Friedrich, 110
Rauff, Willy, 91
Ravenna, 3, 17, 30, 32
Regensburg, 32

Regin, 114, 115, 117, 121, 148, 153
Reginsmäl, 121
Reichert, Hermann, 34, 47, 48, 75, 111, 120, 123
Reinhold of Meilan, 97
Renoir, Alain, 77
Rentwin, 83, 87
Ritter-Schaumburg, Heinz, 73, 75
Robert, Brother, 70
Roðingeir, 118, 154
Roman Empire, 10, 11, 15, 16, 17, 19
Rosenberg, Bruce, 8
Rosenfeld, Hellmut, 88, 140
Rosengarten zu Worms, 70, 90, 93, 98, 99, 105, 106, 127, 128, 129, 146, 148, 149, 150, 152, 158
Rosomoni, 18
Rother, 140, 141, 142, 143, 146, 154
Rüedeger, 77, 79, 80, 90, 91, 95, 103, 106, 112, 118, 148, 149, 151, 154
Rupp, Heinz, 136, 140
rustici, 31
Ryder, Frank G., 107

—S—

Sabene, 135
Sachs, Hans, 130
Saelde, Frau, 96
saga, 5, 18, 44, 68, 69, 70, 71, 72, 73, 74, 87, 108, 114, 115, 116, 117, 118, 119, 121, 137, 148, 150
saints' lives, 40
Salerno, 68
Samples, Susann T., 111, 140
Samson, 68, 70
Schiltunc, 94
Schmid-Cadalbert, Christian, 136
Schmidt, Ernst A, 84

Schmidt, Gerhard, 111
Schmidt-Wiegand, Ruth, 153
Schneider, Hermann, 136
Schnyder, André, 91
Scholler, Harald, 113
Schröder, Edward, 96
Schröder, Walter Johannes, 111, 143
Schröder, Werner, 49, 111, 113, 153
Schröer, K. J., 93
Schulze, Ursula, 140
See, Klaus von, 147
Seemüller, Joseph, 136
Short, Douglas D., 60
Sibeche, 78, 79, 81, 146, 154
  Sifka, 69, 70, 72, 79, 154
Siegfried, 3, 4, 5, 6, 8, 11, 13, 22, 46, 60, 67, 69, 73, 90, 92, 98, 101, 102, 103, 104, 105, 109, 110, 111, 112, 123, 127, 128, 130, 131, 135, 137, 138, 139, 146, 148, 149, 150, 152, 153, 154, 155, 156, 157
  Seyfrid, 42, 99, 129, 130, 131, 149, 155, 156
Sigelind, 156
  Sigilind, 102
Sigenot, 82, 87, 88, 89
Sigibert, 21, 22, 26
Sigmund, 39, 60, 102, 113, 114, 115, 129, 151, 156, 157
Signy, 114, 156
Sigrdrífa, 122
Sigrdrífamál, 121
Sigurð, 5, 60, 69, 101, 113, 114, 115, 116, 117, 118, 119, 120, 121, 122, 123, 124, 126, 146, 148, 151, 153, 154, 156
Sigurðarkviða inn skammi, 122
Sigurðsson, Gisli, 120
Simek, Rudolf, 122

Sinfjötli, 60, 114, 120, 148, 151, 156
  Fitela, 60, 148, 156
singers, 5, 12, 13, 35, 36, 37, 38, 42, 46, 47, 58
skaldic poetry, 44
skaldic verse, 43
Slagfiðr, 63
Slay, Desmond, 74
Smyser, H.M., 62
Snorri Sturluson, 45, 71, 116
  Heimskringla, 45, 71
Sörli
  Sarus, 18
  Serla, 30
Spain, 10, 17, 20, 22, 46, 156
Spielmann, Edda, 108
Splett, Jochen, 111
Stark, Franz, 84
Steche, Theodor, 80
Stein, Peter K., 49
Steinmeyer, Elias von, 89
Stephens, W. E. D., 75, 87
Stout, Jacob, 150
Strasbourg, 31, 98, 99
Stutz, Elfriede, 34, 77
Styria, 32, 92, 146
Symmachus, 21, 26, 29, 30, 32
Symons, B., 139

—T—

Tacitus, 9, 10, 14, 39, 42
Tarnkappe, 92, 102
Taylor, Archer, 14
Tell, Wilhelm, 70
Ten Venne, Ingmar, 140
Terry, Patricia, 14, 120
Thelen, Lynn D., 111
Theoderic, xii, 3, 10, 11, 15, 16, 17, 18, 20, 21, 25, 26, 27, 28, 29, 30, 31, 32, 46, 47, 57, 58, 68, 71, 146, 147

Theoderic Strabo, 20
Thomas, J.W., 135
Todd, Malcolm, 14, 23
Toman, Lore, 123
Toulouse, 17, 30
Tristan, 69, 70, 110, 137, 151
    Tristram, 70
Trûtmunt, 89
Tyler, Lee Edgar, 77

—U—

Überschlag, Doris, 107
Unger, C. R., 72
Unterkircher, Franz, 139
Unwerth, Wolf von, 75
Uodelgart, 85
Ureland, P. Sture, 73
Ute, 102, 103, 105, 112, 128, 136,
    139, 149, 156, 157

—V—

Valentinian, Emperor, 30
Vansina, Jan, 14
Vasolt, 84, 85, 86
    Fasolt, 87
Velent, 63, 64, 65, 68, 70, 72, 157,
    158
Verona, 3, 30, 68
Vestergaard, Elisabeth, 124, 153
Viðga, 57, 64, 68, 72, 157, 158
Virginal, 7, 82, 83, 84, 87, 146
Visigoth, 28
Vogelsang, Heinz, 82
Vogt, Friedrich, 87, 113
Volker, 67, 127, 140, 157
    Folkher, 157
Völsung, 114, 120, 157
Völsungasaga, 5, 13, 18, 45, 60, 71,
    114, 118, 120, 121, 122, 146,
    148, 151, 155, 156, 157
Völund, 63, 64, 157

Völundarkviða, 44, 63, 64, 65, 147,
    157
Völuspá, 44
Voorwinden, Norbert, 79, 80, 113,
    136
Vries, Jan de, 77
Vulcanus, 26, 32

—W—

Wachinger, Burghart, 111, 113
Wagner, Norbert, 79
Wailes, Stephen L., 111, 140
Walberan, 93, 94, 95
Waldschmidt, Anneliese, 109
Walshe, M. O'C., 54
Walther, 60, 61, 62, 63, 69, 88, 127,
    149, 151, 152, 157
    Valtari, 63, 69, 72
    Waldere, 41, 62, 152
    Waltharius, 61, 62, 63, 149, 152
Wapnewski, Peter, 150
Ward, Donald J., 108, 140
Wate, 136, 137, 138, 139, 157
Wayland, 63, 157
Weber, Gerd Wolfgang, 73
Weber, Gottfried, 111
Wenzel, Horst, 111
Wenzelan, 91, 95, 96
Wessels, P. B., 68, 93
Widsip, 46, 47, 58, 63, 151, 158
Wieland, 4, 57, 62, 63, 64, 68, 147,
    157, 158
Wierschin, Martin, 86
Wild Hunt, 33
Wild, Inga, 140
Williams, Jennifer, 91
Wilmanns, W., 84
Wisniewski, Roswitha, 27, 54, 75,
    107, 140
Witege, 57, 58, 62, 77, 78, 79, 81,
    82, 83, 91, 92, 93, 94, 127, 128,
    151, 157, 158

Wolf, Alois, 49

Wolfdietrich, 42, 58, 98, 99, 133, 134, 135, 136, 137, 146, 151, 152, 154, 158

Wolfhart, 77, 79, 92, 94, 95, 106, 127, 128

Wolfram, Herwig, 14, 23

Worms, 6, 18, 46, 61, 70, 81, 89, 90, 91, 102, 104, 109, 112, 127, 128, 129, 130, 146, 148, 149, 150, 152, 153, 155, 157, 158

Wulf and Eadwacer, 59

Wunderer, Der, 96, 97

Wyss, Ulrich, 75

—X—

Xanten, 102, 109, 110, 155

—Y—

Yugoslavia, 37

—Z—

Zatloukal, Klaus, 79, 80, 82, 91

Zeno, Emperor, 30, 32

Zimmer, Uwe, 82

Zimmermann, Günter, 82, 91

Zimmermann, Hans Joachim, 68

Zingerle, I. V., 87

Zink, Georges, 68, 87, 97

Zips, Manfred, 93

Zupitza, Julius, 84, 86, 88, 89, 96

—Þ—

Þether, 69, 158

Þetleif, 68, 146, 147

Þetmar, 68, 147

Þiðrek, 68, 69, 70, 71, 72, 87, 118, 124, 146, 151

Þiðrekssaga, 4, 5, 14, 33, 61, 63, 64, 65, 67, 68, 72, 73, 74, 75, 76, 79, 81, 87, 88, 90, 98, 99, 113, 114, 118, 119, 134, 140, 145, 146, 147, 148, 149, 150, 151, 152, 153, 154, 155, 156, 157, 158